Along Great Western Road

An Illustrated History of Glasgow's West End

Botanic Gardens, Glasgow

Gordon R. Urquhart

Stenlake Publishing
2000

Boer War veterans taking the salute at Wellington Church in the early 1950s.

© Gordon R. Urquhart 2000

First published in the United Kingdom, September 2000,
by Stenlake Publishing,
Ochiltree Sawmill, The Lade,
Ochiltree, Ayrshire, KA18 2NX
Telephone / Fax: 01290 423114
www.stenlake.co.uk
Reprinted November 2000, January 2001

ISBN 1 84033 115 1

Front endpaper: Detail of first edition Ordnance Survey, Lanarkshire VI NW, surveyed 1858, 1:10560.
Back endpaper: Detail of second edition Ordnance Survey, Lanarkshire VI NW, re-surveyed 1893-1894, 1:10560.
Title page: Great Western Road and Botanic Gardens station, *c.*1905.

Introduction

In the mid-eighteenth century, the first country estates of the Tobacco Lords were established along the River Kelvin. A few generations later, James Gibson began feuing his lands of Hillhead for the construction of exclusive suburban houses. Ever since, the area which became known as the West End of Glasgow has been one of the city's most affluent and popular residential districts. Today, the West End boasts some of Glasgow's finest architecture and townscape from the Victorian and Edwardian periods.

Surprisingly, for an area with a legacy of notable residents, important institutions and formidable architecture, there has been comparatively little published on the West End. In fact, more than a generation has passed since the publication of Henry Brougham Morton's classic 1973 work, *A Hillhead Album*. Over the years, in the course of researching history lectures on the West End, it became increasingly apparent to me that there was a wealth of interesting and unpublished material on the West End hidden away in the great libraries and archives of Glasgow and beyond. It also seemed indisputable that these archival photographs should be disseminated, indeed celebrated; hence *Along Great Western Road*.

This book was originally conceived as a photographic study of Hillhead and Kelvinside, the two major estates which straddled the Great Western Road turnpike and which formed the core of Victorian development west of the Kelvin. As interesting material on the periphery of these two estates was uncovered, the boundaries of the study area were expanded slightly to touch upon areas like Park, Dowanhill and Woodlands.

Along Great Western Road is not intended to be a comprehensive or definitive history of the West End. Rather, it is a modest appreciation of the area, a collection of rare and previously unpublished views enhanced by certain classic photographs and accompanied by episodic histories of West End people, places and events. Above all, it is hoped that *Along Great Western Road* will act as a catalyst for further research into this compelling Glasgow neighbourhood.

GRU
August 2000

For Janet, Ross and Callum

The kiln at North Woodside mill, 1955.

Table of Contents

iv

Timothy Pont's c.1596 survey as published in Blaeu's Atlas of 1654.

In the 1580s and 1590s, a young divinity graduate of St Andrews called Timothy Pont undertook the first major cartographic survey of Scotland. More than fifty years later, Pont's manuscript material was incorporated into the greatest world atlas of the age, Joan Blaeu's *Theatrum Orbis Terrarum, sive Atlas Novum*, published in Amsterdam.

Numerous editions of Blaeu's atlas were published in four languages between 1635 and 1658. The fifth volume, *Pars Quinta*, contained 46 separate maps of Scottish counties and regions. Copies of the Latin and German editions of *Pars Quinta* are held in the Special Collection of the University of Glasgow Library. Quite remarkably, scores of Pont's manuscript survey maps still survive and are held in the National Library of Scotland.

Timothy Pont's *c.*1596 survey of the lower Clyde provides the earliest known record of Glasgow and its hinterland. Details of the maps of 'Levinia' or 'The Province of Lennox' (*above*) and 'Clyds-dail' (*below*) contain many ancient place names for the estates, farms and milling sites along the Kelvin which would ultimately develop into the West End of Glasgow. Archaic spellings notwithstanding, many of these names will be familiar to twenty-first century residents of the West End.

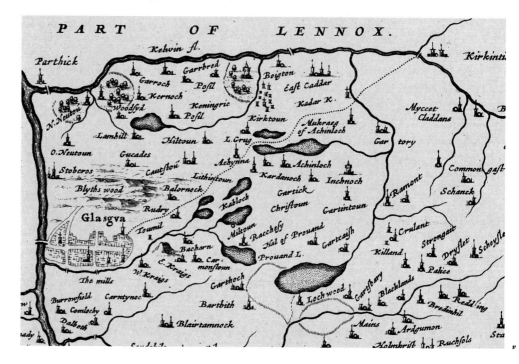

v

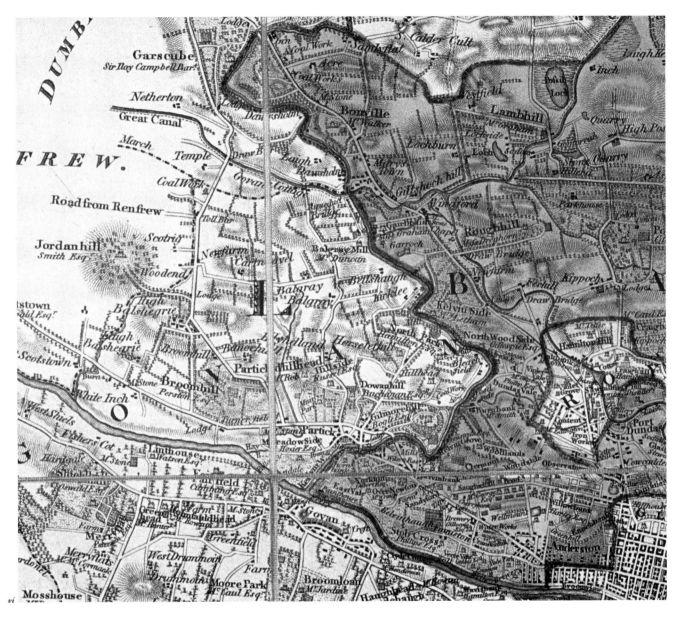

William Forrest's 1816 Map of Lanarkshire.

One of the best records of Glasgow's hinterland prior to the age of suburbanisation is William Forrest's 1816 map of Lanarkshire. Forrest recorded in fine detail the expansion of the gridded city of Glasgow westward towards Blythswood and Anderston, as well as showing the new country estates near the Kelvin (Gilmorehill, Northpark, Dowanhill etc.) which were then appearing alongside the more established retreats of the 'Old Glasgow Gentry' such as Kelvinside, Kelvingrove and Hillhead.

Many ancient place names which were first mapped by Timothy Pont around 1596 are also found in Forrest's 1816 survey. There is a wealth of detail in the map, including topographical shading and locations of country houses and farms, as well as the names of owners of certain estates. Forrest also recorded the locations of mills, coal works and bleachfields along the Kelvin.

Forrest's map is also the earliest record of the old network of parish roads and farm tracks west of the Kelvin. Between the two early turnpikes leading out of Glasgow to the west (which form today's Dumbarton and Maryhill Roads) are many minor local roads which would become major thoroughfares in the Victorian West End. The two most important routes were the old parish road between Partick Cross and Kirklee (later realigned and truncated to become Byres Road), and the old 'Coarse Loan,' or Crossloan Road, which extended from Partick to the Forth and Clyde Canal. Today, the path of this old loan still exists as Hyndland Street/Hyndland Road/Cleveden Road.

The road which would have the greatest impact on the development of the West End — the Great Western Road turnpike — would be laid out across these estates and farm fields to meet the 'Road from Renfrew' at the Anniesland Toll Bar some twenty years after the publication of Forrest's map.

Gilmorehill House, built c.*1802.*

I.

Early History

Documentation concerning the early history of the countryside west of Glasgow is scarce. In the early nineteenth century, several neolithic urns were discovered in a sandstone quarry on Donaldshill (near the site of today's Western Infirmary), and, in 1868, Roman artefacts were uncovered on the estate of Yorkhill by workmen excavating a trench. These discoveries, however, shed little light on the earliest inhabitants of the lands along the Kelvin. The first historical reference to the area pertains to King David's 1136 grant of the lands of the parish of Govan to the see of Glasgow. Govan parish incorporated extensive lands in the lower ward of the county of Lanarkshire on both sides of the Clyde.

After the Reformation, when the church's former holdings in Govan parish were acquired by a small number of powerful Glasgow families, the lands around the Kelvin first appear in the historical records of the modern era. Early town council records of Partick refer to a 'Woodside Mill' in 1608[1], not long after map-maker Timothy Pont's survey of Clydesdale had recorded a place name of 'Woodsyd' on the Kelvin between the lands of 'N[ether] Newton' and 'Garroch.' Pont's 1596 survey was later incorporated into the famous atlas of Scotland by Joan Blaeu (first published in 1654) which contains the earliest known map of the Glasgow area. Other local place names shown on Blaeu's map include the ancient sites of 'Hydland,' 'Garskub,' 'Bagra,' 'Daeshoom,' 'Barshagrie' and 'Partnick.'[2]

The lands west of the Kelvin and north of Partick were undulating, wooded and generally of an agrarian nature. Prior to the mid-eighteenth century, these lands were owned by several old Glasgow families including the Campbells of Blythswood, the Gibsons of Hillhead and Overnewton, and, at Garscube, the

At the time of its demolition in 1935, the picturesque Garrioch Cottage was one of the oldest surviving estate buildings along the Kelvin. Known locally as the 'Half House,' the cottage once served as the lodge on the old parish road leading to Garrioch House, part of a large estate whose lands became the site of Maryhill Barracks in the 1860s. Over the next seventy years, the area around Shakespeare Street and Garrioch Road was feued for tenements and the old cottage was eventually replaced by a Territorial Army building.

3

Campbells of Succoth. Most of the land was leased out for agricultural, light industrial and mineral extraction purposes. The great families established country houses, and there were vernacular buildings housing tenant farmers and other workers. The banks of the Kelvin were dotted with bleachfields and printfields (where patterned cotton cloth was processed), papermaking works, various types of mills, and many small coal workings. Inland were located small sandstone and brick-clay quarries, sometimes with associated brickworks.

As Glasgow's mercantile elite prospered through the mid-eighteenth century, wealthy families bought sizable estates in picturesque locations around the periphery of the city. The wealth which migrated west from Glasgow was by no means all new money. Many of these families were amongst the oldest and most influential families in Glasgow, whose number included generations of provosts and leading merchants. Families which moved to the western lands during the first property boom at the close of the eighteenth century, like the Bogles and Buchanans, often had long Glasgow pedigrees and used their connections to benefit from the city's profitable colonial trade. In the later nineteenth century, these families were often referred to as 'The Old Glasgow Gentry.'[3]

There were three Balgray farms between the Kelvin and Anniesland, two of which appear to have dated from the early seventeenth century or before. The buildings of North or Laigh Balgray (*above*) stood until the 1930s on the corner of Great Western and Beaconsfield Roads. The steading of South or High Balgray stood until *c.*1870 behind the site of No. 1 Devonshire Gardens. These two farms appear regularly in early eighteenth century records. The third farm, called simply Balgray, stood at the corner of Crossloan (now Cleveden) and Kelvindale Roads.

4

Milling along the Kelvin has an ancient history, with records showing that mills were established near Partick at least as early as the mid-1500s. Upstream from Partick, the most important milling site was at South Woodside, the haugh between the Kelvin bridge and Eldon Street Bridge. A grain mill may have operated here from at least the early 1600s, and, around 1790, William Gillespie, a cotton printer from Anderston, constructed Glasgow's first and only water-driven cotton mill on the site (*left*). This oil painting view looks south over the lade; Woodlands Hill rises to the left.

Kelvinside House stood high above the Kelvin on the river's north bank, near the site of today's Botanic Crescent. Built around 1750 by Thomas Dunmore, a prominent Glasgow Tobacco Lord, the mansion was demolished in the Victorian period when the fine ornamental grounds were laid out for the feuing of North Kelvinside.

6

In a picture postcard published *c.*1905, old Kelvinside House was commemorated as the birthplace (in 1836) of the new Liberal Prime Minister, Sir Henry Campbell-Bannerman. His tenure as Premier, however, was cut short after only three years due to his untimely death in 1908.

SIR HENRY CAMPBELL-BANNERMAN.
Prime Minister of Great Britain.

Old KELVINSIDE HOUSE, GLASGOW. Birthplace of Sir Henry Campbell Bannerman.

5

In the early eighteenth century, the lands west of Glasgow were made up of large estates incorporating many smaller units, usually let as tenant farms. One such holding was a farm called Bankhead, lying south of the old Garscube turnpike (now Maryhill Road) and overlooking the River Kelvin. It was part of the expansive lands of Ruchill and Lambhill, acquired in the early 1700s by James Peadie, a leading Glasgow merchant and former Dean of Guild and Lord Provost. In 1749, Peadie's heirs sold Bankhead and part of the lands of Garrioch to Thomas Dunmore, a member of the first generation of Glasgow's Tobacco Lords.

Thomas Dunmore was the first Glasgow merchant of this period to establish a substantial country residence along the banks of the Kelvin. Having changed the name of the estate from Bankhead to Kelvinside, he built a mansion high above the old Garrioch Mill in 1750, and 'originated the ornamental woods which add so much to the picturesque character of the locality.'[4] In the 1770s, Kelvinside was passed on to Robert Dunmore, who, like his father, was a leading merchant in Glasgow, with a wide variety of business interests including iron, bottle and rope manufacture, printing and cotton spinning. The younger Dunmore was also deeply involved in the West Indian and American trade networks.

Robert Dunmore disposed of Kelvinside in 1785, possibly to fund his acquisition of extensive lands in Stirlingshire connected with his cotton mill at Balfron. Dunmore had been a key figure in Glasgow's efforts to help the government put down the rebellion in the American colonies (considered to be a major threat to the city's future prosperity). He not only transported British troops and provisions across the Atlantic, but five of his firm's vessels spent much of the war privateering along America's eastern seaboard.[5]

The next owner of Kelvinside, Thomas Lithan, also had colonial connections, having been a doctor with The East India Company in Rungapore. Lithan resided at Kelvinside until his death in 1807. His widow, Elizabeth Mowbray, eventually remarried, but had left Kelvinside by the late 1820s. During the 1830s, the estate was leased out and a perennial summer tenant was Sir James Campbell, one-time Lord Provost of Glasgow and co-founder of the city's leading warehouse firm, J. & W. Campbell. In 1836, Campbell's younger son Henry was born at Kelvinside House. Henry Campbell, who later assumed his mother's maiden name of Bannerman under the terms of a family bequest, followed his father and brother (a Conservative MP) into politics. Sir Henry Campbell-Bannerman served as Liberal MP for Stirling Burghs for over 40 years, rising through the party ranks to become Secretary of War, and, eventually, Prime Minister.

One of the great names in Glasgow's early mercantile history is that of Patrick Colquhoun. Born in Dumbarton and apprenticed in the Virginia colony at 16, Colquhoun came to Glasgow in 1766 and soon became a leading member of the city's mercantile elite. He not only imported tobacco but also invested in important local industries such as the Verreville Glass Works at Finnieston, the first crystal glass works in Scotland. Colquhoun also established himself as an advocate for Glasgow's merchants. First, he led a successful campaign against a proposed cotton tax which had threatened the fledgling muslin industry, and, after the outbreak of war in the American colonies, Colquhoun sought to protect Glasgow's investments by becoming a major underwriter for the raising of a regiment in the city.

Colquhoun also took advantage of Clyde ships idled by the war, becoming, in 1776, a government subcontractor for 'victualling' the troop ships.[6] When he was elected Lord Provost in 1782, at the age of only 36, Colquhoun acted swiftly to look after the interests of Glasgow merchants as the end of the war approached. He lobbied Parliament to ensure that any peace negotiations kept in mind that 'very large sums' were still owed to Glasgow merchants by 'the inhabitants of Virginia, Maryland and Carolina.'[7]

Like many of his contemporaries, Colquhoun used his newly acquired wealth to obtain the trappings of position and influence. In 1782, the new provost purchased a small estate called Woodcroft on the banks of the Kelvin, about two miles west of the city. It is likely that Colquhoun reconstructed an existing building into the mansion house he called 'Kelvingrove,' which was recalled in the nineteenth century as 'long one of the most beautiful country seats around Glasgow.'[8]

In 1783, in his crowning achievement, Provost Colquhoun helped to establish the Glasgow Chamber of Commerce — the first in Britain and only the second in the world (after New York's). In 1789, he abruptly moved to London where he became a Justice of the Peace, a magistrate and a social reformer, publishing influential leaflets on, among other things, poverty, education and policing. His final work, *A Treatise on the Wealth, Power and Resources of the British Empire in every Quarter of the World* promoted emigration as a means of addressing unsustainable rises in the UK population at the end of the Napoleonic wars. Colquhoun died in London in 1820, and was buried in St Margaret's Chapel in Westminster where a marble plaque commemorates his many civic achievements. In Glasgow, however, he is by and large forgotten.

8

Glasgow Provost Patrick Colquhoun (1745-1820) was one of the most extraordinary men of his generation. A wealthy Tobacco Lord and industrialist, Colquhoun was a co-founder of the Tontine Society (the 'centre of the city's business life for 50 years'[9]), and was also 'sometime Chairman of the Committee of Management' of the Forth and Clyde Canal.[10] Only seven years after establishing the country retreat of Kelvingrove (*below*) in 1782, Colquhoun left Glasgow for a new career in London. His estate eventually formed the nucleus of the West End Park.

9

A hundred years after Andrew Gibson bought Hillhead, the fifth and last generation of this ancient Glasgow family was to inherit these lands along the Kelvin. James Gibson (*above*) became the Laird of Hillhead in 1802, when he was just two years old. In a mere twenty years time, however, young James (1800-1862) set out to develop these family lands into a fashionable residential suburb of Glasgow.

The Gibsons were the most prominent of the old Glasgow families which played a part in the early development of the West End. Early generations of the family were rentallers, or tenant farmers, on the lands of the Bishops of Glasgow in Govan parish (on both sides of the Clyde). The Gibsons were first recorded in 'Mekle Gowan' in 1529.[11] The most notable generation consisted of three of the sons of John Gibson of Overnewton (d. 1679). The elder two, Provost Walter (c.1643-1723) and Captain James Gibson (d. 1700), participated in some of the great events in Scottish history, namely the development of international commerce on the Clyde, the suppression of the Covenanters and, ultimately, the Darien disaster. The youngest son of John Gibson of Overnewton was Andrew (d. 1733), best remembered for his acquisition of the lands of Hillhead in 1702.

It would be fair to say that no single citizen contributed more to the making of mercantile Glasgow than Walter Gibson. Daniel Defoe, after visiting the city in the early eighteenth century, wrote with surprise, 'I find no statue, no grateful inscription to preserve the memory of Walter Gibson!'[12] By 1866, however, it was said that he was 'now scarcely known to our Citizens; although he was the father of the Foreign Commerce of Glasgow, the Originator of its Iron Trade, and the Founder of the Broomielaw Harbour.'[13] It has also been said that Walter Gibson participated in the earliest ventures of the Glasgow merchants to Maryland and Virginia.[14]

Walter Gibson was the fourth generation of Gibsons to reside at Overnewton (the lands between the Kelvin and Stobcross). Later, he enlarged the family holdings by acquiring Gilmorehill, parts of Partick and the massive lands of Balshagray. Gibson also owned salt-making works in Gourock, and coalfields at Camlachie, Bellahouston and around the city. After training as a maltman, Gibson turned to international trade and earned a fortune in the last three decades of the seventeenth century. Around 1668, he hired a Dutch merchant ship, loaded 450 tons of salted herring and sailed to St Martins in France. Gibson famously 'got for each Barrell of Herring, a Barrell of Brandy and a Crown, and the Ship at her return was loaded with Salt and Brandy; and the Product came to a prodigious Sum, so that he bought the great Ship and other two large Ships.'[15]

Not all of Walter Gibson's shipping exploits, however, were such proud moments in Glasgow's history. In 1684, the arch Episcopalian Gibson was hired by the town council to transport the many Covenanter prisoners then languishing in Glasgow's Tolbooth. Thirty-two 'rebel' Covenanters from Glasgow and Dumfries, whose only alternative to exile was execution, embarked for Charleston on Walter Gibson's ship *Carolina*, with Captain James Gibson in command. By all accounts, the prisoners were treated cruelly on the voyage; they were summarily robbed,

beaten and starved. Those wretched souls who survived were virtually sold as slaves, and few ever returned to Scotland.[16]

Walter Gibson was selected as Provost of Glasgow by the Episcopal archbishop in 1687 (the last provost to be so chosen). In those difficult times, the Episcopalian supporters of King James VII and II struggled with the Presbyterian proponents of the House of Orange over the control of the kirks. In February 1689, the provost sent his brother to install an Episcopalian parson in the High Church. Captain James Gibson, his parson and their mob found the cathedral doors locked and guarded by a crowd of some forty women, 'who sternly resisted his entrance.' In the ensuing riot, 'in which fists, sticks and stones were freely used . . . the poor women fought with so much desperation, that many of them carried with them the marks of the injuries they had received till their dying day.'[17]

By 1690, the Presbyterians were firmly in control of the Church, and Walter Gibson's enemies set out to ruin him financially. They soon forced him into bankruptcy and had his vast properties (around 1,000 acres) sequestered. The former provost overcame the bankruptcy, but with substantial outstanding debts to Glasgow Town Council, Walter Gibson was imprisoned for a time in the Tolbooth. Eventually, Gibson's extensive property holdings were sold off and the former provost died in 1723 at 80 years of age, an impoverished, broken man.

Captain James Gibson also died in unfortunate circumstances, seen by many contemporaries as divine retribution for his brutal persecution of Covenanters many years before. In the late 1690s, like many influential Scots merchants, the Gibson brothers were involved in the ill-fated scheme to establish a trading colony at Darien (now Panama). James Gibson captained the *Rising Sun*, which departed from Greenock with three other ships on 18 August 1699, carrying some 1,300 men. Unfavourable winds kept them anchored off Bute until 24 September, and they finally departed only weeks before mainland Scots received word that the first expedition to Darien had utterly failed. A treacherous crossing of the Atlantic prevented the *Rising Sun* from reaching Darien until mid-November. Following the collapse of the colony in 1700, Gibson's ship was chased out by the Spanish fleet. In a storm off the Carolina coast, the *Rising Sun* ran aground, drowning Gibson and 100 men on board.[18]

The third Gibson brother, Andrew, fared better than his older siblings. A maltman in the family tradition, he became the Laird of Overnewton through his brothers' misfortunes. In 1702, he bought the lands he had long been leasing in Hillhead, located on the opposite side of the Kelvin from Overnewton. A century after this acquisition, the last generation of Gibsons would inherit these valuable lands west of Glasgow.

In the early 1950s, during the construction of the new Chemistry building by T. H. Hughes, a deep coal mine was uncovered. This unusual Annan view shows university workers preparing to make the mine safe by walling up between the pillars. Hillhead is pervaded by numerous redundant mines, many dating from the mid-eighteenth century. The last mines in the area were sunk in the 1820s by James Gibson, the self-styled 'Coalmaster of Hillhead.'

Like his forefathers, James Gibson of Hillhead earned an income from his lands along the Kelvin through leases for farming, small-scale coal mining, and some stone quarrying and brick-making. Lands along the river were also leased as a printfield as early as the 1750s.[19] By the end of the eighteenth century, however, the pattern of ownership in Hillhead began to change. In 1799, a year before James Gibson's birth, some 14 acres in the north of Hillhead estate were feued to Glasgow provost and wealthy rum trader John Hamilton. When James was still in his teens, further lands were sold to James Buchanan of Dowanhill.

Early records show that James Gibson of Hillhead was involved in the coal operations around Hillhead from at least the age of 18.[20] In the early 1820s, however, the ambitious young Gibson began developing his family estate for suburban housing. His plans were bold, for at this time the western periphery of Glasgow had barely reached the area around Blythswood Square. Hillhead was another mile across open fields from the Georgian new town, and was difficult to reach due to the poor condition of the old parish loans leading from the city.

In 1822 Gibson built King's Bridge, a timber and iron suspension bridge across the Kelvin. The following year, a feuing plan for Hillhead was drawn up by the prominent Glasgow land surveyor David Smith, and by 1825, a second, stone-arched bridge had been built across the Kelvin near the ancient ford on the Bishop's Road to Partick, just below the South Woodside weir.[21]

From the mid-1820s, the development of the estate seems to have been Gibson's main occupation. Large parcels of land were sold or feued to David Smith, John Hamilton of Northpark and others, but in 1826 the picture changes. It appears that young Gibson had become financially embarrassed, having amassed substantial debts to a number of parties. In 1826, his estates were sequestered by the Court of Session and set aside for the use of his creditors.[22]

The circumstances which prompted the sequestration are not clear, though presumably much of the debt stemmed from capital investment in his estate. The records, however, do show the wide range of creditors in Glasgow and Edinburgh, including several banks (a third of the total being owed to the Royal Bank), various business associates, his closest friends and even members of his own family. Altogether Gibson owed some £8,700, equivalent to about £1m in today's terms.[23] These problems came at a difficult time for James Gibson, who, in 1826, lost his wife of only two years. His creditors acted rather benevolently towards the 26-year-old. Rather than immediately seizing and auctioning off the estate, they established a trust which would manage the feuing of Hillhead on his behalf, allowing him to pay back the money in stages. He was also permitted to retain income from coal leases. Gibson managed to buy back the remainder of the Hillhead estate in 1832, though he would never regain complete control.

An important step in the development of Hillhead was the 1822 construction of a suspension bridge (of rather unusual design, *below*), built over the Kelvin just below South Woodside mills. It was erected, according to a contemporary account, 'for the purpose of connecting the lands of Hillhead and Blythswood. The foundation stone of this bridge was laid with Masonic honours, around the time when His Majesty [George IV] was in Edinburgh. In commemoration of the Royal Visit to Scotland, it was named the King's Bridge. It was designed and executed under the superintendence of John Herbertson, Jun., Architect, on the principle of suspension bridges, with the chains or rods below, and the weight resting on the rods by means of cast iron brackets, on which the beams are placed.'[26]

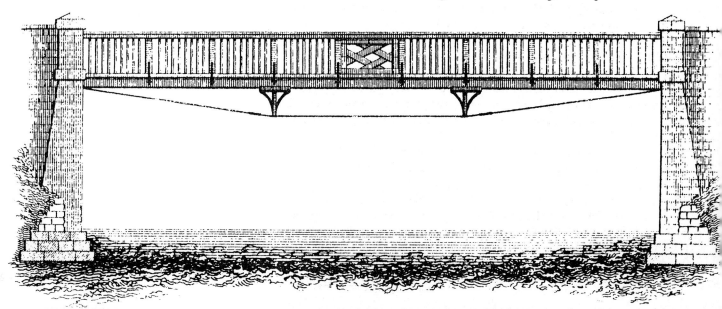

12

Merchant and Provost of Glasgow John Hamilton of Northpark (1754-1829) built his country residence on lands acquired from the Gibsons of Hillhead in 1799. Northpark was, according to an 1870 account, 'a beautiful retired spot. It stood immediately behind Buckingham Terrace, facing towards the north and commanding fine views of the Campsie Hills and the beautiful woods of Kelvinside. At some distance below it ran the clear silvery Kelvin.'[27] John Hamilton was 'a most valuable citizen of Glasgow, and merited, and obtained the respect and affection of its inhabitants.'[28] The wealth and status of John Hamilton and his wife Helen Bogle was such that they sat for portraits by Sir Henry Raeburn. (Helen Bogle's portrait was gifted to the Hunterian Art Gallery by the W. A. Cargill Trust in 1970.)

The first subdivision of Hillhead had come in 1799 when about 14 acres along the Kelvin were feued to the merchant John Hamilton, who developed the lands into a picturesque country seat called Northpark. The Hamiltons were referred to in the Regality Club papers as 'merchants of the highest standing, commercially and socially, and active public spirited citizens.'[24] The father of John Hamilton of Northpark was a minister at Glasgow's High Kirk and had been Moderator of the General Assembly in 1766. Both father and son married members of one of Glasgow's most prominent families, the Bogles of Shettleston. (The uncle of Helen Bogle Hamilton of Northpark, Robert Bogle junior, purchased Gilmorehill in 1802.)

John Hamilton of Northpark was a bailie in Glasgow for six years, the City Treasurer, Lord Dean of Guild and a three-time Lord Provost. In his day, however, this West India trader and rum and wine merchant kept a cellar in Leitch's Close off the Trongate, and was known locally as 'Johnny Sma' Bottles'![25] Over the years John Hamilton acquired additional land from the Gibsons of Hillhead, including a strategically important strip at the western edge of the Hillhead estate, along the march with Horslethill farm. This narrow corridor was laid out with trees and became the formal entrance to Northpark. (Eventually it was taken as the line of the extended Byres Road which was joined to the new Great Western Road turnpike around 1839.)

John Hamilton was succeeded by his son William, also a bailie, City Treasurer and Lord Provost of Glasgow. Apparently, William Hamilton had no use for Northpark at first. He put the estate up for sale in 1830 but eventually let it out for several years, returning to it in 1838 with his wife, their six children and seven servants. Soon after, once the Great Western Road turnpike was under construction, William Hamilton recognised the potential of suburban development. Around 1840, he commissioned a feu plan from the London architect Decimus Burton, lately in Glasgow to lay out the suburb of Kelvinside.

The North Woodside mill was in use for well over two hundred years. It was situated between the River Kelvin and the old Garriochmill parish road (which was spanned in 1870 by the privately-built Belmont Bridge, *above***).**

The picturesque mill at North Woodside was a favourite subject for artists for centuries. When milling operations ceased in the 1950s it marked the end of one of the oldest surviving industrial sites along the Kelvin. The old miller's house itself (*opposite, top***) survived into the 1960s. The mill site, located below Hamilton Drive and Doune Gardens, was recorded in a series of fine photographic views taken in the 1920s by the City Assessor's department (now preserved in the City Archives). In the view** *opposite***, the kiln and heaps of flints are visible through the courtyard.**

The many mills along the Kelvin account for much of the early history of the pre-suburban area west of Glasgow. The ancient village of Partick developed around a series of late medieval mills, and, upstream, from South Woodside to Garscube, there were at least a dozen more mill sites which dated as far back as the seventeenth century. The Kelvin mill sites produced a wide variety of material (including meal, ground flint, timber and paper) over their long and varied careers. The earliest mill of any importance upstream from Partick was called, at various times, Woodside, Mid-Woodside and eventually South Woodside. It is conceivable that the 'Woodsyd' depicted in Pont's survey of 1596 was this site on the Kelvin, located just below Hillhead ford.[29]

The lands at Woodside were acquired by the powerful Campbells of Blythswood early in the eighteenth century, and, around 1784, the mill site was tenanted by William Gillespie of Anderston. Gillespie was one of the greatest figures in the history of Glasgow's cotton industry. A great friend of David Dale, Gillespie began his operations at Woodside soon after New Lanark was established. Gillespie echoed Dale in his efforts to give 'starving Highlanders' decent wages and adequate housing. Like his friend at New Lanark, Gillespie was noted for his benevolence towards his employees. At 'his village of Woodside, then far from kirk and market, Gillespie established a school and a mission church for his tenants and cotton workers.'[30]

William Gillespie's Woodside site was Glasgow's first and only water-powered cotton spinning mill. Gillespie prospered during the last quarter of the eighteenth century, purchasing in 1784 the then barley mill at North Woodside and later acquiring the nearby house and policies of the same name. By the early nineteenth century, however, steam power became the standard for Glasgow's many cotton mills. Eventually, the Gillespie family firm ceased operations at Woodside, preferring instead to let the site to tenants. (In the second half of the nineteenth century, the South Woodside site became a paper mill.)

Just upstream from Woodside, and around the Holme haugh, was North Woodside mill. The origins of this long-time mill site are unknown, but it was described in 1758 as 'all well inclosed [*sic*], with stone dykes and hedges; upon which lands there is a very convenient dwellinghouse and proper office houses, pleasantly situated upon the waters of the Kelvin; and there is also upon the said lands a considerable number of trees of different kinds regularly planted.'[31] According to one source, gunpowder was ground at North Woodside during the Napoleonic Wars.[32]

The mill at North Woodside (and, just upstream, that at Garrioch) changed hands many times in the latter half of the eighteenth century. Around this time North Woodside was operated by a miller called David Jackson, after whom the weir on the Kelvin was named. The mill pond behind Jackson's Dam was a favourite swimming site for local youths. The pond was surrounded by tall trees, 'the green shadows from which on the water were often enlivened by groups of snow-white ducks from the miller's well-stocked poultry yard.'[33] In 1841, the North Woodside mill site was noted on the Decimus Burton feu plan of Northpark as being a 'Corn Mill, lately burnt.'[34]

15

Robert Cochran, owner of the Verreville Pottery in Glasgow, obtained the North Woodside and nearby Garrioch mill sites around the middle of the nineteenth century. Cochran and his partners converted both ancient grain mills to grind flints which had been calcined (*i.e.* burnt) in the kiln at the North Woodside site. (Cochran's Verreville Pottery, incidentally, was the descendent firm of the famous Verreville Glass Works co-founded by Patrick Colquhoun in 1777.) The Verreville Pottery produced 'ironstone china [which] required a much larger proportion of ground calcined flint and Cornish stone than the old white earthenware "bodies."'[35] Verreville closed the site in 1917 but a Paisley firm bought it to produce paste from French and English flints. The Kelvin site was still operating in the late 1950s and was partly demolished shortly thereafter. The ruins were incorporated into the Kelvin Walkway in 1970, though the old kiln had to be dismantled.

Kelvinside Free Church, built 1862.

II.

The New Suburb

2

This classic Thomas Annan view shows the *c.*1825 Hillhead estate bridge surmounted by the high-level Great Western Road turnpike bridge (built 1838-1841) in front of Lansdowne Church. The white cottage alongside the bridges, belonging to South Woodside mills, was once coveted by the turnpike trustees for conversion to a tollhouse (by the addition of another storey). Also visible in this late 1860s view is the cast iron parapet of the extension built to carry the Loch Katrine water pipes. This 1850s extension is seen more clearly in a rare Annan view taken in 1878 (*below*). The chimney seen behind the bridge belonged to Robert Bruce's South Woodside Paper Mills.

The defining moment in the development of the suburban West End came on 19 August 1836 when the New Anniesland Turnpike Act received its royal assent. Prior to the opening of the new road (and its high-level bridge over the Kelvin), feuing had been slow in James Gibson's Hillhead (hindered by its great distance from the city and the poor communication links). Not only did the new turnpike encourage the development of Gibson's lands, but as soon as construction of the Great Western Road began, the neighbouring estates of Northpark and Kelvinside (and, later, Dowanhill) were laid out for feuing as well. Soon, the city's Botanic Gardens and lunatic asylum also relocated to sites along the new turnpike.

It appears that the private turnpike from St George's Road to Anniesland was conceived by James Gibson, no doubt assisted by his neighbour (and future father-in-law), land surveyor David Smith of Westbank. During the summer of 1835, Smith plotted the line of the proposed turnpike and branch roads (to the Forth and Clyde Canal and to Partick). Meanwhile, Gibson personally solicited the views of more than 50 owners and 130 occupiers of land and buildings along the routes (recording only a handful of dissenting or neutral opinions).[1] In February 1836, a 'Petition of Owners of estates, lands, [and] tenements' accompanied the turnpike Bill in the House of Commons. Sir James Oswald of Scotstoun, MP for Glasgow, steered the legislation through Parliament, and authorisation was received on the final day of the Session in August.

In May of 1838, the first meeting was held of the trustees of the so-called 'New Anniesland turnpike,' with James Gibson becoming convener of the construction committee. The financing of the ambitious project, however, was troublesome from the start. David Smith's original 1835 estimate of £5,000 had increased to £9,000 by 1838 (by which time the cost of a stone bridge alone was estimated at £5,560).[2] Credit of £10,000 was obtained from the directors of the ill-fated Western Bank, who, like the turnpike's proponents, 'had little doubt from the local situation of the Road that the Tolls will ere long yield an ample return.'[3]

Construction problems delayed progress on the turnpike, as did the numerous debates over abortive cost-saving proposals (*e.g.* narrowing the roadbed to forty feet, crossing the Kelvin with a bridge of timber rather than stone etc.). One major amendment to the original plans — made early on in the project — was the deletion of the proposed branch road to the canal. This branch would have been extended due north from Horslethill and over a tall stone bridge on the Kelvin near Bellshaugh. Later, further savings were gained by downgrading the Partick branch to the mere widening and straightening of the ancient parish road leading to the Byres of Partick. Other amendments required the acquisition of additional land, and further compensation had to be paid to owners of condemned buildings (including £90 to Kelvinside estate for a barn demolished at North Balgray). Other extra costs were incurred when James Gibson lobbied his colleagues insofar as 'certain parts of the ground through which the Road is to pass are at present under Crop and . . . the tenants must be compensated.'[4] By the time the bridge and turnpike were fully opened in 1841, the project was two years late and well over budget.

Minutes of the Turnpike Trust recorded that progress was slow for a number of

4

reasons, as the 'undertaking has been an arduous one, and [the trustees] have had difficulties to encounter, and have met with much vexatious opposition.'[5] To avoid objections from the millers at South Woodside, the original line of the road was changed from a wide sweep north of their weir across the Kelvin to a direct route that ran to the south of the weir instead. Smith's original levels also required severe revision, notably two additional cuttings, one at Northpark and another to the west of the Botanic Gardens. The spoil from these cuttings provided material to heighten the embankments at Horslethill and South Balgray, as well as for widening the 'Great Bank' west of the Kelvin bridge. Additional spoil came from Hillhead, and was carried along the route of the roadway by wagons on rails.[6]

Further delays to the project arose from frequent minor disagreements over the exact line of the roads. The most significant dispute was with the new owner of Kelvinside, Matthew Montgomerie, who refused to comply with the original perpendicular intersection of the turnpike and the Partick branch (which cut off the north-easterly corner of his lands at Horslethill). After months of squabbling, the trustees agreed to amend the original route and curve the top end of the Partick branch to follow the line of Northpark's tree-lined southerly approach. In the eyes of the trustees, however, the contractors were mostly to blame for the slow progress. Mason James Stewart in particular was frequently criticised for 'the slow and dilatory manner in which his operations have been carried on.'[7]

Throughout 1840, the trustees endeavoured to get the turnpike open so that they could begin collecting tolls and thus pay a return to the Western Bank. A small section of the turnpike near the new Botanic Gardens had opened early in the year to facilitate the relocation of their collection from Sandyford, but the rest of the road did not open to the public until the autumn of 1840. By December, much to the 'astonishment of the trustees,' the new tollhouse on the Great Western Bridge was still awaiting completion, which they thought an 'unpardonable delay.'[8]

The Great Western Road's Gothic tollhouse had to be constructed on the western end of the Kelvin bridge due to the intransigence of the Blythswood estate and other proprietors east of the river. The tolls collected barely covered the turnpike trust's accumulating debts as it struggled on for more than forty years until private turnpikes were abolished some five years after the passing of the 1878 Roads and Bridges (Scotland) Act. This 1873 view shows the new tramlines and the recently completed Rosebery Terrace alongside Lansdowne Church.

5

John J. Blackie (1805-1873) and his father founded the Glasgow publishing firm of Blackie & Son in 1831. John Blackie junior was one of many members of this large family to reside in the West End (his father and brother lived, at various times in Kew, Belhaven and Great Western Terraces). His nephew, Walter Blackie, who once resided in Hillhead, later moved to Helensburgh where he commissioned Charles Rennie Mackintosh to design The Hill House.

espite the regimental nature of David Smith's feu plan of Hillhead, early development of the estate was haphazard at best. Although Smith's grid of small plots was established in the early 1820s, numerous large parcels of land were disposed of in all four corners of the estate after this date. To the north of the Gibsons' old Hillhead house on the crown of the hill stood Northpark, belonging to the Hamilton family. Just to the east of Northpark was the Holme farm, or Kelvinholme, long leased for bleaching and printfields (now the site of Glasgow Academy). To the south-east near King's Bridge was Westbank, belonging to David Smith, and in the south-west of Hillhead were the large villas of Sauchfield and Lilybank, both set in spacious ornamental grounds.

The mansion houses of Sauchfield and Lilybank were probably built in the early 1830s. By 1835, Sauchfield was a country estate of some distinction:

> The House consists of Dining and Drawing Rooms, Parlour, five Bed Rooms, two light Dressing Closets, Store Closets, and numerous other Closets, Cellars etc. There is also a large Garret Room, which could be subdivided into Bed Rooms. The Kitchen contains Milk Room and other conveniences. The Office consists of a three-stalled Stable, Hay-loft, Gig and Cart-house etc.[9]

Sauchfield became the home of prominent Glasgow lawyer John Kerr, who, with his son, the celebrated London judge Robert Malcolm Kerr, eventually bought up much of the remaining lands and feu superiorities of James Gibson. Before being demolished around 1883 (to make way for University Gardens), Sauchfield was for a time the home of James Napier of the Govan shipbuilding dynasty.

Due north of Sauchfield was Lilybank, where feus were taken by Glasgow merchant Robert Allen as early as 1828. Within a few years, Allen amassed extensive grounds and built a small Georgian villa located at the end of a long drive from Hillhead Street. Despite being the most westerly house in Hillhead at the time, Lilybank was easily reached via Gibson Street from King's Bridge. The grounds of Lilybank, which extended westward almost to Byres Road, were planted with ornamental trees and boasted a large walled garden and greenhouses.

John Blackie junior, co-founder of the Blackie publishing empire, first leased Lilybank House in 1857, the same year in which he joined the town council. By 1862, Blackie had become senior bailie and in the next year he was elected Provost of Glasgow. As provost, John Blackie was one of the driving forces behind the City Improvement Trust, a unique civic organisation authorised by Parliament to redevelop the slums around the old High Street and Saltmarket. Model houses for the poor and working class were later constructed in what was one of the earliest examples of urban renewal in Europe. During his term of office, Provost

Architect Alexander 'Greek' Thomson was commissioned to enlarge Lilybank in the mid-1860s. This picture postcard view was taken *c.*1905, when many Thomson details were still evident, most notably the fireplace (which is similar to an example in the architect's Holmwood villa in Cathcart). At the far right of the picture a reflection of the photographer's camera can be seen in front of the window. As Queen Margaret Hall, the house served as a residence for female students for over forty years.

6

7

Blackie entertained Gladstone as well as Queen Victoria's second son, the Duke of Edinburgh, at Lilybank. More notoriously, Blackie is remembered for ordering the execution of the infamous poisoner Dr Edward Pritchard (the last person to be publicly executed in the city). Although the City Improvement Trust went on to reshape the old town of Glasgow over the next few decades, Blackie soon lost his seat in the town council due to public unrest over the increase in rates assessments required to pay for the improvement programme.[10]

After Blackie purchased Lilybank in 1864, he commissioned Alexander 'Greek' Thomson (in one of the architect's many projects for the Blackie family) to enlarge the house by adding a wing at the southern end. Thomson relocated the villa's old central entrance to a new Ionic portico leading to the additional public rooms. The Blackies' new drawing room featured a wall of glazing facing the view to the west, with additional light brought into the room by a mirrored wall opposite.

John Blackie junior was an elder of the Free Church of Scotland, a member of its General Assembly, and an underwriter of the Free Church College on Woodlands Hill (later known as Trinity College). The first permanent church to be built in the new western suburbs (in 1862) was Kelvinside Free Church, opposite the Botanic Gardens. It was promoted in the late 1850s by several members of the large Blackie clan in the West End, including the provost's brother Robert and their father John senior.

John Blackie died of complications of pleurisy in 1873, aged 67, 'an event which will awaken a feeling of sorrow . . . amongst all to whom he was known either privately or publicly.'[11] Within a year of Blackie's death, the lands of Lilybank were laid out for feuing. By 1876, Lilybank Terrace had been built alongside the old villa, and in five years' time construction of Lilybank Gardens was well underway. This street was meant to link through to the new Sauchfield (later University) Gardens then being built on the adjacent estate, but the road was never opened. By the early 1890s, the terraces of Bute Gardens and tenements of Bute Mansions filled up the lands of Lilybank at the top of the hill. In 1894, Lilybank House became a residence for the women students of the new Queen Margaret College, the old mansion having been altered by the architects Honeyman and Keppie.

In this detail from a 1905 Annan photograph looking north-west from the university tower, Lilybank House can be seen hemmed in by University Gardens to the south (lower left), Bute Gardens to the east, and Lilybank Terrace and Gardens to the north and west. The low roof of the Alexander Thomson extension lies to the south of the original villa. The large slate roof above Lilybank House belongs to James Miller's Belmont Church (1894) in Great George Street.

This panoramic view from the early 1860s looks across the site of Princes Terrace and Prince Albert Road to 'Dowanhill Gardens,' the villa development between Sydenham Road (left) and Victoria Circus (right). The massive double villa at the far right, Dowanside House, later became the Convent of Notre Dame. Developer Thomas Lucas Paterson stayed at Newhall, the Gothic cottage second from the left, built *c.*1858. The cast-iron house, Richmond, is pictured just east of Sydenham Road, on the hill behind the two double villas in Prince Albert Road.

The estate of Dowanhill was cobbled together from several plots of land by James Buchanan (1753-1844), a wealthy Glasgow merchant. The lands were between the two old parish roads which led north from Partick (one to Kirklee via the Byres of Partick, the other — the so-called Crossloan — leading to the Forth and Clyde Canal). Buchanan acquired land from Robert Bogle of Gilmorehill, young James Gibson of Hillhead and others from 1812 to 1818.[12] These lands formed a wedge-shaped estate stretching north-west from the Yoker turnpike at Partick Cross to the southern marches of South Balgray and Horslethill farms. Dowanhill also bordered the lands of Hyndland farm.

James Buchanan built his Dowanhill mansion house on the lower slope of the hill (near today's Lawrence Street). It was one of a series of country houses fronting the Yoker turnpike which were built in the early nineteenth century by prosperous Glasgow and Partick merchants. Buchanan was a substantial backer of the Great Western Road turnpike trust, despite the fact that he was an octogenarian by the time the project was underway. Despite his advanced years, he maintained an active interest in the upgrading of the old parish road which had become the turnpike's branch to Partick. He haggled over compensation for land taken off his Dowanhill estate to permit the widening of the branch (now Byres Road), and at one point the 85-year-old complained to his fellow trustees 'of his being charged with toll on the Partick Branch for Carts going from one part of his Lands to another.' The road committee decided to placate Buchanan and ordered that the 'chain presently across the Partick Branch should be removed to the north of Mr Buchanan's back gate and to a position somewhere between it and the Road to Hillhead [now University Place].'[13]

Nearly ten years after James Buchanan's death in 1844, the lands of Dowanhill were acquired by the enterprising cotton merchant and land speculator, Thomas Lucas Paterson. It was Paterson's Dowanhill Estate Company which, over several decades, developed these lands in an interesting variety of villas, terraced houses,

and tenements. Paterson was not always in full charge of the company, for he had occasional battles with insolvency over the next twenty years, and it was eventually left to others to complete his development plans.[14]

From the mid-1850s, Paterson and his successors built the greatest variety of new houses to be seen on a single West End estate. There were working class tenements near Partick and handsome self-contained terraced houses in the centre of the estate along Victoria Crescent Road. At the far end of the spectrum, the grandest properties were the terraced houses in and around Crown Circus and the large villas built in Dowanhill Gardens, at the far north-west part of the estate. The first terraces to be feued by Paterson were Victoria Terrace in 1856 and Crown Circus the following year. The earliest villas were in Victoria Circus.

Most of the villas in Dowanhill Gardens, located between Sydenham Road and Victoria Circus, were designed by architects Boucher & Cousland. They were conceived in a variety of styles, including Italianate, Gothic and various permutations of the classical. Many of these houses are represented in the architects' pattern book, a portfolio of paintings which is now preserved in the National Monument Record of Scotland. Perhaps the most noteworthy Boucher villa was Richmond, surrounded by greenhouses and formal gardens and built c.1855 on a double feu on the corner of Sydenham and Richmond (now Linfern) Roads.

According to Frank Worsdall, who documented the house's demise in the mid-1960s, Richmond was clad with cast iron and had a Daniel Cottier window in the grand staircase.[15] Boucher, favourite architect of ironmaster Walter Macfarlane and his partners in the Saracen Foundry, often incorporated cast iron into his designs (for both structural and decorative purposes). Not only did Boucher design the new Saracen works at Possilpark, but he was also architect for the original interior of Macfarlane's sumptuous house at 22 Park Circus. Not to be outdone, Macfarlane's partner James Marshall commissioned Boucher to design the palazzo he called Carlston (now 998 Great Western Road).

Due to slumps in the housing market, some houses in Dowanhill were empty for long periods before being let or sold. Some had to be extensively modified in order to suit changing market demands (including the villas at either end of Prince Albert Road which both had their roofs raised and a mansard storey added). At the upper right is the Glasgow Observatory, built c.1842 on lands feued jointly from Kelvinside and Dowanhill.

In 1869, Jefferson Davis, former President of the Confederate States of America, was photographed at Benvue in Dowanhill whilst visiting his friend and supporter James Smith. This garden bench was rediscovered in the grounds of Benvue in the 1960s. It was subsequently refurbished and given a place of honour in the front garden (where it remained until it was stolen some years later). The house at the right is Ravensleigh.

Ravensleigh (*opposite*), at the corner of Sydenham and Kensington Roads, was built *c.*1866 by Richard Greenshields Ross, a manufacturer of steam hammers in Cumberland Street, Glasgow. The house had many design features typical of architect James Boucher, such as cast iron cresting, paired round-arched windows and sizeable greenhouses and conservatories. Due to development pressure during the postwar period, Ravensleigh and its large garden were cleared to make way for a large block of flats.

One of the wealthy merchants who came to live in the new suburb of Dowanhill Gardens was James Smith of Benvue.[16] Smith's early life is typical of the fabled enterprising Scot. He was a trained tinsmith who left Scotland from Greenock in 1832 at the age of 16, landing in New York and eventually ending up in Jackson, Mississippi where he established himself in business. His wife's declining health, however, forced the family to return to Scotland where Smith established the famed cooker firm of Smith & Wellstood.

James Smith frequently travelled across the Atlantic, remarkably surviving two shipwrecks. On the second ill-fated voyage, in 1854, the steamer *Arctic* sank in a collision off Newfoundland. Smith was one of only 40 survivors (there were 400 people on board), braving the north Atlantic for three days and two nights whilst squatting in a tin-lined wicker basket! When Smith settled in Glasgow he built a large villa at the corner of Sydenham and Kensington Roads. Called Benvue, it was designed by Boucher & Cousland in 1859.[17]

During the American Civil War, Smith, like many Glasgow merchants with strong ties to the southern states, ardently supported the Confederate cause. One friend sent Smith what was believed to be the first Confederate flag in Scotland, which he proudly 'floated to the Breeze' on the Clyde in 1861. Smith supported the rebels financially, and supposedly also contributed a battery of artillery. Tragedy struck, however, when his younger brother Robert, a colonel in the Mississippi Rifles, died defending a railway bridge in Kentucky. Smith's support for the rebel cause brought him in close contact with Jefferson Davis, the Confederate States' first and only president. Davis was imprisoned after the end of the war, and upon his release travelled to England for health purposes. In 1869, Davis visited Scotland where he was publicly fêted by the Smith family at Benvue. The Smith and Davis families were to keep in close contact until James Smith's death in 1886.

In the centre of this picture postcard view of *c.*1905 stands Victoria Terrace, the first terrace to be built in Dowanhill (in the late 1850s). The second generation of Dowanhill terraces, built in Victoria Crescent Road (*c.*1865-1874) is located to the right, and the last phase of terraces in the area, King's Gate by architects Hugh & David Barclay, is visible under construction at the left.

10

11

Kildowan (*left*) was one of many Gothic houses to be built in Dowanhill, and stood on one of the earliest villa sites to be feued (at the south end of Victoria Circus near Prince Albert Road). Before its demolition in 1973, the house was used for a variety of purposes, including that of a nursery school. The gap site that was left after its removal was used by Notre Dame school for twenty years before being redeveloped for flats in the early 1990s.

12

13

James Brown Montgomerie Fleming (1840-
1899), was the son and nephew of the two
founding partners of the Kelvinside Estate
Company. His mother, Elisabeth Tennent,
was the daughter of the founder of the
Wellpark Brewery. James inherited the
prestigious family law firm of Montgomerie
& Fleming, as well as the estate company.
According to *The Bailie*, 'He has had capital
chances in life from his "fore-bears," but he
has turned these chances into the very best
advantage.'[23]

Following the death of Dr Thomas Lithan in 1807, his widow Elizabeth Mowbray inherited the extensive lands of Kelvinside. Her second husband, Archibald Cuthill, was a Glasgow lawyer who dabbled in property speculation. It is not known when the Lithan-Cuthills resided at Kelvinside House or whether it was let out during the 1810s and 1820s. By 1830, however, after the death of Archibald Lithan-Cuthill, the estate of Kelvinside was being managed by the Leith law firm belonging to Elizabeth Mowbray's brothers.

In July 1830, the Mowbrays tried to sell various parts of the estate, including the mansion house of Kelvinside, Horslethill farm, and the lands of Kirklee and North Woodside. Kelvinside House was described in the *Glasgow Herald* as being

> beautifully situated on the wooded bank of the Kelvin . . . in good condition, and fit to accommodate a genteel family, with an abundance of Offices, and a large and productive Garden. . . . The beauty of this situation is not surpassed in this part of the country; it is now very retired, and as the west end of Glasgow is extending rapidly in that direction, it will soon be in contact with the principal streets at the west end of town, and in consequence become much more valuable.[18]

The lands of Kelvinside went unsold at this time, and thus they were leased through the 1830s. The Glasgow law firm acting as agents for the Mowbrays were Messrs Montgomerie & Fleming of Miller Street.

When James Gibson of Hillhead began his petition for the construction of a turnpike from St George's Road to Anniesland, the Mowbrays were the main financial backers, pledging £1,000 (about a quarter of the total sum obliged by local landowners and speculators in 1835). The Mowbrays never made good on their promise, however, having sold the 462-acre estate to Montgomerie & Fleming's Kelvinside Estate Company in the spring of 1839, leaving the new owners to meet their substantial commitment to the project.

The records of the Kelvinside Estate Company still survive and have been the subject of several recent studies.[19] The Kelvinside story is one of marginal successes and occasional failures over the course of several generations. At the outset, the partnership of Matthew Montgomerie and John Park Fleming included a third partner, James Beaumont Neilson, the wealthy industrialist. Neilson, inventor of the revolutionary hot-blast smelting process, was married to Montgomerie's sister. The partners and their backers had great plans for their picturesque lands, having commissioned the famed London architect Decimus Burton to lay out most of the estate with large detached villas set in a landscape of winding crescents, as well as a number of terraces fronting the new Great Western Road turnpike.

Development in Kelvinside began in the early 1840s, just as the new turnpike was nearing completion. One of the early feu contracts was for some 21 acres given off to the Royal Botanical Institute of Glasgow whose members desired to leave their old premises in Sandyford. The Glasgow Observatory also relocated to a new site in Horslethill in 1842. A few years later, the Kelvinside Estate Company purchased land from the owners of the Gartnavel estate, bringing the assets of Kelvinside to some 576 acres, extending from Garscube Road in the north-east to Anniesland in the west, and spanning both sides of the new turnpike.

Residential development in Kelvinside was slow during the 1840s. The first residential feu was given off early in the decade to Glasgow lawyer (and old school chum of John Park Fleming's) Robert Sword. His house, Marley Bank, was the only villa to be constructed in the lands of Horslethill in accordance with Burton's original feu plan. Around 1847, the estate company began work on its only speculative housing venture, Windsor (now Kirklee) Terrace. For their flagship project, Montgomerie & Fleming commissioned architect Charles Wilson to design a palatial row of houses high on the drumlin adjoining the new Botanic Gardens. Only six houses were built at first, however, and the terrace was not completed for another fifteen years. After this scheme, the estate company abandoned building houses themselves, preferring to feu land for speculative development by others.

A decade after feuing began, the Kelvinside partners were struggling to attract interest from Glasgow speculators, and in 1850 they advertised to feu or sell

[the] farms of Horslethill, Kirklee, North and South Balgray, and Gartnavel. The whole of this Ground is situated at the West end of the City, in the direction rapidly taking up for genteel residences. The surface is varied, mostly elevated, commanding fine views, and securing good air. From the great extent of the Property, and the regulations in the Feu-rights, entire freedom from nuisances is secured; the Public may build with confidence that full omnibus accommodation will be provided so as to render a residence on These Grounds every way suitable. On the Farms of North Balgray and Gartnavel there are beautiful situations for Villas, and there the Ground will be Feued at very moderate prices.[20]

Soon after this advertisement appeared in the *Herald*, Glasgow builder John Christie feued land for the erection of Kew Terrace.

Christie constructed the twenty houses of Kew Terrace throughout the 1850s and early 1860s (during which time he also operated a stone quarry at South Balgray in Hyndland Road). Around the same time, and adjacent to Kew Terrace, there was under construction (according to an 1855 account)

the largest and most magnificent speculation in the way of dwelling houses which the city or suburbs presents at present. This fine range is to be styled Grosvenor Terrace. . . . The interiors promise to be as rich as the exterior; a glimpse we had of the finished plasterwork of one apartment sufficed to shew that no outlay has been spared in the way of ornament. And there will be no lack of light to show the elaborate ornamentation of the interiors, for the dining-rooms have three windows all the width of the apartment.[21]

There were other speculative developments of the early 1850s undertaken along the Great Western Road in Hillhead and Northpark, and terraces and villas also appeared in Dowanhill at this time. Still, the Kelvinside Estate Company was not yet reaping the benefits of its great investment. In 1858, James Salmon senior — in competition with John T. Rochead and Charles Wilson[22] — produced a rationalised feu plan for Kelvinside, but there was little new feuing in the area during the 1860s, other than the start of the Belhaven terraces. Matthew Montgomerie of the Kelvinside Estate Company died in 1868 at the age of 85, and his partner of some fifty years, John Park Fleming, died the following year at 80. In nearly four decades of promotion of Kelvinside, Messrs Montgomerie & Fleming had managed to dispose of only sixty-eight feus.

The first major building project by the Kelvinside Estate Company was the construction of architect Charles Wilson's palatial Windsor (later Kirklee) Terrace. The six houses closest to the Botanic Gardens were built in the late 1840s (Nos. 2 and 5 were the homes of partners James Beaumont Neilson and John Park Fleming respectively). This view was taken from Horslethill, looking across the Great Western Road and the field where Belhaven Terrace would be built in the late 1860s.

A view east from Redlands House *c.*1877 overlooking the Great Western Road at its junction with Kirklee and Horslethill Roads. In the centre is the great embankment which was built to carry the turnpike over a hollow between the drumlins. The newly finished houses to the right of the crossroads are Belhaven Terrace (fronting the turnpike) and Rosslyn Terrace (still under construction behind). At the left, behind Windsor (now Kirklee) Terrace are the early mews houses and a spoil heap of cut stone spilt down the bank. At the right, in the low-lying lands where Belhaven Terrace West was subsequently constructed, there was once a stone quarry (which may account for the sheds seen at the corner of the site).

The dominant figure in the late Victorian development of the West End was James Brown Montgomerie Fleming. A larger-than-life character, Fleming was a successful lawyer, in addition to holding posts of town councillor, Deputy River Bailie, Justice of the Peace and chairman of the County Road Trustees. He was an ardent Tory, as well as being an active campaigner for the expansion of Glasgow's boundaries. Fleming corresponded frequently on this topic, among many others, in the Glasgow papers, where his strong opinions were laced with wit, sarcasm and 'a keen sense of humour.'[24]

When he assumed control of Kelvinside from his uncle and father, Fleming was a mere 28 years old. Fortuitously, when he inherited the estate, Glasgow was on the verge of one of its greatest building booms. Capitalising on the demand for high-quality building land, James B. Fleming was able to continue the work of his late father in selling large parcels of attractive land to developers. The lands hived off by Fleming included parts of the old farms of Horslethill, South Balgray and Kirklee, as well as the area around the old Kelvinside House. By the time a third revised feu plan of Kelvinside was published in 1873, the estate company had sold off nearly all its holdings east of Crossloan (now Cleveden) Road. At this time, the focus of the company's attention was the south side of Balgray Hill, and the remaining lands west of Hyndland Road.

After Fleming's first ten years in control, the Kelvinside estate had been reduced in size by a third, palatial villas and stately terraces lined Great Western Road, and a handsome crescent by John Burnet was under construction on Balgray Hill. Kelvinside was soon attracting some of Glasgow's wealthiest and most influential families, who built some of the grandest suburban houses of the day. In addition to the many ironfounders, shipping magnates and textile manufacturers, there were merchants and businessmen of all descriptions as well as a large number of lawyers, doctors and other professionals.

Shortly before his death in 1868, John Park Fleming began to sell off Kelvinside land for others to develop (a pattern successfully continued by his son, James B. Fleming). The earliest parcel to be sold off consisted of the lands of South Balgray farm which were developed into the area in and around Westbourne Gardens. Developer James Whitelaw Anderson commissioned Alexander 'Greek' Thomson to build at least two terraces, the famed Great Western, and nearby Westbourne in Hyndland Road (*left*). Thomson may also have been associated with a third terrace, in Westbourne Gardens (*centre*), completed after his death in 1875. The house at the end of this terrace was destroyed during the Clydeside blitz in March 1941.

From the 1870s, ranks of terraces along the Great Western Road in Kelvinside were being built in earnest (*below*). Occasionally, villas were also seen fronting the boulevard, such as the massive Windsor House (to the left) standing opposite the Belhaven terraces.

The rapid disposal of large parcels of prime land no doubt brought in much needed cash to James B. Fleming's Kelvinside Estate Company. In the early 1870s, the company began to lay out new streets north of the Great Western Road and undertook a series of major improvements to the existing parish roads. Crossloan (now Cleveden) and Kirklee Roads were widened and straightened, and gradients were improved to facilitate access onto Balgray Hill where the bulk of the best Kelvinside land remained.

During the second half of the nineteenth century, Balgray Hill was often referred to as Collins' Hill due to the fact that three members of the prosperous Collins family lived nearby in the vicinity of their Kelvindale Paper Company. Joshua Heywood Collins, grandson of the firm's founder, resided in a stately pile called Kelvindale House, located near the riverside works. Joshua's brother, Edward, stayed in West Balgray House, located in wooded grounds on the crown of the hill (later the site of Cleveden Secondary School). Joshua's son (also Edward) lived for many years at the nearby Highfield House, built next to the old Balgray farmhouse at the corner of Crossloan and Kelvindale Roads.

Crossloan Road, leading up from the Great Western Road turnpike, was re-levelled and realigned as it reached the crown of Balgray Hill. By the late 1870s, large villas began to appear on the hill. In 1872, the Kelvinside Estate Company sold a large rectangle of land north of the turnpike and west of Crossloan Road to leading Glasgow merchant, Thomas Russell. Russell was a business partner (and brother-in-law) of ironmaster Walter Macfarlane of the famed Saracen Foundry. Russell, a Justice of the Peace and two-time Liberal MP, was active in education in Glasgow, sitting on the city School Board and also helping to found two seats of medicine at the University of Glasgow.

Russell's parcel consisted of plots for around twenty large detached villas in a development formally (albeit temporarily) called 'Kelvinside Gardens.' The first site to be feued was given off to Glasgow Bailie James Morrison, who built Ashcraig (now Balmanno House) at the corner of Great Western and Crossloan Roads. Immediately behind Ashcraig loomed Russell's own house, Cleveden, built on the next corner up the hill. Russell's palatial villa, famous for the carved 'Ruskinian'

An 1883 Annan view looking down Crossloan Road to the Great Western Road and the Kelvinside tram terminus. Above the corner of the Redlands estate are (left to right) Great Western Terrace, Lancaster Terrace and Westbourne House. At the far right, in Hyndland Road, Montague Terrace is visible under construction (being built on the farm-steading of South Balgray). The terrace was never completed, probably because of problems with the old stone quarry on the site. The temporary Hyndland tin church is visible in the distance.

20

William Leslie's *c*.1877 Balgray villa at the corner of Crossloan Road and Montgomerie Drive (now Cleveden Road and Drive) was requisitioned during the last war and abandoned shortly thereafter. After falling into disrepair, it was demolished and replaced by a tall flatted block in the 1970s. The open land to the right, leading down Montgomerie Drive to the new Kelvinside Academy, belonged to James B. Mirrlees of Redlands. This view was taken from the front porch of Cleveden by T. & R. Annan in April 1883.

heads in the gable elevation[25], was built on a double feu along Montgomerie (now Cleveden) Drive. On the next corner up the hill was another early villa, called Montgomerie House, later owned by industrial giant William Beardmore junior.

As Kelvinside expanded slowly westward, there was a gradual extension of the horse-tram lines to Horslethill Road, and, eventually, to Crossloan Road by 1880. By this time, several feus had been developed in Kelvinside Gardens. By far the most impressive house to be built in this development was Carlston (now 998 Great Western Road), designed by James Boucher for James Marshall, another partner in the Saracen Foundry. Carlston occupied a double feu, flanked by a large Saracen conservatory and pedimented carriagehouses.

An 1894 view up Crossloan (now Cleveden) Road, framed by two massive villas. To the left is Thomas Russell's Cleveden, with Arnewood, built for William Neilson of the Summerlee Iron Company, to the right. Up the hill behind Balgray stands Craigmont, built *c*.1882 for ironmaster Gibson C. Smith of the Sun Foundry. This striking house has Flemish gables, an Italianate tower and elaborate interiors with decorative glass attributed to Stephen Adam.

21

22

Mrs J. B. Fleming and her son, James Brown Montgomerie Fleming junior, heirs to the Kelvinside Estate Company. Young Master Fleming lost his father at 14 years of age, then fatally shot a burglar in the family seat of Kelvinside House (*below*) at 23. He lost his own life during the First World War.

When human tragedies occur in the more salubrious districts of a city like Glasgow, they become stories of great public interest. The West End has witnessed many human dramas over the past two centuries, and among the most noteworthy were the fatal collapse of a tenement in Belmont Crescent in 1870 and the 'Kelvinside Tragedy' of 1908.

The crown prince of Kelvinside, Master James Brown Montgomerie Fleming junior (born *c.*1885), was the only son of the flamboyant owner of the Kelvinside Estate Company, James B. Fleming. From 1875, the Flemings lived in Beaconsfield House on Balgray Hill (the mansion was subsequently renamed Kelvinside House). Twenty years later, Fleming senior greatly enlarged the house to the designs of architect James Thomson, making it 'one of the largest and best-known mansions in the fashionable West-End.'[26] After his father died in 1899, Fleming junior carried on the family tradition by studying law, intending to join the firm of Messrs Montgomerie & Fleming. In March of 1908, however, the 23-year-old student was involved in what the newspapers called 'one of the most sensational and dramatic incidents in the criminal history of Glasgow.'[27]

Late one night, whilst up alone preparing for his law exams, young Fleming heard an intruder downstairs in Kelvinside House. After phoning Maryhill police station, he armed himself with a revolver and surprised the lone burglar in the morning room. Fleming challenged the intruder, who then took out a pistol and fired two shots at him, one of which narrowly missed his head. The student quickly returned three shots, one of which fatally wounded the man in the heart. The unfortunate burglar, an unemployed mason named John Macleod, was known to the first police officer arriving from Maryhill, Detective Joseph Trench (later of the infamous Oscar Slater case). According to Trench, Macleod was 'an ex-convict and experienced housebreaker.'[28] The distraught young Fleming fully cooperated with the police during their investigation and the affair quickly attracted great notoriety.

Ten days later, a Fatal Accidents Inquiry investigated the circumstances surrounding 'the tragic death of John Macleod.'[29] The judge, after hearing Fleming's 'thrilling narrative,' directed the jury to find that 'Mr Fleming was entirely justified in acting as he did in the defence of his own life.'[30] He also stated that Fleming should have been exonerated even if Macleod had not been armed, a remark which prompted a flurry of letters to the local papers.

23

During the 1860s, the City of Glasgow Bank began to develop its lands near the Kelvin bridge. By the end of the decade, work on Belmont Crescent was nearing completion. On 20 September, 1870, the north corner tenement block had reached the second storey, with planking laid across the floor joists to provide the builders access to continue. After their morning break, the builders 'had scarcely reached the scaffold when, without a moment's warning, the entire gable and a large portion of the side walls gave way, and fell in a confused heap with a terrible crash, shaking the ground and spreading consternation all over the neighbourhood.'[31] It took two hours to reach all the buried men in the contorted rubble. Altogether, five men were injured and six lives were lost.

The builders, D. & R. Law, were later indicted on charges of culpable homicide. Over fifty witnesses were called (most being workmen employed by the Laws). Many claimed that they knew that there were problems with the building, quite apart from the fact that it was being built on 'forced' or 'made' ground (*i.e.* landfill). The general consensus was that the quality of the mortar and stonework was questionable, due to the fact that the Laws had pushed the men so hard to complete their work. One mason said that David Law 'was such a tyrant on the workmen.' Law, however, was not experienced in building; he relied on advice from his father, David senior, a shipowner and retired builder. There was no supervising architect on site, just the Laws giving instructions. Architect George Bell (of Clarke & Bell) testified that he had merely provided the bank with a feu plan years before, and a report in the *Glasgow Herald* that John Honeyman had designed Belmont Crescent was swiftly and flatly refuted by the eminent architect.

The presiding judge, Lord Neaves, was not moved by the masons' testimony about being pressed by the Laws, stating that 'some of the men who went into the [witness] box looked very much as if they would be much the better of being told to get on.' The jury, after deliberating a mere fifty minutes, agreed with the nature of the judge's direction that they 'could not convict a man for error of judgment, or for inferior work, if it was not proved that there had been recklessness, neglect of duty, and culpability.' They unanimously found David Law senior not guilty, and the charge against his son not proven by a majority of nine to six. According to the papers, 'the announcement of the verdict was received with general applause, mingled with slight hissing from a portion of the audience in the gallery.'[32]

This corner pavilion at Belmont Crescent collapsed during construction in 1870 with the loss of six lives. It was reconstructed after the builders were cleared of charges of culpable homicide the following year. Photographed by the City Assessor's department in 1924, the building eventually succumbed to poor ground conditions and was demolished in the 1970s.

25

In the twenty years following the opening of the Great Western Road turnpike in 1841, the development of the lands west of the Kelvin was slow but steady. The population of Hillhead, for example, increased from 200 in 1841 to 2,244 by 1861. Despite being a growing — if random — collection of villas, cottages, terraces and middle-class tenements, Hillhead of the 1860s was recalled by one writer as being 'largely open country, with hedges, trees and green fields on either hand.'[33] However, the burgeoning suburban district suffered from the lack of any substantial infrastructure and was loosely governed by some fourteen county, parish and sundry other official bodies.

In 1869, a committee of Hillhead residents presented to the Sheriff of Lanarkshire a petition requesting that the district be established as an independent burgh under the 1862 Police Act, on account of 'the disadvantages of indifferently kept roads, inefficient drainage, and expensive tollbars [and the] want of Municipal Government.'[34] The original petition was to include Dowanhill and Kelvinside in the new burgh, but residents in these districts, led by the estate owners, persuaded the sheriff to limit the western boundary of Hillhead to Byres Road. The Burgh of Hillhead was formally established on 15 June 1869, and Robert Bruce, owner of the South Woodside Paper Mills by the Kelvin Bridge, and leader of the petition, was elected chief magistrate, or provost.

The records of the Burgh of Hillhead, which are preserved in the Glasgow City Archives, provide interesting insights into the workings of the new magistrates, or burgh commissioners. For the twenty-two years of the burgh's existence, the commissioners were mostly concerned with providing and maintaining an infrastructure of roads, lanes, pavements, gas street-lighting and sewers. Only the many battles to prevent annexation by Glasgow occupied the minds of the commissioners to the same degree.

Among their other important tasks, commissioners joined forces with the burghs of Partick and Maryhill to construct and operate a fever hospital in Knightswood. In the early years, the commissioners also had to arrange for the construction of a Burgh Hall. More mundane matters in the records include overgrown thorn hedges, excessive carpet-beating and the nuisance caused by 'cows trespassing on or otherwise obstructing the pavement.'[35] With the exception of occasional letters from disgruntled ratepayers, the burgh commissioners seemed to have satisfied most residents, providing adequate cleansing, policing and fire services whilst maintaining relatively low rates. They were hardly the buffoons depicted by James B. Fleming of Kelvinside and his friends in the Glasgow establishment who regularly ridiculed the city's satellite burghs as being amateurish and parochial, if not parasitical. In fact, Fleming used to refer to Hillhead and the other small burghs as the 'warts on Glasgow's nose.'[36]

The leader of the campaign to establish the suburb of Hillhead as an independent burgh was local papermaker Robert Bruce (*above*). Bruce later became the new burgh's first provost. In addition to the obligatory committee rooms and public chambers, Hillhead Burgh Hall also included facilities for Lanarkshire county police constables and the part-time fire brigade (the latter remaining long after Hillhead's annexation by Glasgow in 1891). In this 1914 view, the last Hillhead fire engine horses, Tweed and Kelvin, are introduced to their modern replacement.

26

27

During the twenty-two years of Hillhead Burgh's existence, there were at least a dozen different campaigns, petitions, movements, Bills, amendments or Acts proposing alterations to the boundaries of Hillhead and the other suburban burghs and districts around Glasgow. As early as 1870, Hillhead's first full year of existence, Glasgow attempted to expand its own boundaries by annexing all the neighbouring 'small imperfect police districts.'[37] In 1872, a Municipal Extension Bill succeeded, annexing the new university site at Gilmorehill and also that part of the West End Park on the Partick side of the Kelvin.

Over the next few years, as Glasgow battled on to annex the nine suburban burghs, there were skirmishes amongst the suburbs themselves. At one point, the burghs of Partick, Hillhead and Maryhill considered joining forces to form a 'super-burgh' of some 35,000 inhabitants. Also, Kelvinside once sought a merger with Partick, and Hillhead tried twice to annex Kelvinside and Downhill. In 1885, James B. Fleming supported a committee of Kelvinside and Hillhead residents campaigning for a Hillhead & Kelvinside Annexation Bill. The debate carried on for nearly two years in the City Chambers, the various burgh halls, in local newspapers, as well as in Parliament. In early 1887, however, the Lords' Select Committee finally killed the Bill, primarily because it could not justify the abolition of a local authority without that authority's consent.

The matter did not end there. A Boundaries Commission was established for the Glasgow region, and after months of testimony, it recommended that Glasgow should annex the three West End and six South Side burghs (Govan, Govanhill, Crosshill, Pollokshields, Pollokshields East and Kinning Park), as well as several suburban districts. In 1890, elections for new commissioners in Hillhead brought in a majority of annexationists who promptly overturned the position of the previous administration. Subsequently, Maryhill and two South Side burghs withdrew their opposition to the annexation Bill. Partick and Govan, however, continued to resist and in the end Glasgow refused to carry on without them. Shortly thereafter, the Lords threw out the Bill. In the next year, however, the revised City of Glasgow Act of 1891 was passed with relatively little difficulty, and the Burgh of Hillhead, as well as the districts of Kelvinside and Downhill, were incorporated into Glasgow.

Hillhead Burgh Hall was constructed in 1872 on an old quarry site near the top of Byres Road. It was designed by architects (and local residents) William Clarke and George Bell, who were also responsible for the Western Baths Club built a few years later on an adjacent site. Few expenses were spared on the new Burgh Hall. In the mid-1880s, for example, the premises were wired up with the latest convenience of the day, a so-called 'telephonic communication system.'[38] After the annexation of Hillhead, the building was used as a community hall for several generations before its demolition in 1970. The site is now occupied by Hillhead Library.

BURGH OF HILLHEAD.

NOTICE IS HEREBY GIVEN that the Commissioners of Police of the Burgh of Hillhead have resolved to alter the level of the Street known as Great Western Road from the western termination of the Bridge over the River Kelvin to a point at or near the east side of Otago Street.

That a Plan and Sections of the said Street showing the alteration proposed have been prepared, and will lie for inspection for seven days from this date within my Office at No. 54 West Nile Street, Glasgow.

That any person considering himself aggrieved by the proposed operations may appeal to the Sheriff in manner provided by the General Police and Improvement (Scotland) Act, 1862.

That, in the event of no appeal being presented within seven days from this date, the said operations will be proceeded with.

JAMES MUIRHEAD,
Clerk.

BURGH CHAMBERS,
HILLHEAD, 1st March, 1880.

28

The proposal to enlarge the boundaries of the city of Glasgow was a persistent source of controversy during the last two decades of the nineteenth century, and passionate views were held by both camps. Proponents of the suburban burgh zealously defended their independence from the sprawling city of Glasgow. Annexationists, on the other hand, believed that

> the suburban districts . . . are occupied almost exclusively by persons whose business is in Glasgow, but who are necessitated by the increase in population to reside beyond the municipal boundaries. Though thus resident, however, and in the enjoyment of all the advantages of citizenship, including water, gas, public parks, museums, galleries of art, etc., they are not subject to the taxation and obligations which those within the [city] boundaries . . . have to bear.[39]

Hillhead, with its high rateable values and relatively modest civic administration, could afford to keep its rates low. Glasgow, on the other hand, had a predominately working-class population and was required to provide facilities for a half a million inhabitants (as well as servicing a debt of £6m). Naturally, the Corporation coveted the high rateable values of an area like Hillhead.

Both Hillhead and the district of Kelvinside were policed by constables of the Lanarkshire county force (based in the Burgh Hall). Despite the fact that Hillhead had more officers per capita than Glasgow, several prominent annexationists played up public disquiet over potential mob violence in order to strengthen their arguments in favour of annexation. James B. Fleming told a Commons Select Committee that 'the houses in Hillhead and Kelvinside are of the very class that would be most readily attacked and would suffer most during a riot.'[40] His Kelvinside neighbour, Glasgow Bailie James Morrison of Ashcraig in Great Western Road, testified that he particularly feared the large population of miners who lived and worked out by Anniesland as they 'are subject to periods of excitement, and I have seen them passing my house in periods of wage agitation in a very excited state, and I have shrunk back from the window in fear lest they should be tempted to do violence to the house.'[41]

The sanitary condition of the burgh was also a concern for both sides. For example, Hillhead jointly operated a fever hospital in Knightswood, but critics like James B. Fleming remarked that it possessed 'a fever van, but no horse or man. The horse and the man are provided when wanted by . . . a cabman in Hillhead, and the man who has driven the fever van in the morning is perhaps employed to drive a Cab-full of children in the afternoon, a very serious source of danger.'[42] In 1878, Glasgow's eminent Medical Officer, Dr James B. Russell, investigated a serious typhoid epidemic around Woodside and Hillhead in which 153 cases led to 12 deaths. Russell testified that he believed that the source of the outbreak 'emanated from milk which was being distributed out of a dairy within the burgh.' Russell testified that in *his* jurisdiction, an inspection of all the houses and all the potential sources of infection would be warranted. The little burgh of Hillhead, however, did not have the necessary staff to cope with such a problem.[43]

The commissioners of Hillhead Burgh were intensely proud of their daily refuse collections, a vast improvement on the usual clearing of ashpits every fortnight. Still, the refuse had to be tipped somewhere, and for many years the Hillhead Cleansing Department used a coup literally in their own backyard — the old stone quarry and brick-clay pits near the Burgh Hall. According to James B. Fleming, however, 'the sanitary condition of the Burgh . . . never has been good. For years, the Commissioners allowed a "Tip" to exist in the heart of the Burgh for all sorts of filth and rubbish, including the offal from the fish shops.'[44] Provost Robert Bruce did not recall this site being a nuisance. Although Bruce acknowledged that it produced 'an abominable smell in summer time,' he was pleased to state that 'the moment the Commissioners got any complaint they attended to it.'[45]

Glasgow Corporation was slightly more conscientious, sending its rubbish to the outskirts of the city near South Woodside. One Hillhead resident, during his daily commute into Glasgow from Buckingham Terrace in the 1860s, recollected watching 'every abomination from the city' being tipped into the old Woodside quarry between Great Western Road and Woodlands Road. He recalled that 'vegetable matter [was dumped] in such a condition that the boys used actually to set fire to it, and, when the quarry was full, instead of being properly covered with soils, it was covered with horse dung and other refuse.'[46]

Annexationists also castigated Hillhead for the delay in improving the old Kelvin bridge. Due to the increase in traffic during the third quarter of the century, in particular the introduction of horse-drawn trams, the old stone bridge (even with its iron extension of 1858) had become dangerously constricted, with tramcars passing perilously close to the pedestrian pavement. For most of the life of the burgh, there had been constant wrangling between the city, the county and the commissioners over the apportioning of costs for a new bridge. At first Hillhead agreed to contribute one-third, only to renege later on.

A bigger bone of contention was the suburbanites' use of the city's facilities. Glasgow Corporation noted that its citizens were 'especially bitter' at the free use made of city parks, most of which were situated nearer the suburbs than the city.[47] Hillhead residents were accused of acting as if the West End Park was their park too. According to one Glasgow businessman, 'West End Park is used as a thoroughfare between business places in Glasgow and Hillhead. I have frequently used it myself in walking out in that direction. It is kept up at great expense; . . . and business gentlemen living in Hillhead going to business in the morning pass through a flower garden on their way to their businesses.'[48]

For many years the lands of Woodside just east of the Kelvin were used as an extensive quarry, providing cream sandstone for the city and its suburbs. In the second half of the nineteenth century, residential development crept westward toward the Kelvin and eventually the quarry was filled in — largely with Glasgow's refuse. This *c.*1867 view looking north from Park Quadrant, shows new tenements along Great Western Road, and a newly laid out Park Road to the left alongside the old workers' houses from William Gillespie's Woodside cotton mill. The empty space at Holyrood Crescent (upper right) had been filled by the Episcopal cathedral of St Mary by 1874 (pictured *below*, long before the spire was added in 1893).

Ancient Order of Foresters at Kelvingrove House Museum, 1873.

III.

Early Institutions

The Kibble Palace (*opposite*) opened as a public venue in June 1873, and was most famously the site of two great addresses by University Rectors Gladstone (*above*) and Disraeli. After John Kibble's lease was terminated, the palace was made into a winter garden.

Glasgow's Botanic Gardens at Kelvinside have their origins in the Physic Gardens and the Chair of Anatomy and Botany at the Old College in High Street. Following the founding of a botanical society in Glasgow by Mr Thomas Hopkirk of Dalbeath in 1816, a campaign was started to form a proper botanic garden in the city. Hopkirk 'secured the cooperation of numerous wealthy citizens, and from the University there was obtained a grant of £2000, under the conditions that the garden should always be available for the teaching purposes of the College.'[1] Within three years, the society had acquired 8 acres at the western end of the old Sauchiehall Road at Sandyford and established itself as the Royal Botanical Institution of Glasgow. The institution's first president was Islay Campbell of Succoth, Laird of Garscube. Under the direction of the university's eminent Professor William Hooker, the gardens flourished.

By the early 1830s, however, it had become apparent that the restricted site at Sandyford was inadequate. As the gardens prospered, the collections began to outgrow their existing premises. At the same time, the city's western extremities were beginning to encroach upon them. When the gardens were first established at Sandyford, the expanding city was still years away from reaching the summit of Blythswood Hill. By the 1830s, however, the lands of Woodside (between the Blythswood and Kelvingrove estates) were being laid out for feuing. 'As property in the neighbourhood of the Garden had been built upon,' states an 1832 entry in the institution's minutes, 'thereby greatly increasing the value of the Garden Ground it would be desirable as early as convenient to be on the look-out for a beneficial site for a new Garden . . . with sufficient ground to prepare it for receiving the extensive rich treasures of the present garden.'[2]

After five years of informal searching, the pressure mounted for a new site. A committee of the institution 'were requested to bear in view the new site for the Garden and to be on the out look [*sic*] for an eligible and advantageous one.'[3] Meanwhile, the institution took steps to dispose of the Sandyford site, but early advertisements failed to attract any interest. By the end of 1838, the situation was so desperate that the directors pleaded that a relocation was 'the absolute necessity.'[4]

Overtures were made to three of the leading landlords in the Glasgow area, namely James Davidson of Garrioch, the Mowbrays of Kelvinside and Sir John Maxwell of Pollok. The latter, the predominant landowner south of the Clyde, showed no interest, but Davidson and the Mowbrays responded to the institution's initial enquiries and offered various lands on either side of the Kelvin. Garrioch farm, on the north bank of the river, was considered to be best suited for the purpose, but on the other hand was thought to be too far along the Garscube turnpike to attract sufficient subscriptions and entrance fees from Glaswegians. The Mowbray brothers from Leith, who managed the Kelvinside estate on behalf of their sister, the widow Elizabeth Lithan-Cuthill, offered the institution nearly 22 acres of Horslethill farm (whose ancient lands had just been severed in two by the Anniesland turnpike).

The institution immediately negotiated with the Mowbrays, and Curator Stewart Murray reasoned that even if the relocation failed, the lands at Horslethill would still be a good investment either as a nursery (plant sales were their main source of revenue), or for later feuing. Murray stated in a report that 'an acre of Ground on Mr Gibson's property of Hillhead and within 130 yards of Horslet Hill was lately bought at Six hundred pounds,' that is, three times the price of the land offered by the Mowbrays.[5]

Two months after the initial offer by the Mowbrays, however, the institution had to deal with Kelvinside's new owners, Glasgow lawyers Matthew Montgomerie and John Park Fleming. Through the course of 1839, the institution corresponded, negotiated and generally haggled with the new owners about boundaries, feudal restrictions and conditions. At one point, the institution threatened legal action against the current and previous owners of Kelvinside unless the terms of the original agreements were met.[6] By December 1839, differences had been resolved and plans for the relocation from Sandyford were well underway. During the course of 1840, Stewart Murray and staff endeavoured to enclose, drain, trench, lime and manure the 22 acres between the turnpike and the Kelvin prior to transfer of the plant stock. This preparatory work continued throughout 1840 and 1841, during which time the institution engaged architect Charles Wilson to design the lodge (now demolished), the curator's house and other buildings. (There has been some speculation that Wilson may have contributed to the layout of the gardens, but this has never been substantiated.)

Even before the new Botanic Gardens had opened, Montgomerie & Fleming were promoting the attractions of 'Queenstown' at Kelvinside, destined to become the most fashionable suburb of Glasgow. In the summer of 1840, they advertised in the *Glasgow Herald* and distributed lithographs of the picturesque feu plan by Decimus Burton as a prospectus for potential investors.[7] It is interesting to speculate as to when Messrs Montgomerie & Fleming first considered acquiring Kelvinside, having acted as the agents for the Mowbrays from at least 1830.

By 1844, the original greenhouses and much of the plant material had been transferred from the old garden at Sandyford (with several specimens lasting well into the twentieth century). The Sandyford site was sold to building speculators, though feuing was so slow that much of the land remained an informal wooded park for many years (complete with pond and popular archery range).[8] The new Botanic Gardens at Kelvinside opened in the spring of 1842, not long after the completion of the Great Western Road turnpike.

Overleaf: **A panoramic view *c.*1905 looking west over the Botanic Gardens, Great Western Road and Grosvenor Terrace, taken from the spire of the former Kelvinside Free Church. This dramatic photograph actually consists of two views spliced together, with some additional figures and shadows drawn in by hand. In the late 1920s, the original side gardens to No. 1 Grosvenor Terrace were truncated and the Botanic Gardens gates moved back in conjunction with the opening of the new Queen Margaret Bridge.**

For well over a century, the Botanic Gardens relied on horse power for carrying out heavy work. Additional horses were taken on to improve the lands when the gardens were first established in Kelvinside in 1840-1842, and as late as 1970 a horse called Donald (shown here with friend, Hugh McNeish) was used throughout the grounds.

6

When it reopened at Kelvinside in 1842, the Glasgow Botanic Gardens remained a private institution (with annual members), though it maintained its formal links with the university. The site was also open to day visitors who paid a nominal entrance fee. The arrival of the Botanic Gardens, and the subsequent erection of the new observatory in Dowanhill, helped to legitimise the fledgling suburbs west of the Kelvin. Over the next generation, as Hillhead, Kelvinside and Dowanhill developed, the gardens became an important local fixture. Still, the institution failed to thrive in its new location, partly due to lingering debts from the transfer and high operating costs at Kelvinside.

Around 1873, the institution leased about 2 acres to the entrepreneur John Kibble of Glasgow and Coulport. Kibble, a wealthy eccentric whose interests included engineering, photography and inventing, originally offered to transfer his large cast iron conservatory from Coulport to the city of Glasgow for use as a performing arts venue. A plan to reassemble it in Queen's Park failed to attract support, and Kibble ultimately struck a deal to operate his 'Crystal Art Palace' at the Botanic Gardens. Though presented to the institution *ex gratia*, Kibble kept a long lease on the structure as a place for public meetings, concerts and 'entertainments of an elevating character.'[9] Despite the palace being the scene of many important civic events in the 1870s, the nature and frequency of John Kibble's activities did not always satisfy the directors of the gardens. Eventually they bought out Kibble's lease and converted the Crystal Art Place into a winter garden. Further expenditure which was required to replace the original greenhouses from Sandyford

The great greenhouses of the Main Range were constructed from teak and cast iron in the late 1870s, replacing the original glasshouses which had been relocated from Sandyford. Today, the Main Range houses a wide variety of exotic plants, including the garden's national collection of begonias, as well as the famous tropical orchid collection. This picture postcard view dates from the mid-1920s. The Main Range glasshouses were substantially reconstructed in the 1990s.

7

8

exacerbated the institution's debt burden. The city, as the main bondholder, soon took over effective control and subsequently had to subsidise the gardens in order to save the collections on behalf of the university.

In the late 1880s, the fate of the Botanic Gardens became a major factor in the last of the many boundary squabbles between Hillhead and Glasgow. While the annexation debate raged in the city, suburbs and in Parliament, Glasgow's town council closed the gardens to the public for several years. Although the city wished to turn the gardens into a public park, the site was impossible to police effectively while it was located beyond the boundaries of the independent Burgh of Hillhead. Annexationists were quick to accuse the obstinate Hillhead Commissioners of risking the future of an invaluable local amenity.

Amid the great clamour surrounding Glasgow's perpetual expansion, the city operated the gardens on a care and maintenance basis for several years. The town council, however, never denied that it might sell the gardens for development if the annexation legislation failed. According to the 1888 testimony of the esteemed City Architect John Carrick, making the gardens into a public park was 'the main object' of the boundaries Bill then before Parliament.[10] When the City of Glasgow Act was passed in 1891, the Botanic Gardens, Kelvinside, Dowanhill and Hillhead finally came under Glasgow's jurisdiction. The city soon opened the Botanic Gardens to the public and made many important improvements, including the installation of new cast iron railings around the perimeter, new gate lodges at the main entrance and a new gate at Kirklee. Before the end of the century, additional lands along the Kelvin had been purchased, including 'Montgomerie's Woods' on the north bank which was set out with rambling paths across a new iron footbridge. With the acquisition of the lands at Kirklee, 'one of the most picturesque spots in the immediate vicinity of Glasgow [was] preserved for all time.'[11]

Behind the Main Range stands a large number of sheds and outbuildings including this picturesque pot-washing shed. Many of these buildings have been in constant use since the Kelvinside site opened. Following its relocation, the Glasgow Botanic Gardens remained a private institution funded by annual memberships (*below*) and daily admission charges. In the mid-nineteenth century, William Campbell of Tullichewan, one of the directors, personally subsidised the free opening of the gardens during the annual Glasgow Fair holidays. The gardens were eventually taken over by the Corporation of Glasgow and reopened as a public park.

9

A rare (*c.*1875) view of the Tudor-style teaching buildings at the observatory on Dowanhill, built by the private Astronomical Institution of Glasgow in 1841-1842. The main approach to the observatory followed part of the course of the old parish road though Horslethill farm (still known today as Observatory Road).

10

The study of astronomy at the University of Glasgow dates back to at least the 1690s, when the subject formed part of the Natural Philosophy curriculum. In the 1750s, Jamaica merchant Alexander Macfarlane's bequest of valuable astronomical equipment prompted the establishment of a new Chair of Practical Astronomy and the construction of the university's first purpose-built observatory near the Old College in Glasgow's High Street. When Macfarlane's equipment arrived in the city after the long sea journey, certain pieces which had suffered corrosion were given over to a young Glasgow instrument-maker and engineer named James Watt to refurbish.

In the early nineteenth century, the popularity of astronomy led to the establishment of the Glasgow Society for Promoting Astronomical Observation. This private body erected an observatory on Garnethill where popular astronomy courses were held for many years. In the early 1830s, the society tried and failed to entice the university to rescue the financially-troubled private observatory, then being encircled by the expanding city. At the time, the university was still using the Macfarlane building east of the High Street campus, then considered to be 'the most ancient Academic Observatory in the British Isles.'[12]

The year 1836 marked a turning point in the history of astronomy in Glasgow due to the appointment of the charismatic John Pringle Nichol as the new Professor of Practical Astronomy. Nichol rekindled popular interest in astronomy, and upwards of a thousand people thronged to hear his public lectures.[13] Soon, a new private association was founded to promote the study of the subject and erect a new observatory. Around 1841, the Astronomical Institution of Glasgow obtained an eminent site on the crown of Dowanhill, about two miles west of the city. The oval-shaped site was feued jointly from the estates of Dowanhill and Kelvinside, and by 1842 the new buildings were 'finely situated on the highest ground in the neighbourhood, and were surrounded by open farmlands in all directions.'[14]

Professor Nichol was appointed Observer at the Dowanhill premises and proceeded to furnish it with new equipment. As early as 1843, however, financial problems beset the institution and soon the university was compelled to pay off the debts and take control of the facilities at Dowanhill. Nichol then transferred the most valuable equipment from the ageing Macfarlane Observatory, and by 1845 Dowanhill had become the site of the university's first teaching facility west of the Kelvin (some 25 years before the move to Gilmorehill).

Nichol died in 1859 and was succeeded by Professor Robert Grant, who expanded the observatory's remit by providing the first accurate time signal for shipping on the Clyde. Under Grant's direction, a one o'clock signal was erected at Yorkhill Quay to permit ships to set their chronometers before embarking downriver. The time clock was powered by an underground electric cable from Dowanhill, with the observatory's own clock being set according to the passage of the stars. Over a twenty year period, the paths of over 6,400 stars were charted at

Dowanhill and the findings were incorporated into Grant's 1883 work, popularly known as the *Glasgow Star Catalogue.*

Grant was succeeded in the Chair of Practical Astronomy by Ludwig Becker. This German academic was very popular with his students over his long career at the university, though during the First World War he went on a leave of absence until anti-German sentiment subsided. Becker's ultimate successor, William Smart, was appointed in 1937 and soon determined that serious astronomical study could no longer be undertaken at the antiquated and restricted facilities at Dowanhill. Threatened with the downgrading of the Chair, Smart persuaded the University Court to dispose of the Dowanhill site and erect a small teaching observatory on open land at the western end of University Gardens. The Dowanhill site was then sold to the Glasgow Corporation Education Authority for the proposed new Notre Dame High School. Architect Thomas Cordiner drew up plans in 1939, but the outbreak of war postponed the completion of the striking Scandinavian-modernist building until 1953.[15]

During the 1950s, the University Gardens observatory was used to trace the Sputnik satellite, and the data gathered there was sent on to the Smithsonian Astrophysics Observatory. By 1964 the observatory site was required for the new Queen Margaret Union, and the astronomy students were relocated to a house in Ashton Road. A new observatory was built in 1969 on the Garscube estate, though urban development of the 1970s caused the usual problems of excessive light and smoke. In 1984, the university moved its facilities outside of the city boundaries once again, building a new observatory in the Kilpatrick Hills.

12

Professor Ludwig Becker (*below*, seated next to tripod) surrounded by his students at Dowanhill. For many years, these buildings were situated in a rural setting (*above*), but during the course of the nineteenth century the suburbs of Glasgow gradually encroached upon them.

11

The 66-acre estate belonging to the Glasgow Royal Asylum at Gartnavel contained a wide variety of structures including a chapel, farm buildings and several recreational pavilions. From the main gate at Great Western Road (*right*), the roads and paths rambled around picturesque grounds, through woods and pastures. Panoramic views were available in all directions, a feature that was considered beneficial to the well-being of the patients.

13

14

Recovering inmates at Gartnavel were often brought outside to enjoy the surroundings of the 'fresh-air wards' in the gardens below Charles Wilson's East house (*centre*). There were several classes of patient at this private charitable institution. The wealthy had private rooms and many leisure facilities, whereas the 'parish poor' had only basic amenities and were required to work to contribute to their upkeep. Patients occupying the lower-cost private wards (*right*) were somewhere in between.

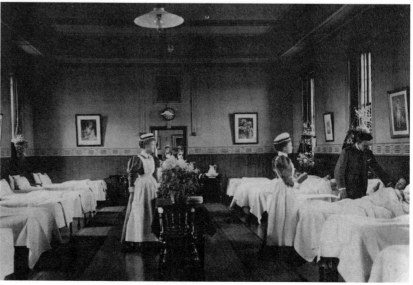

15

16

The farm-steading of Gartnavel appears in historic records of Glasgow from at least the second half of the seventeenth century. The Gartnavel farmlands and mineral workings were once part of the extensive Balshagray holdings of Provost Walter Gibson, whose lands were later owned by generations of Crawfords, Oswalds and Donaldsons. Gartnavel farm-steading was located on a rise high above the old parish road from Jordanhill to Balgray (now Shelley Road). (Its buildings still survive in Whittinghame Drive, although the farm was renamed Flemington in the late nineteenth century.)

When construction of the Great Western Road turnpike began in the late 1830s, the wooded and arable drumlins west of the Kelvin suddenly became accessible to the city of Glasgow. Not long after the new road opened, Horslethill farm became the site of both the Royal Botanical Institution of Glasgow and the city's new observatory. Further west along the turnpike, part of the ancient farmland of Gartnavel was selected to become the site of the city's new state-of-the-art lunatic asylum.

By the 1830s, architect William Stark's famous and inventive panopticon building of four radiating wings (dating from 1810) was considered to be inadequate for the needs of the city's mentally ill. Furthermore, the asylum at Dobbies Loan in Townhead had become dangerously overcrowded, and could not be expanded due to new development surrounding the site.

In 1840, before the Great Western Road had opened, the asylum directors purchased some 66 acres of Gartnavel from James Donaldson of Thornwood (a leading sponsor of the turnpike). A young Glasgow architect named Charles Wilson, already employed locally on the new Botanic Gardens, was appointed to design the new asylum complex. Wilson was only 30 years old at the time, and the Gartnavel project was his first major commission. (Not long afterwards he also designed nearby Windsor Terrace for the Kelvinside Estate Company.) In order to conceive a thoroughly modern institution, Wilson travelled to England and the continent to inspect the latest asylums there.

The foundation stone of the new asylum at Gartnavel was laid in June 1842 with full Masonic rituals. The ceremony included a grand procession from the City Halls in Candleriggs complete with a 'full military band and a regiment of Artillery.'[16] Wilson chose a Tudor Gothic style for his main buildings on the eminence at Gartnavel, sitting in stark isolation between the drumlins of Jordanhill and Dowanhill. The two residential blocks, known as the West and East houses, were originally meant to be linked by a central chapel with a tall campanile. Cost overruns resulted in Wilson's chapel being omitted from the finished building.

A detail from the famous Hyndland farm view of the 1890s shows how prominently the Gartnavel Asylum featured in the local landscape. This westerly view over Hyndland Road shows Wilson's looming Tudor pile surrounded by open farmland. The chimney at the right was built for the recently opened works of the Kelvinside Electrical Company, a private venture supported by many prominent local citizens, including Kelvinside's James B. Fleming.

17

18

19

20

Activities for the residents at Gartnavel were many and varied, and staff often joined in as well. Private patients enjoyed various sporting, cultural and social events, whilst the parish patients helped pay for their keep by working in the grounds. Note the asylum's extensive greenhouses behind the tea party scene; beyond the 1906 bowling green (*top*) loom the tenement roofs of York (now Novar) Drive in Hyndland.

Despite the omission of architect Charles Wilson's campanile from the finished scheme, the new Glasgow Royal Asylum soon became a notable landmark on the western outskirts of Glasgow. Wilson's massive complex, with Tudor chimneys and pointed arch windows, was constructed in sandstone quarried at Cowcaddens. The popular author Hugh MacDonald wrote in 1854 that on the hill at Gartnavel

> stands a melancholy thing, apart from the noise and bustle of the neighbouring city. This benevolent establishment is indeed most appropriately situated here, in a quiet and secluded place, where ministration to the "mind diseased" is completely undisturbed, as in an urban locality it would necessarily to some extent be by the distractions of discordant external influences.[17]

The expansive grounds provided a buffer between the asylum and the nearby suburban houses, there being no gates or perimeter walls until the late nineteenth century.

The Wilson scheme incorporated a West house for voluntary, or fee-paying, patients and an East house for paupers paid for under parish relief. The West house was finely furnished, each inmate having a small private room off a central drawing room or lounge. These lounges were richly appointed in the latest fashion, and were furnished with parlour palms, stuffed armchairs and the occasional grand piano. The wards in the East house were far more basic. According to an early inmate, however, 'although everything there is upon a plainer and cheaper scale, yet, when the restoration of reason or the preservation of life is involved, the rate of board does not enter in the Superintendent's calculation.'[18]

Many of the private patients in the West house were placed there by middle or upper class families who could not cope with an agitated or troubled child, sibling or other relation. A large number came from outside Glasgow (including a significant proportion from England) as it was common for family members to be sent away from home, ostensibly to aid their recovery. More common, however, was the desire of well-to-do families to avoid the social stigma associated with mental illness. Many others were voluntary inmates who could come and go as they wished. It was not unknown for 'cured' patients to return, years after their original dismissal, and readmit themselves for a time 'in order to have the threatened attack [of insanity] warded off, or speedily removed.'[19]

Private patients in the West house were encouraged to recover from what was termed 'the saddest of all maladies' by the latest theories of rest and relaxation, fresh air and exercise, and general social and cultural entertainments. Over the first few decades, the private inmates enjoyed a score of activities in, around and outside Gartnavel. Sports facilities were numerous, and included a cricket pitch, small golf course, croquet lawns, curling rinks, and most importantly two bowling greens. The Gartnavel bowling club not only competed against local Glasgow clubs but also travelled to other sites for events. Staff often participated in sporting activities with the West house inmates, and there was a separate croquet lawn for ladies only (where tea parties were also held).[20]

On the cultural side, the private patients enjoyed a lending library, produced a hospital newspaper, had series of lectures and concerts, formed a debating society and even put together a brass band. The East house patients, on the other hand, tended to provide the domestic labour in the buildings, and also undertook farm and garden work outside. Gartnavel, like nearly all UK asylums of the day, grew much of its own produce in order to keep costs low. The hard labour, of course, was also considered to be therapeutic for the parish paupers. Gartnavel's farm occupied around 40 of the 66 acres and included greenhouses, byres and a piggery.[21]

During the first few decades at Gartnavel, the Royal Asylum struggled to pay off its debts. One of the institution's early goals had been to reduce the number of parish poor it took on, and this figure was cut from 472 in 1874 to a negligible

number by the 1890s. The subsequent increase in fee-paying patients ushered in a new era of prosperity for Gartnavel and, around the turn of the century, many improvements were made. Electric lighting was installed, new staff were hired, ancillary buildings were constructed and a second bowling green added. There was also a new lodge built at the main entrance at Great Western Road, which was funded by the Lanarkshire & Dumbartonshire Railway in part-payment for a right of way along the eastern march of the Gartnavel grounds.

The asylum continued to prosper through the first half of the twentieth century, although overcrowding was a perpetual problem. In the 1920s a house at No. 2 Princes Terrace in Dowanhill became a nursing home for elderly Gartnavel patients, as did the former Collins mansion of Kelvindale House soon thereafter. In the 1930s, financial problems returned to the asylum, with wage costs spiralling and income falling.[22] In 1947, Glasgow Royal Asylum became part of the new National Health Service. Although access to Gartnavel was made freely available to the public, it still admitted fee-paying patients for a time.

At the end of the 1960s, the government's health policies led to a redevelopment of many Victorian hospitals and asylums throughout the UK. Gartnavel's ornamental grounds soon became the home of a nine-storey general hospital and other new buildings. Many old sites were lost, including the main gate lodge, the hay fields, various cottages and the 1906 bowling green. New buildings were built throughout the postwar era, the most significant being the new Glasgow Homeopathic Hospital constructed near the site of the asylum's home farm in 1999. In the early twenty-first century, the asylum's mental health facilities are currently being phased out and gradually supplanted by the expansion of the general hospital and the relocation of facilities from the Western Infirmary.

This aerial view of *c.*1929 looking north shows the extent of the Gartnavel Asylum site prior to the major postwar developments. The original Wilson complex and other later buildings are surrounded by extensive wooded and arable lands. Across the North British Railway line in the foreground are the lands of Broomhill. Part of Flemington farm — to the north of Gartnavel and west of Bingham's pond — had been built upon by this time. Across Great Western Road stands the newly built estate of 'New Kelvinside' on the southern slope of Balgray Hill. At the far right, St John's Renfield Church, in Beaconsfield Road, can be seen under construction.

The Stewart Memorial Fountain, pictured here in 1955, was designed by architect James Sellars and sculptor John Mossman as a memorial to Provost Robert Stewart of Murdostoun, one of the leaders of the campaign to bring Loch Katrine water to the city in the mid-nineteenth century.

The history of Kelvingrove or West End Park has been recounted many times over the past century-and-a-half. One of the earliest accounts is found in Hugh MacDonald's *Rambles Around Glasgow*. 'This is a recent acquisition of the municipality,' wrote MacDonald in 1854, 'and one which must be considered a decided ornament, as well as a sanitary benefit to the city. The rapid extension of the town in this direction rendered such a breathing space necessary; and if the opportunity had been once neglected, a lasting injury would undoubtedly have been inflicted on the community.'[23]

Prior to the 1850s, the city's only public park was the ancient Glasgow Green. At the time, the town council had not created any new public open space in its 160-year history; meanwhile the city's population had increased from 66,000 to 330,000.[24] It was evident that if the council did not act to obtain some parkland for its citizens, residential, commercial or industrial development would eventually engulf the city's rural hinterland.

In 1852, the town council purchased the rustic estates of Kelvingrove and Woodlands, along with parts of the Clairmont, Woodside and Blythswood estates. A municipal account of 1896 recorded that 'certain portions, embracing the crest of the hill and the slopes towards Woodlands, were reserved for feuing, and are now covered by the dwelling-houses of Park Terrace, Park Quadrant, Park Circus and Park Gardens, etc.'[25] The layout and elevations would be the crowning achievement in the career of architect Charles Wilson, who had been commissioned by the town council to produce the original feu plan back in 1851.

The remainder of the lands along the River Kelvin were made into Kelvingrove Park, 'or as it is [in 1872] more popularly called, the West-End Park.'[26] Several further parcels were subsequently added to the park, including the riverside lands of Gilmorehill and the site of the medieval Clayslaps mill (added in the 1870s). From its earliest days, Kelvingrove Park was a favourite retreat for Glaswegians. Hugh MacDonald wrote that

> these fine grounds are situated on the eastern bank of the classic Kelvin, which, under a fringe of trees, flows somewhat lazily past. . . . From a design by Sir Joseph Paxton, the surface is beautifully intersected with walks and carriage drives, turning and twisting in every direction — now gliding under stately trees — now meandering amidst blooming borders and gay parterres, and anon winding in the sunshine around terraces of smoothest and freshest green.[27]

The exact role of Paxton has never been adequately clarified, and Wilson is generally given credit for the overall design of the park.

The old estates along the Kelvin bestowed the new park with mature grounds, with many trees dating back to the eighteenth century. A popular 1872 guide to Glasgow stated that 'the fact that the Park formed a portion of the old estates of Woodside and Kelvingrove has been greatly to its advantage, for to that it owes much of its wooded beauty.'[28]

In the 1870s, the West End Park underwent its first major period of transition. First it was substantially enlarged by the addition of the lands on both banks of the Kelvin near the old Clayslaps mill. In 1872, the Stewart Memorial Fountain was inaugurated (after many delays) to commemorate the greatest civic achievement in nineteenth-century Glasgow, the establishment of the Loch Katrine water supply. Robert Stewart of Murdostoun was not only responsible for promoting the water Bill in Parliament, but during his term as provost (in the early 1850s) the plans for Kelvingrove Park and Woodlands Hill were enacted by the town council. The early 1870s also saw the old mansion of Kelvingrove opened as Glasgow's first civic museum. Finally, in 1872 an Act of Parliament was passed which extended the city's boundaries around the new university site on Gilmorehill, as well as the future home of the Western Infirmary on Donaldshill.

Prior to the realisation of Charles Wilson's final design for the terraces on Woodlands Hill, there was an interesting 1854 submission by architect James Smith for a cruciform-shaped Crystal Palace on the crown of the hill.[29] Smith is best known for being the son-in-law of prominent architect David Hamilton and the father of the notorious Madeleine Smith, accused of poisoning her lover with arsenic. Her 1857 trial was the most sensational of the age, ending spectacularly with a verdict of not proven. Charles Wilson's housing scheme of 1855 was finally accepted by the Corporation of Glasgow and construction of Park Terrace (*below*) began soon afterwards. This 1860s view from inside Kelvingrove Park was taken prior to the completion of Park Circus.

23

25

The Kelvingrove Museum was opened around 1872 in Provost Patrick Colquhoun's former mansion. Within a few years the collection far outstripped the display space in the old Georgian house (*opposite*), and in 1876 a new extension (*above*) opened. The first curator of the museum was John MacNaught Campbell (*below*).

24

Having sat empty and forlorn in the centre of the West End Park for some twenty years, the old Kelvingrove mansion was opened in the early 1870s as the city's first museum. One of the best early descriptions of the new museum is found in Tweed's 1872 *Guide to Glasgow*.

The large white house at the end of the beech avenue, and standing with its back to the Kelvin, is old Kelvingrove House, now converted into a very interesting Museum, where the lounger in the Park may pass an hour very pleasantly in a saunter through the galleries. For many years after the opening of the Park, this house was unoccupied, but in 1868 steps were taken to fit it up as a Museum, of Art and Natural History. Its interior was remodelled, with four fine galleries being fitted up inside. . . . The two lower galleries are devoted expressly to specimens of Glasgow manufacture. . . . In the gallery upstairs, we find models of the famous Elgin marbles, ancient Roman coins, ancient glass and pottery, and a number of fine paintings. . . . Altogether, the Museum adds greatly to the interest of the West End Park.[30]

By most accounts, however, the old mansion was never well-suited to its role as a major civic museum. The limited space in the building, according to a 1914 municipal guide, 'was subjected to very severe strain by the manner in which all sorts of objects began to be accumulated. . . . The smallness of the building soon became very obvious.'[31] As early as 1874 the city resolved to build an extension. A public appeal was launched and £7,500 was quickly raised (the Corporation adding another £500). City Architect John Carrick designed a large extension to the south-east, which, according a writer in 1878, 'dwarfs what remains of the fine old mansion.'[32]

The new extension by Carrick, however, still failed to provide enough room for the museum's burgeoning collection, and 'the space available made it quite impossible for any systematic classification or arrangement of its contents to be carried out; ultimately it came to be looked upon more as a store than a museum suited for educational or scientific purposes.'[33] By the end of the century, however, old Kelvingrove House had been superseded by the immense new art gallery and museum built at nearby Clayslaps.

26

Behind the old Kelvingrove Museum were several industrial exhibits, including this large beam engine, rescued from a property in the Gorbals by the City Improvement Trust. Often referred to as a James Watt engine, investigations in the 1870s by the Council of Engineers and Shipbuilders in Scotland indicated that it may have been an early copy of a Boulton & Watt patent, but had, over generations of use, become 'a patchwork of styles of different dates.' Until a real Watt engine could be obtained, it was decided 'that in the meantime the old engine at present there be allowed to remain.'[39]

27

Venerable Kelvingrove House, despite its physical limitations, remained the city's chief museum until the new art gallery and museum building opened in the park in 1901. In 1888, during the first International Exhibition in Kelvingrove Park, the old mansion was used to display more than 800 of Queen Victoria's jubilee gifts. These diverse presents, from all corners of the Empire, had not previously been seen outside London and were therefore a main attraction of the Glasgow Exhibition.[34]

Between the 1888 and 1901 exhibitions in Kelvingrove Park, the old mansion reverted to its former use as Glasgow's main civic museum. With the prospect of the profits from the first exhibition being used for a new purpose-built art gallery and museum, the future of Kelvingrove House was suddenly in doubt. The old museum's fate was sealed when architect James Miller's masterplan for the proposed 1901 exhibition plotted the Grand Concert Hall and a restaurant on the approximate site of the Colquhoun mansion.

News that the beloved Kelvingrove House was to be demolished to make way for a temporary exhibition structure led to a public outcry. The subject was not only debated in the Glasgow press, but even London-based trade journals commented that this proposed act of 'vandalism . . . for the mere convenience of a passing show pitch,' would be 'a most deplorable blunder.'[35] The strongest challenge to the exhibition plans came from architect and antiquarian Peter Macgregor Chalmers and his fellow members of the Glasgow Archaeological Society. Chalmers wrote letters to the *Herald* and lobbied the Corporation Parks Committee, suggesting that the mansion would become a welcome addition to

A 1920s picture postcard view looking over the new bowling greens and tennis courts and showing an earlier generation of courts located on the site of the old Kelvingrove House Museum.

28

29

The amenities in Kelvingrove Park made it a favourite destination for generations of Glaswegians. The new bandstand (*left*) between Kelvin Way and the river was constructed in 1924 by the Corporation Public Parks Department.

the 1901 exhibition if it could be 'repaired and decorated in the style of the eighteenth century. . . . It could be filled with old furniture, pictures, prints, books, etc. illustrative of the history of Glasgow, and so become, not only for the period of the International Exhibition, but for all time to come, a museum of Glasgow antiquities.'[36]

The City Chambers was also lobbied by the prestigious Glasgow Art Club, some 140 members of which submitted a petition to save the mansion. Among the signatories were such important Glasgow artists and architects as James Craig Annan, Alexander Nisbet Paterson, John A. Campbell, Thomas L. Watson, John Keppie, David Gauld, R. Macaulay Stevenson and Fra Newbery. These artistic luminaries, though labouring under the misapprehension that the original mansion was the work of the celebrated architect Robert Adam (a claim they never substantiated), considered that the antiquity of Kelvingrove House and its association with the famed Provost Patrick Colquhoun made it worthy of preservation. In their petition they wished the lord provost and the Corporation would understand 'the importance of conserving the best of those types and mementoes of the past which once destroyed can never be restored.'[37]

In the end, the exhibition planners won the battle and Kelvingrove House was 'ruthlessly destroyed.'[38] In an added twist, however, the Carrick extension of 1876 was retained, painted white and converted for use as the Japanese Pavilion during the 1901 exhibition. For the following ten years, the old museum extension was adapted to house the Jeffrey Reference Library prior to the opening of the new Mitchell Library building in North Street.

In 1911 the Scottish National Exhibition was held in Kelvingrove Park, and the Carrick extension was once again called into service, this time becoming part of the large Palace of History pavilion. After the end of the exhibition, the old museum extension was finally demolished and during the course of the twentieth century the site of Patrick Colquhoun's Kelvingrove House was used successively for football pitches, tennis courts, an open-air dance floor, a roller rink, and, ultimately, as Scotland's first skateboard rink.

Glasgow Academy Pupils, c.*1910.*

IV.

Education

John Baird I (1798-1859) was the architect behind the plans for the University of Glasgow's proposed relocation to Woodlands Hill in 1846. Baird's Jacobean scheme (*right*) was delayed by the Treasury in London, where Pugin and Barry (architects for the new Palace of Westminster) had levelled criticisms at the design. After the university's deal to sell the High Street site fell through, Woodlands Hill was bought by Glasgow Town Council and in the 1850s became the site of Charles Wilson's Park Circus development.

2

The University of Glasgow has a long and esteemed history which dates back to the famous papal bull of 6 January 1451 and the early lessons in the chapter house of the cathedral. Since 1870, the university has made the West End its home, though the original campus has expanded well beyond the confines of Gilmorehill into Hillhead and beyond.

The early history of Gilmorehill, prior to its acquisition by the university in the 1860s, includes the names of many of Glasgow's great landowning families. A member of the Hamilton family was granted the lands of Gilmorehill in the seventeenth century, and, in 1720, the venerable Walter Gibson added these grounds to his massive holdings of Overnewton and Balshagray. Some fifty years later, the site was acquired by Thomas Dunmore of Kelvinside. When Robert Dunmore sold Kelvinside to Dr Thomas Lithan in the 1780s, Gilmorehill was included in the deal. Lithan, however, showed little interest in holding on to this asset; the lands and printfields of Gilmorehill were repeatedly advertised for sale over the following twenty years. It was not until the Yoker turnpike and its new bridge over the Kelvin were constructed that Gilmorehill finally found a buyer.

In 1800, the lands of Gilmorehill were purchased by Robert Bogle junior, the scion of one of the great families of Glasgow. Two branches of Bogles, belonging to Shettleston and Daldowie, were at the forefront of Glasgow's civic and mercantile activities for centuries. One Bogle was a founder member of the Merchants House in 1605, and later generations were among the original sponsors of the Chamber of Commerce.[1] When Robert Bogle of Shettleston bought Gilmorehill, the lands had long shown potential as the location for a country retreat suitable for a member of the Old Glasgow Gentry. As early as 1789, the 30 acres of land above the Kelvin were advertised as being 'all enclosed and subdivided with thriving hedges, belts of planting, and a stone dyke. The situation is most delightful, and commands a most extensive and pleasant prospect — a very eligible situation for setting down a house, the avenue to which is already formed.'[2]

Within a couple of years of his purchase, Robert Bogle built the mansion house of Gilmorehill, which 'from its elevated position, as well as its imposing style of architecture, formed a conspicuous and attractive object.'[3] Bogle soon acquired the adjacent lands of Donaldshill which extended westward to the old parish road from Partick to Kirklee. According to an 1870 account, 'Mr Bogle laid off a large portion of the grounds in the vicinity of the mansion, in ornamental plantings, shrubberies and walks; while extensive walled gardens contained grape, peach, and greenhouses, besides other accessories to a gentleman's country residence.'[4]

Robert Bogle was succeeded by his son Archibald in 1822. Archibald Bogle remained at Gilmorehill for another twenty years, but all four of his sons left

Glasgow and the estate was sold in 1845 to a group of speculators who hoped to build a private cemetery, or western necropolis, on the hill. Nothing came of this scheme, nor of the ten or so feuing plans for villa and terrace development which appeared in the 1840s and 1850s. Eventually, the mansion of Gilmorehill was leased out for a variety of purposes, including a hydropathic retreat run by a Mr Hunter.[5]

By the early nineteenth century, the university's presence in the High Street was becoming increasingly untenable. Glasgow's mercantile expansion had led to the streets of its ancient medieval core becoming

> the dwelling places of dense masses of the lowest of the population, among whom filth and fever never cease to be, [and thus] it is not surprising that the professors should be anxious to transfer their academic halls and dwelling-houses from this polluted locality to "fresh fields and pastures new."[6]

The railway mania of the 1840s presented the university with an opportunity to sell its High Street lands and use the proceeds to relocate to a more desirable site in the city's West End.

In 1846, Parliament authorised the university to sell its High Street lands to the Glasgow, Airdrie & Monklands Junction Railway in order to pay for 'a new College upon an improved scale on a site on the property of Woodlands.'[7] The scheme also included a new teaching hospital at the corner of North and Sauchiehall Streets. Glasgow architect John Baird was engaged to provide plans for the new college on Woodlands Hill, most likely aided by his chief assistant, Alexander Thomson.[8] Baird's Jacobean scheme was rejected by the Treasury (which was to provide about half the funding), and despite revisions the project was delayed for several years. By the time the Treasury approved the scheme, the railway company, like many ambitious speculative ventures of the 1840s, had run into financial difficulties and was not able to buy the High Street site. The university sued prior to the railway's liquidation and were able to salvage a nest egg for the future.

It was nearly twenty years after the failure of the Woodlands Hill scheme that Glasgow University finally saw its new West End home rise from its foundations. In this 1868 view looking west from Kelvingrove Park, Sir George Gilbert Scott's buildings on Gilmorehill are taking shape. The wooden bridge in the foreground was constructed to carry the royal procession of the Prince and Princess of Wales to the foundation stone ceremony on 8 October 1868. The procession (*overleaf*) attracted tens of thousands of spectators hoping to catch a glimpse of the future King Edward VII and his new wife Princess Alexandra. Lining the route from the High Street to Gilmorehill were 'Yeomanry Cavalry, Hussars, the 25th Regiment, [and] thousands of Volunteers in grey, green, red and blue uniforms.'[9]

The construction of the university buildings took four years (a year longer than anticipated), with much time being lost because of a stonemasons' strike. 'This dispute was not about wages or working hours,' reported the *Glasgow Herald*, 'but simply in consequence of three men being employed who had rendered themselves obnoxious to the trade's union. Their instant dismissal was demanded, and when this was refused there was a general strike of the masons.' The contractor 'at considerable expense was forced to import masons from all over Scotland, England and Ireland to the number of 1,000' in order to complete the work.[11] Some of these masons were photographed preparing the two ceremonial foundation stones for the Prince and Princess of Wales in October 1868.

Despite the collapse of the plan to relocate to Woodlands, the University of Glasgow persevered in its goal of leaving the High Street for more salubrious surroundings to the west of the city. The university was so desperate to relocate that it seriously considered selling off the Hunterian coin collection (thought then to be worth nearly half the sum expected from the sale of the High Street lands). In 1863 a new railway partner emerged, and within a year a new Act of Parliament authorising the university's relocation had been passed. By that time, however, the site at Woodlands was already being feued for housing, and architect John Baird was dead.

The university was fortunate in that Gilmorehill House and its picturesque 43 acres were available for purchase in the 1860s. The institution went ahead and bought the old Bogle lands of Gilmorehill, along with 14 acres of Donaldshill to the west and around 5 acres of Clayslaps on the opposite bank of the Kelvin. By 1866 plans for a new building drawn up by the eminent London architect Sir George Gilbert Scott had been accepted, much to the dismay of Baird's old assistant, Alexander 'Greek' Thomson, and other members of Glasgow's talented architectural fraternity. Scott's thirteenth-century style Scottish-French Gothic building would soon dominate the landscape of the West End, but not before the contractors had reduced the height of Gilmorehill by nine feet in order to provide a level site.

Needless to say, the budget and programme for the construction of Scott's buildings far exceeded original expectations. Nearly one third of the total cost of the project (including the new teaching hospital on Donaldshill) was raised by public subscription, and donations were still being collected long after the buildings had been completed. Some money was saved by using sandstone obtained from

6

Sir George Gilbert Scott's 'Scottish-French' building was far from complete when the first classes were held there in 1870, with neither the spire nor the Bute Hall added until the late 1880s. When Gilmorehill was first acquired, there was much opprobrium surrounding the university's decision to engage a London architect rather than offering the commission to local firms. After 'Greek' Thomson's highly critical lecture at the Glasgow Architectural Society in 1866, 'an interesting and prolonged discussion followed,' involving such local luminaries as John Honeyman, James Boucher, H. K. Bromhead, Daniel Cottier and William Leiper, in which 'almost all were agreed' that 'a slur had been cast on the Glasgow architects.'[12] It was not long, however, before the new university building became the West End's best-known landmark. Its tower formed a dramatic backdrop to popular events such as the 1901 International Exhibition in Kelvingrove Park (*left*).

quarries on the site, which provided the squared rubble used for main walling stone (the finer dressed stones came from Bishopbriggs and Giffnock). The contractors were also able to use coal found on the site to fire the steam boilers of their derricks. Meanwhile, university geologists were delighted to find no less than five fossil tree stumps in the Gilmorehill quarries.[10]

Without doubt, the relocation of the university to the banks of the Kelvin provided an important boost to the development of the West End, an impetus that was only surpassed by the opening of the Great Western Road turnpike a generation earlier. In actual fact, when the university buildings were formally opened on Gilmorehill in 1870, these lands were outside the municipal boundaries of Glasgow. It was not until 1872 that the city obtained the Parliamentary Act required to wrest its ancient university from the neighbouring Burgh of Partick. This Act was Glasgow's first annexation of lands west of the Kelvin, and no doubt put fear into the hearts of residents in the fledgling Burgh of Hillhead next door.

7

Architect John Burnet senior's Western Infirmary opened in 1874. The original site for the university's teaching hospital was meant to be at Clayslaps on the south bank of the Kelvin, but an *ex cambion* deal with Glasgow Town Council gave the university the necessary additional lands in Donaldshill for the infirmary, and in exchange the city was able to expand its West End Park, with the Kelvingrove Art Gallery & Museum ultimately being built at Clayslaps. Burnet's building was gradually superseded during the infirmary's postwar expansion and was ultimately demolished in the early 1990s.

A fire in the top floor of Glasgow Academy on Christmas Eve 1954 (*right*) was quickly extinguished. During the subsequent repairs, however, the opportunity was taken to make certain improvements to the facilities. Large dormer windows were added, forever altering the original appearance of Hugh and David Barclay's design of 1878. The 1902 science block, situated behind the main building, was the first addition to the academy's campus and was also designed by Hugh Barclay.

Below: Glasgow Academy boys in the rooftop gymnasium in 1914. They have 'just finished dumb-bell exercises, and are about to begin marching exercises.'[23] *Bottom*: A group of academy pupils display the variety of dress that was permitted in the early years before uniforms were made compulsory. (The crown spire behind belongs to the Kelvin-Stevenson Memorial Church in Belmont Street.)

8

9

10

Prior to the 1872 Education (Scotland) Act, primary and secondary education in the West End of Glasgow was a strictly private affair, with most schools organised by churches or charitable bodies. During the early years of the western suburbs' existence, most children (primarily boys) ventured into the city for their education. In 1845, a group of leading Glasgow businessmen, all with strong affiliations with the new Free Church of Scotland, formed a private company to establish a school 'for the purpose of teaching youth the various branches of secular knowledge, based upon strictly evangelical principles and pervaded by religious instruction.'[13] The founders of the new Glasgow Academy included publisher John Blackie senior, warehouseman William Campbell of Tullichewan and merchant James Buchanan of Dowanhill.[14]

In one of his early commissions, architect Charles Wilson designed the original academy buildings in Elmbank Street. Following the passing of the 1872 Act, the Glasgow School Board purchased the buildings for its new High School. The academy company was accordingly wound up, but quickly reformed with a remit to find a new site. After considering lands in Woodlands Road, University Avenue and Kelvingrove, the directors purchased the 'made' ground belonging to the City of Glasgow Bank near the Kelvin bridge.[15]

Upon the recommendation of John Burnet, architects Hugh and David Barclay were invited to prepare four plans. The directors selected the simplest and least expensive scheme, but the Barclays successfully prevailed upon the directors to choose a more prestigious design in order to project the correct image for the new school. The handsome classical structure, splendidly situated some sixty feet above the Kelvin, was completed in a mere sixteen months.[16]

The academy struggled financially during its first few years in the West End. Not only did the new Kelvinside Academy open on the same day in October 1878, but the Govan School Board established Hillhead School only seven years later. It was not until the Kelvinbridge subway and railway stations opened in the 1890s that the academy was able to attract boys from further afield.[17]

In 1903, the *Glasgow Academy Chronicle* surveyed the careers of members of its Latin class some fifteen years after leaving the school, enumerating 'two advocates, one barrister, one Indian Civil servant, three clergymen, one assistant professor, one soldier, one civil engineer, two accountants, one banker, one naval architect, four electrical engineers, three stockbrokers, two merchants, five manufacturers, two master tradesmen, three shipowners, two farmers, two artists, two with no occupation, seven clerks, and three unclassed. Five members could not be traced, thirteen had gone abroad to various occupations, and twelve had died.'[18]

Despite the creation of Board schools in and around Glasgow following the 1872 Education Act, the West End lacked its own public school for many years, and private schools of various sizes continued to be established to serve the growing suburban population. One of the most prominent private institutions from this era was the 'Westbourne Gardens School for the Education of Young Women,' established in September 1877 by the six Levack sisters of 34 Westbourne Gardens.

By the time the third Miss Levack became headmistress (during the First World War), the school had outgrown its Westbourne premises despite having acquired No. 33 at an early stage. The girls (and their younger brothers in the preparatory school) were not only forbidden from playing in the communal pleasure ground in the central triangle of Westbourne Gardens but one pupil at the turn of the twentieth century also recalled how 'she was asked to go to Miss Levack's room to be told that she must not hop when in the Gardens on her way to school.'[19]

In 1921, the school acquired Kelvinside House in Crossloan (now Cleveden) Road, the former home of the James B. Fleming family. The mansion — originally known as Beaconsfield — was prominently sited on the west edge of Balgray Hill, on what its flamboyant builder claimed to be 'the best site of the Estate, and certainly the view from the house can hardly be surpassed by any suburban residence within a radius of three miles from the centre of a great commercial city.'[20] Former pupils fondly recalled the early days at Kelvinside House, where they enjoyed the mature rose garden and the original grass tennis courts. The flagpole, which was reputed to be the highest in Glasgow, spectacularly crashed whilst being removed some years after the Second World War.[21]

With Kelvinside House still occupied by the army when the Westbourne girls returned from their wartime evacuation, the school obtained a lease on No. 1 Winton Drive just over the road. When the army left in 1946, this annexe was kept, to be augmented in 1952 by the purchase of the other half of this semi-detached villa of c.1884. No. 5 Winton Drive was acquired later, and a large extension was constructed behind to link the three properties.

Through the 1960s and 1970s, education in the UK underwent a period of great upheaval, with the number of single-sex schools declining in both the public and private sectors. By the late 1980s, the West End could still boast five independent single-sex schools, though pupil numbers were generally in decline. In early 1990, an approach from the directors of Glasgow Academy proposing an amalgamation of the schools was accepted by the governors of Westbourne. An era ended in 1992 when the Westbourne girls removed to the academy. A year later, when a new science block was opened at the Kelvinbridge site, it was named the Levack Laboratory to commemorate the founders of the original girls' school in Westbourne Gardens.[22]

12

The elegant main staircase of the Westbourne School's Kelvinside House, as recorded in 1964. The mansion, infamous as the site where James B. Fleming junior shot dead an armed intruder in 1908, acted as the junior school when the villas in Winton Drive were acquired after the Second World War. When the school first moved into Kelvinside House, part of the property was occupied by the headmistress Miss Neilson, her family and their 'staff of resident cooks and maids.'[24]

11

When James B. Fleming of the Kelvinside Estate Company built his new mansion in 1875 he called it Beaconsfield (the original c.1750 Kelvinside House of the Dunmore family was still standing at the time). Fleming subsequently commissioned architect James Thomson to double the size of the building by adding a baronial extension (complete with tower). This 1956 view from the west shows the construction of the Ann Fraser Hall, erected by Hugh Fraser (later Baron Fraser of Allander) and located on the site of the Flemings' old walled kitchen garden. This sports hall was demolished in the mid-1990s when the property reverted to residential use.

Kelvinside Academy.   *Glasgow.*

13

Architect James Sellars was only 34 years old when he designed the Kelvinside Academy in 1877; his plans for Hillhead Parish Church in Huntly Gardens and Belhaven United Presbyterian Church (Dundonald Road) date from around the same time. The academy building was described by Gomme and Walker in *Architecture of Glasgow* as a synthesis of typical 'Greek' Thomson forms and the famous Royal High School on Edinburgh's Calton Hill (by Thomas Hamilton, c.1825).[28]

In the mid 1870s, in the absence of a public 'Board' school in the area, and with the demise of the private Glasgow Academy in Elmbank Street apparently imminent, a group of prominent West End lawyers, merchants and bankers formed a limited company to establish a new school 'to supply education of the highest class to the large and increasing population in the Western Suburbs of Glasgow.'[25] Among the founding directors of the Kelvinside Academy Company Ltd. were James B. Fleming, owner of the Kelvinside Estate Company, the engineer James Buchanan Mirrlees of Redlands, and James Marshall, a partner in the famous Saracen Foundry, who resided at Carlston (998 Great Western Road).

Soon after the Kelvinside Academy Company was formed, share capital was raised and lands at Kirklee were feued, with Glasgow architect James Sellars commissioned to build the neoclassical buildings. The viability of the scheme, however, was immediately threatened by the decision of the Glasgow Academy directors to re-form their school on a new site in the West End. Both schools opened on the same day in September 1878. There were other private schools around the West End at this time (with several located in Partick), but in the vicinity of Hillhead, Dowanhill and Kelvinside they were very small and usually located in the homes of the owners/teachers. Kelvinside Academy was the first new school of substantial aspirations to have a purpose-built site in the West End.

The original expectations of the Kelvinside Academy directors were no doubt tempered by the relocation of the 'new' Glasgow Academy near the Kelvin bridge. According to the outspoken James B. Fleming,

after the erection of these two private-venture Schools, which had been started not for profit but to supply the wants of the District, the Govan School Board suddenly awoke to a sense of its supposed duty and built a Board School in Cecil Street, Hillhead, just about halfway between the Glasgow Academy and the Kelvinside Academy, thus greatly and very unfairly injuring the prospects of both.[26]

14

Kelvinside Academy's club sports were initially organised by the students themselves on an area of waste ground in Prince Albert Road, Dowanhill (*left,* just west of Princes Terrace). One former pupil recalled, 'A cricket pitch had been laid down some years before by an athletic club, but the rigs which the last ploughing had left were still over all the rest of the ground. . . . [As it was] about the lowest point in the district, it was always muddy, and often flooded in parts.'[29] Corporation flats were built on this site after the Second World War.

In addition to the new Hillhead School which so annoyed Fleming, the Govan School Board also opened the Hamilton Crescent School in Partick in 1885. A few years previously, Glasgow School Board had opened its large Woodside School in Woodlands Road in order to serve the growing population at the western extremity of the city. Altogether, these three Board schools contributed to the financial difficulties experienced by the Kelvinside Academy in its early years.

Much of the early history of Kelvinside Academy pertains to the struggle of the fledgling institution to clear its debts whilst attracting sufficient numbers of boys. The original share capital of 1878 was not sufficient to pay for the new buildings and other start-up costs, and even the feu duties to the Kelvinside Estate Company were soon seriously in arrears. The quality of the school, however, could not be faulted. As early as 1894, Kelvinside Academy was ranked alongside its much older rival from Kelvinbridge in an Educational Institute of Scotland guide which noted that both academies had

> extensive recreation grounds and gymnasiums, affording every facility for the physical training of the pupils. The fees charged place them beyond the reach of the many. They, however, do most valuable work as Higher Class Schools, and the public confidence they enjoy is justified by the reports of the Scotch Education Department, and the University successes of their boys.[27]

In the 1880s, the academy's formal sporting and cadet activities took place in a field just across from the school which was rented from the Mirrlees family of Redlands. Around 1900, the academy's sports clubs moved to (North) Balgray farm in Great Western Road. In the early years, visiting teams made do with changing facilities at the skating house at nearby Bingham's pond. The school later purchased the redundant Press Pavilion from the 1901 exhibition and moved it to Balgray (to the right, *below*). Behind the pavilion in this 1920s view is the newly laid out Leicester Avenue leading to the Kelvindale estate.

5

Glasgow.
Hillhead Academy.

17

This *c*.1905 view shows 'Hillhead Academy,' designed by Hugh and David Barclay, soon after the north wing (towards Alfred Terrace) had been built and an extra full storey was added to the top of the building. Within a few years, persistent overcrowding led to a large mansard being added to provide science laboratories. Hillhead's second headmaster, Duncan Macgillivray, is pictured below in 1928 at the recently established War Memorial Recreation Ground at Hughenden. To the left is the rear elevation of Marlborough (now Devonshire) Terrace.

16

The 1872 Education (Scotland) Act, which made education compulsory for all children between the ages of five and thirteen, led to the establishment of school boards throughout the country. The new western suburbs of Glasgow, being in the parish of Govan, were the responsibility of the Govan School Board. Despite the fact that the burgeoning suburb of Hillhead had been declared a 'populous place' back in 1869, and was thus established as an independent burgh, the Govan Board made no immediate provision for a new school for the local population. Through the middle decades of the nineteenth century, and for more than ten years after the 1872 Act, Hillhead and its environs had to rely on the established private schools in Glasgow and the two private academies which had opened in 1878. In the late nineteenth century a number of small private schools opened west of the Kelvin, such as the one operated by a Mrs J. L. Sutherland in the Gibsons' old Hillhead mansion house prior to its demolition in the 1870s.

The Govan Board finally opened a school in Cecil Street in Hillhead in 1885. It was an immediate success, with 200 pupils enrolling when the school opened in April, and the number rising to 500 by the time the summer term ended in June. By 1892, the roll had increased to over 800, and by 1910, following two phases of extensions (to the north and on top of the roof) in the previous decade, the school was still desperately overcrowded with more than 1,200 students. There were even annexes formed in nearby houses at 8 Alfred Terrace and Nos. 12 and 40 Cecil Street.[30]

In the years prior to the First World War, the situation worsened. Despite students being transferred to the new Hyndland School, countless numbers were still refused admission to Hillhead. The Inspectors' Report of 1911 'complained that a hundred infants were being taught in one room.'[31] By 1913, it was decided that a new school was required (an idea first mooted back in 1907) and, despite the outbreak of war, a site was acquired a few streets away. The new location was a large rectangle between Glasgow Street, Great George Street, Ann Street (now Southpark Avenue) and Wilson Street (now Oakfield Avenue). The new Hillhead High School required the compulsory purchase of two short terraces and several

Authoritative School Kit.

Hillhead High School Outfit:

Regulation School Cap, 3/6.
,,   Blazer, Silk Badge on Pocket from 25/-.
,,   Blazers without Badge and Braiding from 10/6.
,,   Knicker Hose from 3/11.
,,   Knitted Tie, 10½d., 1/6.
,,   Elastic Belt, 1/-, 1/6.
,,   Serge Shorts, 4/11, 6/11, 10/6.
,,   Club Stripe Knitted Wrap.
,,   Football Shorts, 2/6, 3/6.
,,   Swimming Costumes, 2/6, 3/6.

Girls' Academy Straw Hat, 3/6, 4/11.
(New Egg Oval Crown)
Regulation Silk Hat Band, 2/-.

*Estimates given for Lawn Tennis
Posts and Nets.   Tennis and
Cricket Requisites.*

*Special Wholesale Prices for Club
Blazers and Caps.*

D. M. HOEY,   ST. GEORGE'S CROSS, GLASGOW.

18

Hillhead School, although a public 'Board' school, was a fee-paying institution until the era of Comprehensive Education reforms in the 1970s. The fees, however, were considerably less than those at the so-called 'private-venture schools' in the West End. In 1887, shortly after Hillhead School opened, the fees amounted to £5 or £6, only a fraction of the £12 to £14 levied at Glasgow and Kelvinside Academies.[33] There were extra costs for parents, of course, such as school uniforms, as depicted in this 1920s advertisement for the old family firm of D. M. Hoey (still trading in 2000 in Dumbarton Road, Partick).

villas, one of which was the home of a popular private girls school called Laurel Bank.

The war halted the project's progress, and it was not until 1921 that an architectural competition was held. A 'butterfly' scheme with open balcony corridors by architects Wylie Shanks & Wylie was selected, but it was not until the late 1920s that work began on site (by which time the top floor and swimming pool had been omitted from the plans).[32] The new Hillhead High School finally opened in 1931, nearly 25 years after it had first been proposed. The old Cecil Street building became Hillhead Primary School, though for decades the links were so strong that the pair were still considered by many to be a single institution.

Architect E. G. Wylie's competition-winning entry for the new Hillhead High School was not completed until a decade after the design was selected. During the intervening years, many alterations were made to the architect's original scheme (*below*). Much of the grand architectural ornamentation was toned down, the attic storey and swimming pool were omitted, and the therapeutic open-air corridors were relocated to the east elevation facing Oakfield Avenue.

19

Although established as a girls' school, Laurel Bank also admitted boys up to the age of seven (by which time they were eligible for Glasgow Academy). Around 1910, Laurel Bank apparently commissioned a series of picture postcards recording the school building and grounds, as well as the students in their respective forms and sports teams. *Right*: Miss Eglin and her kindergarten charges posing in the tree-lined garden. *Centre*: The school's playground behind Tyrefield, recalled one former pupil, 'was covered in pink blaes and formed the centre of feverish activity twice in the morning at ten minute breaks.'[36] The gable of the original school building, the villa of Laurel Bank, is seen at the far left.

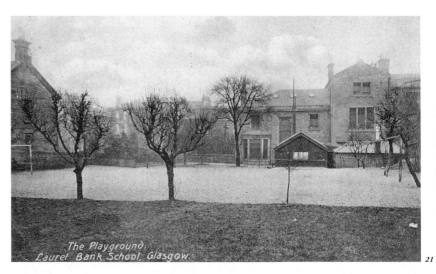

The spacious garden behind Tyrefield 'was surrounded by a hedge and between the hedge and the path the previous herbaceous border had been divided into plots to form individual gardens planted and kept by ourselves — each plot the focus of keen rivalry.'[37] *Right*: Pat Dixon, Irene Dixon, Winnie Gordon and Constance Ellis tend their patch under the watchful eye of Miss Janet Watson.

Laurel Bank School was the first school to be established by Scottish women graduates. Founded in 1903 by Miss Janet Spens MA (Glasgow) and Miss Margaret A. Hannan Watson MA (St Andrews), Laurel Bank is now the sole surviving private girls' school in the West End of Glasgow (having merged with the Park School of Lynedoch Street in 1997 to become Laurel Park School).

When the Misses Spens and Hannan Watson set out to establish a new private school in the early years of the twentieth century, they did not immediately consider locations in Glasgow's West End as they thought there would be too much competition from existing girls' schools, such as the 25-year-old Westbourne Gardens School. Instead, they looked for appropriate sites in places as far afield as Bearsden, Pollokshields and Kilmarnock, but in the end, Miss Hannan Watson recalled, 'we found the right house and garden, just across the street from my own house, [named] Laurel Bank, a semi-detached villa that was to let, convenient in every way, near the car-route, and within hearing of the University Bell.'[34]

The new Laurel Bank School was immediately successful, with thirty students enrolled on the first day in September 1903, ten more joining before the end of the summer term, and a total of fifty registered for the start of the second year (with even more hoping to enrol). The school's proprietors immediately went to see their landlord, former Hillhead Provost John King, who also owned the more spacious villa of Tyrefield next door. According to Miss Hannan Watson, 'We went through [Tyrefield], saw that painting was all that was needed to make it a very desirable successor to our little villa, and immediately arranged an exchange. At the beginning of October, when all was ready, there was one very busy day when each child in School helped in carrying chairs and books from one house to the other.'[35]

24

The villa of Tyrefield (*above*), built *c.*1850 in Wilson Street (now Oakfield Avenue), became the second home of Laurel Bank School a year after the latter's founding in 1903. Tyrefield, along with the neighbouring Thornville Terrace (abutting to the left) and the nearby villas of Laurel Bank and Thornville were all cleared in the 1920s to make way for the new Hillhead High School. Tyrefield's big bay window (*below*) faced onto unfeued ground which served as the school's garden and playing field. This photograph of the school roll was taken in 1909.

Lilybank House has been used for many purposes since its construction in the late 1830s. Originally a small country house for wealthy Glaswegians, it later became Queen Margaret Hall, a residence for women students at the University of Glasgow, and in recent years has been the home of various university departments. For much of the twentieth century it also acted as an elegant backdrop for group portraits of the girls of Laurel Bank School. In the 1950s view below, the alterations undertaken for Provost John Blackie by architect Alexander 'Greek' Thomson around a century earlier can be seen. Thomson moved the original entrance from the centre bay of the main block to the Greek Ionic portico of his asymmetrical extension to the south. In 1894, architects Honeyman and Keppie altered the interior and added a first floor to the stable wing to the north.

By its third year, Laurel Bank's roll had trebled to 95 pupils. Over the next decade, the school continued to thrive in its pleasant home at Tyrefield. One early pupil remembered that Tyrefield was 'delightfully large,' whilst Miss Hannan Watson recalled that it was a 'bright, roomy house. It had one advantage which we all enjoyed — a second staircase, so that at the walk-around between classes, the girls went down the wide stair and up the narrow one.'[38] In 1915, however, Laurel Bank School was suddenly forced to leave Tyrefield.

Just at the time that Miss Hannan Watson was considering purchasing both Tyrefield and Laurel Bank, she received a letter from the Govan School Board informing her that the site was required for the proposed new Hillhead High School and that her school would have to leave forthwith. She managed to extend her lease of Tyrefield until the end of the term, and in the meantime she 'started looking for a suitable house and was very fortunate in finding No. 4 Lilybank Terrace, which was for sale.'[39] Ironically, despite Laurel Bank School being evicted so hastily by the Govan School Board, construction on the new Hillhead High School did not begin for some fifteen years.

Laurel Bank left Tyrefield with great regret, mostly due to the loss of its large and picturesque gardens. 'Everyone is sorry about the move,' wrote Miss Hannan Watson to her girls in 1915,

> for the old house is to be pulled down, though a brighter, airier house is not to be found in Glasgow. From every window the outlook is pretty, . . . from the day when the lofty old pear-tree clothes itself in snow-white blossom, life for those classes whose windows look out on the garden, is a succession of joys: cherry blossom is followed by apple blossom, and then the white lilac and laburnum appear, but the sweetest of all is from the side window of the old drawing-room, when the pink hawthorns are in bloom and the masses of foliage of the taller trees hide all trace of town from sight.[40]

Headmistress Hannan Watson chose to move the school to Lilybank Terrace partly because of the spacious grounds in front of Lilybank House next door, which the owner, Mr J. B. MacBrayne 'would most certainly be willing to lease or sell.'[41]

Within three years of moving to Lilybank, Miss Hannan Watson purchased a second house in the terrace. Around the same time, Laurel Bank underwent a major transformation, though the practical effect on the daily affairs of the school was negligible. Rather than remain a privately-owned and independent school, Miss Hannan Watson decided to relinquish her sole ownership of the school and

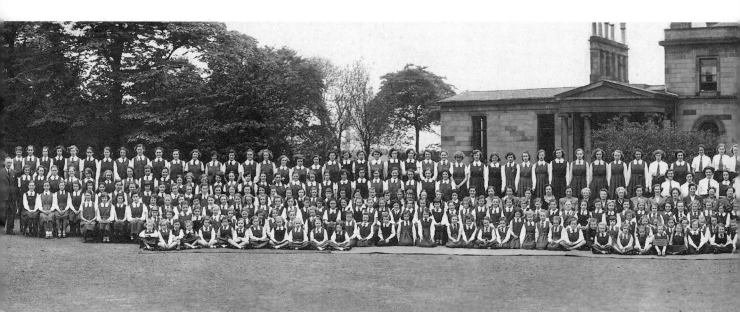

Laurel Bank girls in their playground in front of Lilybank House, which became the site of the University of Glasgow's Adam Smith building in the late 1960s. The school buildings in Lilybank Terrace are at the rear left of the picture.

26

its assets in order to comply with the terms of the Education (Scotland) Act 1918. Under this new Act, Laurel Bank would become a part of the statutory provision of education in Glasgow, though the ownership and direct control of the school would be transferred to a newly formed private limited company. Miss Hannan Watson remained, however, as headmistress, as well as being a governor and a director of Laurel Bank (which, incidentally, was the first private school in Glasgow to be involved in the scheme).[42]

Laurel Bank School continued to prosper under the new arrangements. A third house in Lilybank Terrace was purchased in 1929 and new sports grounds were acquired in Scotstounhill to replace the old playing fields shared with Queen Margaret College at the top of Crossloan (now Cleveden) Road. After the last war (during which Laurel Bank girls, like many other students around Glasgow, were evacuated to the countryside), the school still prospered. In 1952, Laurel Bank obtained its own hall by purchasing the neighbouring Belmont Parish Church (built *c.*1894 by architect James Miller), whose congregation had recently merged with Hillhead Parish Church in Huntly Gardens. The new acquisition was appropriately named The Hannan Watson Wing. In 1964, the school's expansion in Lilybank Terrace was completed when the fourth house in the terrace was obtained from the University of Glasgow.

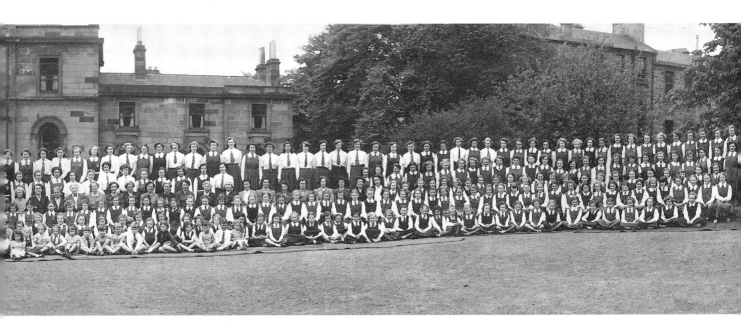

The second Northpark House (*right*), built c.1870 by John T. Rochead for John and Matthew Bell of the world-famous Glasgow Pottery, is not to be confused with the original Northpark of Provost John Hamilton which stood nearby from 1800 to c.1864. From 1883 to 1935, the Bells' Northpark House was the home of Queen Margaret College, after which it became the Scottish headquarters of the BBC. Northpark came under threat in the 1920s when Glasgow Corporation was planning a new bridge across the Kelvin. Three options were proposed: one scheme put the approach road through Northpark House, another went through the Kibble Palace, and the third plan threaded the road between the two structures.

Queen Margaret's College.   Glasgow.

27

The history of the development of women's education in Scotland has, until recently, been a neglected field of study.[43] Prior to the middle of the nineteenth century, the educational opportunities for girls in Glasgow (and Scotland) were poor. After the 1850s, an increasing number of private schools for girls were opened in areas such as the West End, but tertiary education was still a solely male domain. From the 1860s, however, the question of the education of women suddenly became a major topic of social and academic debate.

In Glasgow, the first positive steps in the campaign to educate women came in 1868 when Mrs Jessie Campbell of Tullichewan organised a series of 'Lectures for Ladies' in the McLellan Galleries. The success of the first series led to them becoming an annual event, with several distinguished professors from Gilmorehill participating over the years. Jessie Campbell was the wife of the prominent Glasgow businessman James Campbell (nephew of a former Lord Provost of Glasgow and cousin of the future Liberal Prime Minister Sir Henry Campbell-Bannerman). In her campaign to educate women, Jessie Campbell garnered support from Principal John Caird, his brother Edward Caird, Professor of Moral Philosophy, and other prominent staff at the university.

Although Jessie Campbell appreciated the encouragement of prominent local academics, much more practical and sustained work was required. 'These and other broad-minded men remained valiant supporters of the new educational movement, although the burden of its promotion,' she would later recall, 'was borne by the women themselves.'[44] To this end, the Association for the Higher Education of Women in Glasgow and the West of Scotland was formed in 1877. Principal Caird chaired the first meeting and Queen Victoria's daughter, Princess Louise, said to be 'the clever woman of her family,' was nominated as president.[45] Most important, however, was the appointment of Miss Janet Galloway as one of the acting secretaries of the association.

In 1883, due to the hard of work of Jessie Campbell and Janet Galloway, the association was incorporated as Queen Margaret College, named after King Malcolm Canmore's wife St Margaret, the woman responsible for bringing formal education to Scotland in the eleventh century. The aim of Queen Margaret College was 'to perform for women work similar to that done by Colleges and Universities for men.'[46] Janet Galloway was secretary of Queen Margaret College from the college's opening in 1883 until her death twenty-six years later.

Janet Galloway's tireless dedication to the college was legendary. Not only did she organise the educational programmes, but also encouraged the women students to form debating and dramatic societies, learned and social clubs, and their own union. When the college first opened, overcoming the attitude of local landladies towards providing accommodation for single women was a major issue. Marion

Gilchrist, an early graduate, recalled that 'everywhere we were met with the answer, "We take only single gentlemen." Here again Miss Galloway did trojan work. She not only found rooms, but visited the students and saw that they were properly looked after.' She also recalled that about once a week Miss Galloway took lunch with the women students, 'and that was always a very pleasant social event.'[47]

Despite the determined work by Jessie Campbell and Janet Galloway, had it not been for the generous financial support of Mrs Isabella Elder, Queen Margaret College would never have become a reality. Mrs Elder, widow of John Elder, the shipping magnate and owner of the Fairfield yard in Govan, was one of the great philanthropists of nineteenth-century Glasgow, financing, among other things, Elder Library and Elder Park in Govan, as well as Glasgow University's Chair of Naval Architecture. She also successfully managed her late husband's empire for many years. Mrs Elder's resolute dedication to the provision of education for women was such that she acquired the extensive property of Northpark and offered it free of charge to the fledgling college on the condition that it raise an endowment fund amounting to £20,000.

Mrs Elder supported the college for many years, and in the early 1890s provided the necessary funds to ensure that the new medical college would be an appropriately substantial and prestigious building. Unfortunately, several years after the 1892 incorporation of Queen Margaret College into the University of Glasgow, Mrs Elder fell out with the university over the latter's apparent failure to maintain its declared commitment to the concept of equal opportunities for the women students (which was, in fact, a contravention of the conditions of her original gifts to the college).

Queen Victoria visited Glasgow for the final time in August 1888 to formally open the new City Chambers and view the International Exhibition in Kelvingrove Park. Her Majesty also paid a fleeting visit to Queen Margaret College, no doubt at the behest of her daughter Louise, the Marchioness of Lorne (who was the college's president). Victoria was received at Northpark House by philanthropist Mrs Isabella Elder and Mrs Jessie Campbell of Tullichewan. Mrs Elder is seen (*below*) on the steps of Northpark House standing to the right of Mrs Campbell, who is holding a piece of paper most likely bearing the address to Her Majesty.

In the late 1880s, the issue of women's education was still being debated widely across Scotland, and in 1889 a Royal Commission was appointed to consider, among other things, 'the question of provision by Universities for the teaching and graduation of women.'[48] Legislation in that same year permitted Scottish universities to admit and graduate women students, and to this end the council of Queen Margaret College negotiated with the University of Glasgow over the future relationship between the institutions.

After the success of its early years, Queen Margaret College was justly proud of its independence. Still, the college wanted its women to obtain graduate degrees and thus it had to decide whether it wished to become 'affiliated' with or 'incorporated' into the university. Affiliation would bring official recognition by the university, though the college would retain responsibility for its own financial arrangements. If incorporated into the university, the latter would assume these burdens. In 1892, the college's council decided to seek incorporation.

As recalled by Francis Melville, the college's mistress for twenty-five years, incorporation was finalised in July of 1892, when the

> deed of gift was approved by the College Council, which handed over to the University Court of the University of Glasgow, to its government and administration as the Women's Department of the University, the whole property and buildings of the College, together with a "dowry" of £25,000, on condition that these were "to be held and used in all time coming as an integral part of the said University premises for separate University education of women equal to that of men." By this change, neither the College nor its students lost identity.[49]

As of 1892, the women of Queen Margaret College were also fully matriculated students of the University of Glasgow.

After 1892, Queen Margaret College students continued to take their women-only classes at Northpark, but there were also mixed classes held on Gilmorehill. Medicine, however, was still to be taught separately and thus a new medical college had to be built at Northpark. Boarding for women students remained a problem, and at the instigation of Janet Galloway a company was formed in 1894 to acquire Lilybank House and convert it into the first women's residence (known as Queen Margaret Hall). The alterations were undertaken by Honeyman and Keppie.

The history of Queen Margaret College came to an end in 1935. After many years of increasing student numbers, it became clear that Northpark was at capacity. Also, more women were choosing to attend mixed classes at Gilmorehill. According to one historian, 'once absorbed into the university life the women gradually lost their taste for separate instruction,' and, eventually, 'the separate teaching of women, which had become both irksome and expensive, dwindled away, until, in 1935, it ceased altogether.'[50]

The ornamental grounds of Northpark House were used for many fêtes, galas, bazaars and other events, not only for Queen Margaret College but also for Laurel Bank School, Redlands Hospital and other local institutions. Eventually, most of the gardens were built over by the various extensions to the BBC from the 1930s onwards.

29

As early as 1888, the Queen Margaret College Council sought to establish medical classes for women. Following the 1892 legislation which permitted women to study in Scotland's universities, Queen Margaret students were permitted to attend any established classes in Gilmorehill except medicine, which it was thought best to keep an all-male affair. With the assistance of Isabella Elder and the Bellahouston Trust, new medical college premises (*left*) were built at Northpark by architects Honeyman and Keppie. It is believed that much of the building was by John Keppie, but that considerable input came from his senior assistant Charles Rennie Mackintosh. In the 1960s, the medical college was enveloped by a major extension of the BBC.

Northpark was designed to house a major private art collection and thus contained a lofty gallery space. Matthew Perston Bell, a widower, died around the time work on the house was begun, so it was actually the vision of his bachelor brother John Bell which saw the project to its completion. John Bell, however, died intestate, and his massive art collection was broken up and sold at auction. The Corporation of Glasgow, despite a public outcry, failed to launch a bid to acquire this important collection.

Lady tram driver at the Botanic Gardens, c.1915.

V.

Transport

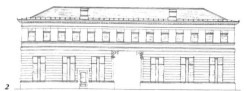

2

Despite the fact that Glasgow's horse-tram network was set to start operating in 1872, omnibus and cab operator John Ewing Walker commissioned Alexander 'Greek' Thomson around the same time to design handsome new stables, the so-called Royal Horse Bazaar, in Smith (now Otago) Street, near Gibson Street, Hillhead. In Thomas Gildard's famous eulogy of Thomson, he declared that here the architect had produced 'an admirable work, the highest art most happily bestowed on what, by some, might be deemed a mean object.'[11]

Previous page: **During the First World War, manpower shortages led to the employment of women tram drivers. One of the five young 'lady drivers' trained in 1915 was a Miss Mary Campbell, who drove a Green route standard along Great Western Road. Interviewed about the demands of her new role, Miss Campbell said, 'speaking candidly I don't consider the task beyond women folks. I prefer driving to conducting; there may be occasions when dilatory carters make me wish that my command of the King's English could be more forceful and still be lady-like, but taking it all over, it is a grand life. Out in the open air, with no one to bother you as long as the work is going on and the wheels revolving to time.'[12]**

O f all the major transport improvements in the nineteenth century, it has been argued that the Great Western Road turnpike was the only one which preceded, rather than followed, suburban development in the West End of Glasgow.[1] Most often, when the omnibus, tram, railway and subway services were established, their routes and stations were located well within built-up areas. It was also the case that residents in outlying areas often had to petition the transport companies to extend services to reach them.

The first form of public transport in the West End came in 1847 when the Kelvinside Estate Company subsidised a regular omnibus service between Glasgow Cross and the Botanic Gardens in order to demonstrate to potential feuars that the new suburb was easily accessible from the city centre. 'This was at first a one-horse affair,' wrote James B. Fleming many years later, 'but very shortly after, a two-horse omnibus was put on, and it was a great event on the Road when the omnibus with three horses abreast was started.'[2] The service ran every two hours at first, and was then enhanced to an hourly and later a half-hourly service. The fact that the first omnibus had only appeared in Glasgow two years previously illustrates how progressive the Kelvinside estate proprietors were.

This original omnibus service on the Great Western Road was operated by James Walker, one of the great Glasgow liverymen of the day. The tenacious Walker fought with the trustees of the Great Western Road turnpike for nine years to have the tolls for omnibuses reduced (finally succeeding in gaining a reduction from 1/6 to 9d in 1856).[3] Within a few years, however, Walker had to compete on the Great Western Road route with his great rivals Wylie & Lochhead, who had started a similar service at the behest of the turnpike trustees.[4] James Walker's perseverance was such that, at his death around 1866, it was recorded that he left 'a great Establishment to the Management of his Son, Mr John E. Walker, who appears to be carrying on the Business with equal energy and success.'[5]

As early as 1870 it was generally anticipated that Glasgow would soon have trams, or as described by the *Glasgow Herald*, 'Street-Cars running smoothly in Iron Grooves, after the American model.'[6] Legislation was soon enacted which authorised the Corporation of Glasgow to construct tramlines throughout the city. These lines were then leased to the private Glasgow Tramway and Omnibus Company until 1894, after which the Corporation decided not to renew the lease and instead took control of the service. Within two years, 'nine depots had been built, 3,500 horses purchased, 244 cars built, and the necessary stores and workshops prepared.'[7] Also, advertisements were removed from cars, the use of different colours for different routes was established, and the famous ha'penny fare was introduced.

In the first seven years of Corporation management, the number of tram passengers city-wide rose from 54 million to 140 million annually.[8] Within four years of the Corporation takeover, it was decided to adopt electric traction in order to ensure that Glasgow's network remained one of the best in Europe (where many systems were already electrified). Most of the Glasgow system was electrified by 1901 (in time for the International Exhibition in Kelvingrove Park) and the last horse-trams finally disappeared the following year. Many old horse cars were converted for use under electric traction and remained in active service for several decades.

For the emerging West End middle class, the trams enabled families to reside in the comfortable suburbs whilst the male breadwinners continued to work in the bustling city. Author J. J. Bell, who grew up in Hillhead in the 1870s, later recalled the regular weekday scene along the Great Western Road.

About 8:30 began the pilgrimage of Hillhead's papas into town for the purpose of making pennies [,] . . . some running after a tramcar and nimbly boarding it, without troubling the horses to stop, others making up their minds to walk into the city for the good of their health. A considerable number of them wear black coats and silk hats. Such a garb is certainly a

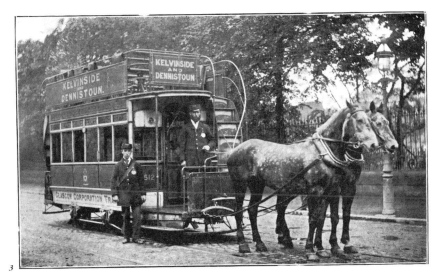

The West End's first tramway opened in 1872 and ran along Great Western Road to the terminus at Kirklee Road. When the Corporation of Glasgow took control of the system in 1894, it inherited not only the staff and horses, but also the original open-top cars. Over the next twenty years, the top decks of most of these old cars were enclosed, and after 1901 many horse cars were also converted for electric traction. Here, car No. 512, its driver, horses and conductor pose outside the Botanic Gardens in the late 1890s.

sign that the wearer is a banker, or a lawyer, or a member of the Royal Exchange, or, of course, a cabby.[9]

Soon after the establishment of Glasgow Corporation's tram company, the network became recognised as one of best in the world. The Glasgow tramcars were an endearing feature of the city streets for generations, and in the decades since the procession of the last tram in 1962 there has been an extraordinary amount of historical research and much passionate eulogising on the subject.[10]

Persistent lobbying by local residents led to the 1880 extension of the Great Western Road tram line to Hyndland Road, Lancaster Terrace and Westbourne House. This c.1885 view shows the team of horses being 'turned' for the return journey to Glasgow. Note also the many adverts on the car (later to be banned by the Corporation).

The year 1901 saw great changes to the Corporation's tramways as the network was electrified and many routes were extended. In the West End, a new terminus was established for the Green cars on Great Western Road at Anniesland Cross, and new lines went up Byres Road and Gibson Street. This enclosed Standard tram (*right*) was photographed in Great Western Road outside Red Hall, near the corner of Beaconsfield Road. The 1880 terminus opposite the newly built Lancaster Crescent (*centre*) was marked by the end of the elegant central trampoles. The 1901 extension to Anniesland was powered by wires on poles in the pavements (*right*).

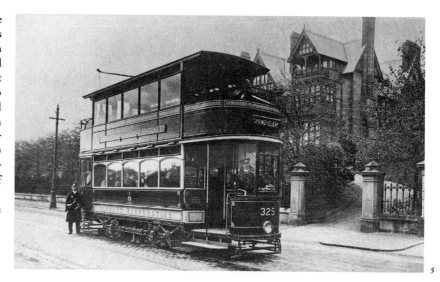

5

6

A 'Hex Dash' Standard tram on the Yellow route turns into Byres Road from Highburgh Road. When this new route was proposed, there was great opposition from Highburgh residents who were concerned about the noise of tram traffic.

7

8

9

10

Top: An open-top Yellow car proceeds up a relatively empty Byres Road just across from the Hillhead subway entrance in this *c.*1905 picture postcard view. *Centre*: A White car enters Gibson Street en route to Pollokshields. Immediately behind the tram is Bloomfield Place, the first range of tenements to be built in Hillhead (*c.*1840s). *Left*: An early view of the White car terminus in University Avenue in front of Anderston Free Church, designed by James Sellars *c.*1877 (though his proposed corner tower was never built). After being used for many years as an examination hall, the church was converted into the university's arts complex in 1998.

From the 1920s, motorbuses made gradual inroads into the domain of the tramcar. Many of the tramlines that were proposed or authorised prior to the First World War were put on trial with motorbuses in the 1920s in order to assess passenger popularity. One long-planned West End tram route was meant to link Great Western and Garscube Roads, crossing the new Queen Margaret Bridge near the Botanic Gardens. After motorbus trials in the 1920s, however, it was decided that the route was not viable and no tramlines were ever laid on the wide new bridge. *Right*: increased congestion caused by trams, automobiles and motorbuses eventually led to the use of traffic policemen at the corner of Byres Road.

11

Following the end of the First World War, Glasgow's tram network entered a period of gradual and inevitable decline. Despite expansion of the system (*e.g.* Great Western Road's tramlines were extended to Knightswood in 1924 and Blairdardie in 1949), and the introduction of newly-designed cars (Cunarders appearing as late as 1952), the famous Glasgow tram was doomed for a variety of reasons. In the late 1940s, staff shortages, rising wage and maintenance costs, falling revenue (despite fare increases) and the increasing age of much of the city-wide network prompted a series of studies and reports into the future of Glasgow's trams. There was much criticism of the increasing road congestion caused by the old trams, and the two fatal accidents in the 1950s along Great Western Road no doubt hastened the demise of the system.

Depending on the value of scrap metal at the time of the tramways' phased closure, redundant rails were either lifted or simply buried under asphalt. This mid-1960s view looking up Byres Road (taken from a similar vantage point to the one on the previous page) shows the traffic congestion of the day.

12

13

In the end, the main trouble the tram network faced was the great age of the majority of the fleet. Hundreds of cars were decades old, and some which were in constant operation in the 1950s had been in service since the early years of electrification. The introduction of motorbuses in the 1920s and trolleybuses from 1945 paved the way for the replacement of trams with buses to reduce maintenance costs for the Corporation. In June 1957, it was determined that to replace the ageing tramcar fleet would have cost over £11 million, but replacement motorbuses would cost the Corporation half that amount.[13] Within six months, the first West End route had been abandoned (the Yellow, or No. 5, along Byres Road). Further closures came in the following three years, and the final West End tram, the Blue route (No. 10) along Great Western Road, ceased to operate after 4 June 1960.

The increase in vehicular traffic in postwar Glasgow brought about a spate of fatal accidents involving trams. In May 1950 seven people died and 43 were injured when a bus overturned in the path of an oncoming tram in Great Western Road near Beaconsfield Road (*above*). Five years later, a tram derailed further east at Byres Road and caused a collision with a bus, a car and a motorcycle with sidecar, killing two people. By 1958, the decision had been taken to cease operation of Glasgow's tram network.

14

The Green line was extended to Anniesland in 1901, and beyond to the Corporation's new garden suburb of Knightswood in the 1920s. Around this time, Great Western Road was widened west of the entrance to Gartnavel Asylum and the tramlines were placed on a central reservation. This view looking east near Kelvindale was taken in the late 1950s, shortly before the trams were removed from Great Western Road. The central reservation was eventually planted over.

In order to pass through Kelvinside on its route between Partick and Bellshaugh, the Lanarkshire & Dumbartonshire Railway acquired a right-of-way along the eastern boundary of Gartnavel Asylum. A shallow cutting (*above*) was constructed to permit the line to pass under Great Western Road and into the tunnel to Bellshaugh. This cutting was partly filled in and built over with houses in the late 1980s, though a short section is still visible today behind John J. Burnet's Kelvinside station building (now a restaurant). Behind the steam-powered cranes in this rare construction view of the early 1890s can be seen the old North Balgray farm and the massive Tudor mansion of Red Hall at the foot of Beaconsfield Road.

Soon after the Great Western Road turnpike opened, a railway boom swept the country. The 'railway mania' of the 1840s initiated radical new patterns of development in Glasgow and most other British towns and cities over the next fifty years. Railways facilitated industrial expansion and established convenient links between burgeoning residential and commercial districts. Although this transport boom coincided with the development of Glasgow's new western suburbs, it was another half-century before the first railway was extended into the heart of the prosperous residential quarter beyond the Kelvin. By the time the railways began to provide a proper service to the growing populations of Dowanhill, Hillhead and Kelvinside in the mid-1890s, the ever-popular tramway network was on the verge of electrification and the new cable subway system was under construction.

Although the so-called 'golden age of railways' and the West End's own boom years neatly overlapped, the railways had little direct impact on the development of the western periphery of Glasgow. As in the case of the tram network, new railways lines (with the exception of the Hyndland spur) never preceded the steady development of these residential neighbourhoods. Rather, the railways only came to the West End 'when it was two-thirds complete.'[14] Even the ebullient James B. Fleming, who in the 1860s fought against a proposed North British goods line through the centre of his family's Kelvinside estate, was surprised at the inability of the railway companies to provide Glasgow's most exclusive suburb with a railway connection to the city. 'It is rather an extraordinary thing,' wrote Fleming, 'that upon an Estate such as Kelvinside, situated between the Two-mile and Three-and-a-half-mile radius from the centre of a great City, there is not up to the present day (April, 1894) such a thing as a Railway in working operation.'[15]

There are many reasons why no railway company was interested in constructing a line through the West End during the decades following the railway mania of the 1840s. First, nearly all the major companies were busy competing for the most advantageous routes into the city centre and the best sites for their terminus buildings. For example, the original scheme to relocate the University of Glasgow from the High Street to Woodlands Hill was predicated on the high value of city

A view north from the site of Kirklee station shows the new plate girder bridge for Kirklee Road being built above the split in the Glasgow Central Railway. Here, branches diverged northwest to Dawsholm (left) and northeast towards Maryhill Barracks (right). The triangular sidings between these two branches and the River Kelvin were used as a mineral yard for many years, and later became the site of a car showroom. At the turn of this century, the area was redeveloped for housing.

16

centre land for railway development. Upon the collapse of this first deal, some fifteen years passed before another railway company successfully negotiated with the university for the High Street site. Between the building of Queen Street station in the early 1840s and the Caledonian's Central station in the late 1870s, the city centre remained the chief interest of the major railway companies.

Another reason why the West End was bereft of rail connections for so long was that in this age of great industrial development in Glasgow, great profits could be made in the movement of goods and minerals, rather than passengers. Many of the greatest railway projects of the mid-nineteenth century included the establishment of goods yards and connections between important quays and industrial sites along the Clyde. Although there was railway activity west of the city from the 1850s onwards, particularly around Stobcross, Partick and Maryhill, this early traffic was almost exclusively commercial. Hillhead, Kelvinside and the adjacent districts, being developed as high-quality residential areas, were not considered to be worth the investment.

The construction of the Glasgow Central Railway was a great engineering achievement, tunnelling under 'certainly the busiest streets in the city' before reaching the open air by the River Kelvin.[16] Between Kirklee and Dawsholm, engineer Charles Forman built a robust infrastructure of cast iron bridges and viaducts constructed in local sandstone. This view of a stone arch under construction near Bellshaugh was probably taken by Forman himself. [17]

17

Glasgow has always been a densely populated city. In the Victorian period, even as the population grew exponentially, most people still lived within walking distance of their workplaces. Residents of the new suburbs west of the Kelvin, despite their apparent isolation, could still easily reach the city centre by carriage, omnibus or on foot along the Great Western Road. From 1872, horse-trams also provided easy access to the city.

There was a limited amount of suburban railway development on the northern fringes of Glasgow during the middle decades of the nineteenth century, but the new lines circumvented the West End to link the city (via Maryhill) with more distant residential enclaves. A railway line to Helensburgh first opened in 1858, followed by a spur to Milngavie five years later. Despite the West End's steady population growth in the second half of the century, it was not until the mid-1880s that the first passenger railway skirted the area.

The first attempt to construct a railway across the Kelvin was made by the North British Railway in the early 1860s, when it proposed to create a branch from its Cowlairs/Helensburgh line at Maryhill, and take it down through Kelvinside and Partick and over the Kelvin to Stobcross. The quays at Stobcross were of crucial importance to the economy of the upper Clyde, yet by this time no company had managed to provide a direct rail link to the waterfront area. This roundabout route via Maryhill was the most logical at the time, for it avoided the problem of driving a line through the built-up areas immediately west of Glasgow (*e.g.* Grahamston and Anderston).

Parliamentary authorisation for this Stobcross branch was obtained in August 1864, only leaving the NBR with the task of settling compensation claims from landowners along the route from Maryhill to the Clyde. For the most part, the claims were settled quickly; two major estates, however, caused severe problems for the railway company. After protracted adjudication, one landowner, Jane Graham-Gilbert of Yorkhill (wife of the famed portrait painter John Graham-Gilbert), managed to extract an award nearly three times the amount originally offered by the NBR.[18]

The Stobcross branch was authorised to follow the line of the Hay Burn (which ran between the drumlins of Partickhill and Broomhill) before sweeping east behind

In the hollow between the drumlins of Hillhead and the Botanic Gardens, the 'cut and cover' method was used to excavate the section of the Glasgow Central Railway which connected the two deep brick-arch tunnels driven through the local bedrock and boulder clay. Here, by the Botanic Gardens station, engineer Charles Forman spanned the platform area with massive roof girders (some 52 feet long) set on five-foot thick walls of concrete faced with brick.[21] At the upper left of this fascinating photograph taken below Great Western Road (looking west towards the station) is the hazy outline of Kelvinside Free Church's landmark spire on the corner of Byres Road.

18

the old farmhouse of South Balgray near the intersection of Great Western and Hyndland Roads. At this point the line was intended to continue north-east through the prime feuing land of Kelvinside before crossing the Kelvin near Bellshaugh. Despite taking a path through lands destined for residential development, the Stobcross branch was never intended to be a passenger line. Having been strictly planned as a goods line, it offered no benefit to Kelvinside and the other affected estates.

Needless to say, the Kelvinside Estate Company contested the NBR proposals with great vigour. James B. Fleming was able to elicit the support of such Glasgow notables as architect James Sellars and City Architect John Carrick during the jury trial. Most of the lands affected by the railway were still in the hands of the estate company, but 10 acres along the Great Western Road had been feued to the Free Church many years before. As trustees of the church, publisher John Blackie senior of Kew Terrace, and wealthy landowner John Bain of Moriston, brought the compensation claim against the railway company. The supporting evidence for the claim provides an interesting insight into the lofty aspirations of the estate company, which tried to 'preserve the lands for houses of the best description.'[19]

After many years of wrangling, the NBR was faced with a court judgment which imposed severe restrictions on the scheme, as well as requiring costly investment in improving infrastructure (new bridges, sewers etc.) along the path through Kelvinside. In the end, having paid out handsomely to Mrs Graham-Gilbert of Yorkhill, the NBR decided to abandon this route. Instead, in 1870 it sought to obtain new parliamentary authorisation for a revised Stobcross branch (which deviated from the original line before reaching Gartnavel). Rather than heading north-east to cross the Kelvin at Bellshaugh, the revised line swept to the west of Kelvinside, crossing the Great Western Road by Anniesland before tunnelling under the Forth and Clyde Canal at Dawsholm. The line opened for goods in 1874, and having been linked to lines to Clydebank and Helensburgh, opened for passenger services by 1886. New stations were opened at Yorkhill, Partick (later called Partickhill), Jordanhill and Great Western Road (called Anniesland from 1931), and a short spur was built to a new terminus at Hyndland Road.[20]

The Caledonian Railway was renowned for its impressive station buildings, and few were finer than architect James Miller's Botanic Gardens station, pictured soon after completion in 1896. It was described at the time by the London-based journal *The Builder* as a 'pretty little red brick tiled building with white woodwork and half-timbered gables, a strange sight in Glasgow; it has two tall turrets on the roof with gilded onion-shaped domes, is very well grouped and detailed and looks too good architecturally for what it is.'[22] It has often been said that this whimsical station was a precursor to Miller's flamboyant Main Hall at the 1901 International Exhibition in Kelvingrove Park.

The collapse of the North British Railway's plans to branch through Kelvinside in the 1860s did not deter the company — or its chief rival, the Caledonian Railway — from pursuing other routes west of the Kelvin in due course. There was, however, little progress in the early 1870s, and the collapse of the City of Glasgow Bank at the end of the decade led to a depression which stagnated the city for several years. It was not until the early 1880s that formal proposals were made for new railway lines into the West End of Glasgow.

In 1881, when the North British Railway finally announced plans to provide the suburb of Hillhead and its environs with a direct line to Queen Street, the *Glasgow Herald* commented that it was not before time. 'It does seem somewhat remarkable,' reported the *Herald*, 'that while all the other districts of the city are accommodated by railway, the western district, which contains the greater part of the wealth and population, and especially of the travelling public, should have been overlooked.'[23] The route proposed in this Bill went west from Queen Street to Woodlands Road (via Cowcaddens), and crossed the Kelvin at South Woodside before reaching stations at Bank Street, Byres Road, Hyndland Road and Partick.

Within weeks of the North British plans being promoted, the Caledonian Railway also started planning a route through the western suburbs from its Buchanan Street station. The Caledonian plan proposed stations at Woodside, Kelvinside Free Church at Byres Road and at Great Western Terrace.[24] The NBR

After passing through the longest railway tunnel in Scotland,[26] the Glasgow Central line emerged from beneath Kelvingrove Park to cross the Kelvin before entering a second, deeper tunnel under the Great Western Road. The platform of Kelvinbridge station (*below*) spanned the river just below the station building in Caledonian Crescent. The large brick warehouse next door to the station was built in Otago Street *c.*1888 for Peter Hepburn's furniture company, one of Hillhead's earliest businesses.

20

scheme of 1881 went to Parliament for authorisation but was subsequently withdrawn, whereas the Caledonian scheme does not seem to have advanced beyond the planning stages. The *Glasgow Herald* stated that it was a propitious time to form a railway route through the west, not only because property prices were still low in the wake of the bank crash of 1878 but also because 'the whole district would welcome it.'[25]

The one scheme from 1881 which did succeed was the Glasgow City & District Railway, an independent venture promoted by a group of Glasgow businessmen and landowners. The City & District company put up the capital to construct the line which was then operated on their behalf by the NBR (who paid a return on each ticket sold). The new line created a low-level route under NBR's Queen Street station, extending west to join the Stobcross line. Further west, the City & District company not only built a spur to Hyndland Road, but also added new passenger stations to the 1874 goods line between Stobcross and Maryhill.

Despite the addition of passenger stations to the Stobcross to Maryhill goods line, and the new spur to Hyndland, the bulk of the population of the West End was not well served by commuter railway links for many years (unlike similar neighbourhoods in Glasgow's South Side). Not until 1888 would Parliamentary authorisation be obtained by the Glasgow Central Railway Company to tunnel directly through the heart of the West End. This complicated line from Dalmarnock to Dawsholm would not, however, be completed until 1896.

Having won a competition to design Belmont Parish Church in Great George Street in 1893, young architect James Miller resigned his position in the civil engineering office of the Caledonian Railway and set up his own practice in Glasgow. He continued to work with the railway company for many years, producing many fine buildings such as the exquisite Wemyss Bay station, built *c*.1907. At Kelvinbridge (*above*), Miller produced a modest station house of brick and red sandstone, tucked neatly behind his exuberant Caledonian Mansions in Great Western Road. For many years Miller stayed in Hillhead Street, almost equidistant between his station buildings at Kelvinbridge and the Botanic Gardens.

Emerging from the Botanic Gardens tunnel, the Glasgow Central line reached the rustic station of Kirklee, where architect John J. Burnet's picturesque red sandstone buildings appear to be chiselled into the hillside above the Kelvin (*above*). Construction of the railway dramatically changed the topography of the area around Kirklee, with the station standing on the legendary trysting spot of the Three Tree (or Pear Tree) Well. At the left of this *c.*1896 view are the upper floors of Kirklee Quadrant. In the foreground is the Ha'penny Bridge, built in the 1880s to replace an ancient timber crossing. This iron bridge survived, though closed for some time, until it was swept away in the great flood of December 1994.

In 1896, after many years of delay and failure, two railways finally started running in the West End of Glasgow. After six long years of construction, the Glasgow Central Railway opened fully for passenger services in August 1896. The Lanarkshire & Dumbartonshire Railway also served the West End, if only peripherally, in its circuitous route running north and west from Stobcross to Bellshaugh and Maryhill. Like the Glasgow Central Railway, the L&D was a private venture which had backing from (and was eventually absorbed by) the powerful Caledonian Railway Company. Though authorised by Parliament three years after the GCR, the Lanarkshire & Dumbartonshire opened to West End passengers in October 1896, only a few months after the Glasgow Central line.

These two Caledonian subsidiaries were the last railways to be constructed in the West End. Of the two, the L&D had the more marginal impact on the development of the West End. Both lines ran west from Stobcross, with the L&D forming stations at Partick Central (where a high-level ticket office on Benalder Street Bridge still remains), Partick West and Crow Road, before passing underneath the NBR's Stobcross branch near Gartnavel Asylum. The line's most impressive station was built by John J. Burnet in Great Western Road, near Gartnavel. Kelvinside station, as it was called, was very much in keeping with the palatial villas then being built along the Great Western Road. North of this station, the L&D tunnelled under Balgray Hill to emerge near the Kelvindale Paper Works, before sweeping eastward along the river to Bellshaugh and up to Possil.

When the two lines opened in 1896, the Glasgow Central Railway's three stations at Kelvinbridge, Botanic Gardens and Kirklee were much better placed to serve Hillhead, Dowanhill and Kelvinside than was L&D's peripheral Kelvinside station by Gartnavel. Burnet's handsome station was located too far out along the Great Western Road and thus had very little population in its catchment to the east (and practically none to the west). Although the GCR fared better than its rival, the opening of the subway (also in 1896) and the electrification of the Corporation tramways in 1901 prevented either railway line from thriving.

The ceremonial first sod for the construction of the Glasgow Central Railway was cut at Kirklee in June 1890, only weeks after the company had been absorbed by the mighty Caledonian Railway. Without the financial clout of the Caledonian, it is probable that the ambitious Glasgow Central line would not have been built. Construction of the line was arduous and expensive, involving lengthy excavated sections through the centre of Glasgow. Engineer Charles Forman, who had been instrumental in driving legislation for the project through Parliament, had to contend with difficult ground conditions near the Clyde and delicate Georgian buildings in Argyle Street, Trongate and other busy parts of the city. Temporary decking was also required to permit the tramways to function as normal.

Most of the Glasgow Central line was constructed by the cut and cover method (whereby deep trenches are excavated, and brick arches formed, before the cut is backfilled and the road surface reinstated). West of the city, however, much underground tunnelling was required. Squads of 'six miners and four labourers, on a twelve hours' shift,' drove a tunnel beneath Great Western Road between Kelvinbridge and Botanic Gardens stations. Within the Botanic Gardens, two shifts of men took twelve months to cut a curving tunnel lying some forty feet beneath the crown of the drumlin. After emerging high above the Kelvin at Kirklee, the line split and continued to termini at Dawsholm and Maryhill. These two West End tunnels formed the steepest ascent in the line, with a gradient of 1 in 80 raising the level of the railway to more than a hundred feet above the Clyde.[27]

The line west of the Kelvin was not wholly underground. Ventilation shafts had to be constructed above the Botanic Gardens station to permit the escape of the sulphurous smoke from the engines. There were warnings, however, that this smoke would be 'destructive to the valuable collection of trees, shrubs and plants therein.' Similarly, there were grave concerns about the proposed open cuttings in Kelvingrove Park. 'This park is the West End Park of Glasgow,' stated the town council's petition, 'and the construction of the Railway through the same in the manner proposed by the Bill, will to a great extent destroy the amenity and enjoyment thereof.'[28] Consequently, in the end, the tunnel from Stobcross was extended under Kelvingrove, submerging the line until it reached South Woodside.

At the north end of the Botanic Gardens, the Glasgow Central line left the tunnel through a massive sandstone portal which opened out into a deep cutting high above the Kelvin. Kirklee station was just beyond the cutting. Maryhill Barracks, built from 1870 on the lands of Garrioch, can be seen in the distance of this expansive view, taken from above the portal. The buildings on the horizon are at Gilshochill, and at the lower right the River Kelvin can be seen through the trees.

The Glasgow Central Railway line emerged from beneath Kelvingrove Park and ran in the open air for a few hundred yards before passing Kelvinbridge station and returning underground into the Great Western Road tunnel. Upon construction of the railway, the South Woodside mill site was cleared for use as a goods and mineral yard. (It is possible that the mill lades were filled with rubble from the nearby tunnel excavations.) Although passenger services to Kelvinbridge ceased in 1952, the mineral yard remained in use until shortly after this photograph was taken in 1964. James Miller's station building at Kelvinbridge was destroyed by fire in 1968. Later, the yards were landscaped and a car park built to serve the reconstructed subway entrance near the river.

The Glasgow Central Railway's West End stations enjoyed some early success, but never really thrived. Despite the parent Caledonian Railway's best efforts to attract custom, the stations at Kelvinbridge, Botanic Gardens and Kirklee struggled to compete with the new subway line and, later, the electrified trams. The Caledonian had invested substantial amounts in the Glasgow Central Railway, commissioning appropriately elegant stations for the West End from some of the city's leading architects such as John J. Burnet and James Miller.

Miller also designed the richly-detailed Caledonian Mansions alongside Kelvinbridge station. The mansions were not, as is popularly believed, built as an annexe to the Caledonian's Central Hotel. Recent research in the railway company's archives shows that the shops and the flats above were built purely for rental income.[29] Further Caledonian Railway investment in the area included bearing nearly half the cost of constructing the splendid sandstone and granite Kirklee Bridge of 1901, built to improve accessibility between the station and the developing lands of North Kelvinside.

Despite its superior facilities, the Caledonian Railway's Glasgow Central line could not compete with the tramways following their electrification in 1901. The railway may have provided a faster journey into Glasgow from the West End, but the travelling conditions were hardly comparable. The trams were more cramped and provided a less smooth ride, but travelling on the railway between the West End and the city centre could be extremely unpleasant. The distinguished architecture provided for its passengers above ground belied the 'somewhat stygian conditions below,'[30] where the great length of the tunnels and the infrequency of ventilation shafts compelled Glasgow Central passengers to suffer 'choking smoke in the dim and dismal environment below ground.'[31] To make matters worse, the noise in the tunnels was often deafening.

Within a few years of the introduction of electric trams, the number of passengers on the Glasgow Central line dropped dramatically. At Kelvinbridge station, the number of bookings fell from some 373,000 in 1897 (the first full year of operation) to only 78,000 in 1908. At the next station, Botanic Gardens, the decline was even steeper: from 109,000 in 1900 to barely 11,000 in 1911.[32]

Although the Glasgow Central Railway and its sister line, the Lanarkshire &

Dumbartonshire, eventually succumbed to the popularity of the tramways, both railways had faced the prospect of other competition from the very start. Even before these railway lines were first mooted, a Bill had been presented to Parliament for an underground cable railway running from St Enoch's Square to Byres Road in Partick. This Bill ultimately failed in the Commons, but in 1888 (the year of the Glasgow Central's authorisation), another Bill for a cable subway system was promoted. The robust objections to this Bill came from many quarters in both the city and the suburbs. Among the property-owners and businesses in Buchanan Street who strongly opposed the subway were the department stores of Wylie & Lochhead and their rivals, J. & W. Campbell. All along the proposed route under Great Western Road, property-owners feared that the tunnelling for the subway would cause subsidence if old flooded coal mines were disturbed.

This 1888 subway Bill ultimately failed, mostly due to the concerns of the Clyde trustees (who feared that tunneling under the river might threaten shipping and dredging operations). Strong opposition also came from the Caledonian Railway and its supporters, including James B. Fleming of Kelvinside, who argued that the proposed subway would diminish the amenity of his estate and could even damage buildings along its route (Grosvenor Terrace, in particular). What Fleming did not state in his petition of objection was that he was also a promoter of the Glasgow Central Railway.[33] By the time a revised but outwardly similar subway Bill was presented in 1890, the Glasgow Central Railway had already commandeered the most desirable route beneath Great Western Road, forcing the subway to excavate its deepest tunnel in the system, more than 110 feet below the crown of Hillhead between Kelvinbridge and Byres Road. This circular cable-powered underground railway opened in December 1896.[34]

25

The Glasgow District Subway opened late in 1896, some four months after the Glasgow Central Railway. Initially advertised as 'the only underground cable railway in the world — no smoke, no steam, perfect ventilation,'[35] the Glasgow subway has experienced many peaks and troughs of popularity over the past century. The system was taken over from its original private operators by Glasgow Corporation in 1922, and was electrified in 1935. Originally there were meant to have been three stations with passenger lifts, but the only one to be installed was at Kelvinbridge. The lift, which took passengers from Great Western Road down through a shaft in the corner tenement, fell out of use in 1938 but was reinstated some thirty years later. Stairs into this station were located at the foot of the cast iron staircase (*left*). This entrance and the lift were lost in the system's 1977-1980 refurbishment, when they were converted into an emergency exit from the platform below. New station buildings were constructed in the old mineral yards at the same time.[36]

A diesel passenger train from Rutherglen to Possil crosses the Kelvin in 1963, not long before this section of the old L&D line was finally closed. When this massive sandstone viaduct was constructed between Bellshaugh and Kirklee in the 1890s, it completely transformed one of the more picturesque parts of the lower Kelvin valley, once the site of rustic farm cottages, bleachfields and pastures. The tall building on the central horizon is Redlands, and Kelvinside Academy can be seen to the left of the locomotive. At the far right, the University of Glasgow's new Queen Margaret Hall is visible under construction on an old allotment site in Bellshaugh Road.

Declining business caused problems for all West End stations during the interwar years. Despite the fact that Glasgow's population was reaching its maximum of around one million, and the existing tram and subway systems were showing their age, the railways could not attract the numbers of passengers that their survival required. The first stations to close were the Glasgow Central's Botanic Gardens and Kirklee buildings in 1939, with the Lanarkshire & Dumbartonshire's Kelvinside station near Gartnavel shutting in 1942. Kelvinbridge struggled on to serve passenger traffic through the last war, but was finally made redundant in 1952.

Of the two Miller and two Burnet stations in the West End, only the latter's Kelvinside building still survives, having suffered the indignity of temporary closure during the First World War and having withstood nearly forty years of dereliction after its final closure in 1942. Several earnest attempts were made to rescue the building from the brink of demolition in the 1970s, but British Rail was only interested in leasing, not selling the decaying structure. The scale of repairs required was far too onerous for any prospective tenant, and it was only when BR decided to sell the building outright that a developer undertook a project to refurbish the ruin and convert it to a restaurant. In the mid-1990s, a serious fire destroyed the upper floors and roof, leading to another period of closure until new owners repaired and reopened the building in 1998.

James Miller's elegant stations at Kelvinbridge and the Botanic Gardens were tragically lost to fires in August 1968 and January 1970 respectively. Both sites were cleared not long afterwards, leaving few visible traces of the landmark buildings. There are a few remnants at Kelvinbridge (including a small plate girder bridge over the river) and the old platforms beneath the Botanic Gardens can still be seen though the long ventilation cuttings. At Kirklee, Burnet's buildings survived for some years after the line closed. Although there were several proposals to reopen the line for railway use during the 1970s, development pressures in the

The Kirklee area was very slow to develop, with many gap sites being used as allotments during (and well after) the wartime years of 1939-1945. The last allotment at Kirklee is seen in this *c.*1970 Henry B. Morton photograph, just to the right of the point where the old Glasgow Central line emerged from under Kirklee Road. Dinwoodie & Little's coal yard was displaced by a car showroom soon afterwards. (Not far away, between Mirrlees and Cleveden Drive, are the only extant allotments in Kelvinside.)

27

West End and the lack of a strategy for the future of such redundant lines led to the unfortunate redevelopment of this site a decade later.

Interestingly, when the Strathclyde tram (a light rail network) was proposed for Glasgow in the mid-1990s, there were plans to make use of the Great Western Road and Botanic Gardens tunnels, including a proposed station on the site of Miller's onion-domed masterpiece. At Kirklee, however, the loss of the right-of-way to new housing a few years previously forced the engineers to divert the proposed tramline from the Botanic Gardens, taking it down onto Addison Road behind the new flats before rejoining the old Glasgow Central line near the Kirklee allotments. In the end, the tram scheme failed to gain support in Parliament and the entire project was abandoned.

The redundant Kirklee station buildings of John J. Burnet stand forlornly as a passenger train bound for Maryhill Central passes by in 1959, some twenty years after this station was closed. This section of the Glasgow Central Railway remained in use for goods purposes until the 1960s when the line was finally dismantled. Kirklee station was eventually demolished and the area was redeveloped for housing in the 1980s and 1990s.

28

It is not surprising that in Victorian Glasgow, the industrial powerhouse of the British Empire, engineers were experimenting with the development of motorised vehicles as early as the 1880s. By the turn of the twentieth century, Glasgow was the home of some of the greatest names in Scottish motorcar manufacturing, including Arrol-Johnston, Argyll and the last survivor, Albion of Scotstoun. During the early period of hand-built dog carts, voiturettes and tourers, the number of car-owners among wealthy Glaswegians grew steadily.

By 1906, car ownership in Glasgow was such that the Royal Scottish Automobile Club (established in Edinburgh in 1899) decided to relocate its headquarters to the city in the west. In addition to its campaign to 'promote, encourage and develop Automobilism in Scotland,' the RSAC also began to survey and catalogue the condition of Scottish roads as well as rating the quality of the country's hotels.[37] RSAC members also undertook rigorous trials on the more strenuous roads, such as the route from Arrochar up to the Rest and be Thankful in Glen Croe. Reaching the summit of Ben Nevis, of course, became a popular test for many early motorcar drivers. For Glaswegians, the 1920s extension of Great Western Road (to meet the old Dumbarton Road near Bowling) provided a convenient motor route from the city centre to Loch Lomond and the West Highlands.

29

Around 1922, architect Charles McNair designed a new three-story garage complex in Julian Avenue, just behind Redlands House (then a women's hospital). Called Kelvinside Garage (*right* and *above*), the building was fronted in sandstone and had a pedimented entrance to the top deck. Of the new garage buildings in the West End, the most prominent was Wylie & Lochhead's in Byres Road (illustrated on page 185). This 1930 building replaced the company's old horse-cab stable on the site.

30

Good use was made of vacant ground in the West End in the early decades of the twentieth century to meet the growing demand for garages and lock-ups. Only a small minority of West End houses had existing mews buildings to convert to garages, so enterprising companies established storage garages either in former livery stables or, more rarely, in new-build premises. Some garages also provided repair services as well. The oldest surviving custom-built motorcar garage in the West End is the Botanic Gardens Garage in Vinicombe Street (*left*). It is also the most interesting architecturally. Built *c.*1912 by architect David V. Wyllie, the garage has a steel skeleton, a front facade of green and white faience (blocks of glazed terracotta), and a side elevation with large expanses of glazing.

31

32

33

The upper level of the Botanic Gardens Garage was reached by a ramp in the pend of the adjacent tenement (*left*). This top-floor storage area was spanned by barrel-vaulted steel trusses, with one section being glazed (*centre*). Unlike its later rival in Julian Avenue (with its stable-like stalls), the private lock-up spaces here were simple concertina cages. Like most other buildings around Cranworth Street, the garage took advantage of the low-lying land (a legacy of nineteenth-century stone, brick-clay and coal extraction) to form a valuable basement level. Although the Botanic Gardens Garage became part of the Arnold Clark empire in 1964, the painted sign on the tenement gable above (*top*) was faded but still legible until it was finally painted over in the mid-1990s.

The Wedding party of Marion Mirrlees at Redlands, 1891.

VI.

The Golden Years

In 1869, James B. Mirrlees acquired 24 acres in Kelvinside and employed architect James Boucher to build the massive villa of Redlands fronting Great Western Road. This *c.*1870 Annan view looking north from Great Western Terrace shows the new mansion still surrounded by the unfeued lands of Kelvinside. By the early years of the twentieth century (*opposite*), these open lands had been covered with villas and small terraces. The later view also shows an enlarged conservatory (probably by Boucher) and the main roof following substantial reconstruction after a fire in 1882. Mirrlees had four daughters whose wedding parties were photographed at Redlands in the 1880s and 1890s, including Marion, who married Ivor Phillips in 1891 (*previous page*). Phillips was a career soldier who later became Liberal MP for Southampton, and was knighted in 1917.

The start of the West End's 'golden years' can be dated from the late 1860s, when James Brown Montgomerie Fleming took effective control of the Kelvinside Estate Company and Hillhead was established as an independent burgh. Prior to this time, Hillhead had been growing steadily, but still had many large gap sites. Burgh status brought a degree of civic orderliness to the area, as roads, lighting, cleansing, policing and fire protection came under local control. These improvements led in turn to further development around the suburban West End.

After 1868, James B. Fleming radically altered the pattern of development in Kelvinside. He hived off large parcels of land along the Great Western Road, and many of the greatest names in Glasgow's mercantile community moved in and constructed some of the grandest houses in the area. In the decades to follow, the West End enjoyed its greatest period of sustained growth. Land was feued for substantial new houses; churches and schools were established; and the area became the most salubrious suburb of Glasgow.

Fleming's first major disposal of Kelvinside land was a triangle of some 16 acres south of the Great Western Road which was sold in 1868 to James Whitelaw Anderson, a sewed muslin manufacturer from Govan. In the following year, construction began on the first terrace west of Horslethill Road when the first feus of Alexander 'Greek' Thomson's Great Western Terrace were given off. Other lands sold by Fleming in the late 1860s included old Horslethill farm (sold to the Victoria Park Feuing Company, which subsequently built Athole and Huntly Gardens) and the extensive lands on the north bank of the Kelvin (including the 1750 Kelvinside House) sold to omnibus operator John Ewing Walker.

In 1869, not long after the North British Railway abandoned its proposed goods line through the heart of Kelvinside, wealthy Glasgow businessman James Buchanan Mirrlees acquired a 24-acre site north of the Great Western Road, the largest parcel of land ever developed for a single steading in the West End. Mirrlees commissioned architect James Boucher to build a classical palace, complete with conservatory, stable block and greenhouses. The luxurious mansion, called Redlands, was prominently sited on the highest section of the Great Western Road turnpike and set in an enclosed walled precinct in the centre of the roughly triangular plot between Kirklee and Crossloan (now Cleveden) Roads.

James Buchanan Mirrlees came from an old Glasgow family which figured prominently in the city's mercantile development.[1] Mirrlees' father and grandfather were Burgesses of the city, and he himself was a member of Glasgow Town Council, a one-time bailie and Lord Dean of Guild. James B. Mirrlees, an engineer, amassed a fortune in the manufacture of various types of engineering machinery. His firms were particularly known for their sugar refining equipment. Mirrlees was an important philanthropist in his day, contributing generously to the campaign for the university's removal to Gilmorehill. He was also a founder director of Kelvinside Academy and an ardent supporter of the Free Church of Scotland.

After removing from their previous residence at Sauchiehall House, James B. Mirrlees and his second wife Helen Gumprecht raised their family of nine children at Redlands. In a remarkable series of photographs preserved in the Greater Glasgow Health Board Archives, the grounds and interiors of Redlands are seen in their high Victorian splendour. The two Annan views of the mansion from Great Western Terrace (illustrated here) were taken around 1870 and 1901 and show the dramatic increase in development in Kelvinside during the West End's golden age, while further interior views reveal fine furniture, *objets d'art* and curiosities, and many portraits of eminent Mirrlees ancestors. Most telling, perhaps, are the formal group portraits of the wedding parties of four of the five Mirrlees daughters, all of which display the ultimate trappings of late Victorian wealth in Glasgow.

3

James Buchanan Mirrlees (1822-1903) came from a family of important Glasgow merchants. In 1871 he moved his family of nine children from a large Georgian villa in Sauchiehall Street to a palatial Italianate mansion on the western outskirts of the city at Kelvinside.

4

5

In the early 1870s, the first terraces constructed on the former Kelvinside lands south of the Great Western Road turnpike and west of Horslethill were built to the design of Alexander 'Greek' Thomson. Westbourne and Great Western Terraces were Thomson's last great residential buildings. Thomson may also have been an investor in the speculative construction of Great Western Terrace, by most accounts his finest terrace design and by far the most significant of all the imposing buildings along the Great Western Road. The builder was John McIntyre, a friend and occasional business partner of Thomson's.[2]

The early residents of Great Western Terrace included some of the most important names in Glasgow commerce at the time. One prominent Glasgow family (which, coincidentally, had many connections with Alexander Thomson) was the Blackie publishing dynasty. Robert Blackie (brother of Lord Provost John Blackie junior) was the original owner of No. 7 Great Western Terrace, and in 1872 commissioned Thomson to design the interior of the house, a project which caused the architect 'such frustration and some irritation.'[3]

After Great Western Terrace was completed, no more speculative terrace construction took place along the Great Western Road turnpike until the local economy had recovered from the City of Glasgow Bank crash in 1878. The decade between 1868 and 1878 had been good for the Kelvinside Estate Company. The sale and feuing of large parcels of land had enabled James B. Fleming to return to the company's former policy of feuing small plots for single or multiple steadings (e.g. villas and small terraces). Around 1873, Fleming not only commissioned a third revised feu plan for the estate, but also used his new capital to pay for infrastructure improvements such as the making of new roads (mostly on the east slope of Balgray Hill). The company also paid for the widening, straightening and re-levelling of Crossloan (now Cleveden) Road, the old parish road to the Forth and Clyde Canal. Streetlights were also installed throughout the estate.

Among the second generation of elite proprietors in Great Western Terrace was shipping magnate William Burrell, who moved to No. 8 after his marriage in 1901. (Previously, Burrell had stayed at No. 4 Devonshire Gardens with his widowed mother.) Burrell, now best remembered for his prodigious career as a fine art and antiquities collector, and as a great benefactor of his native city of Glasgow, was one of the dominant figures in Clyde shipping. He and his brother amassed a fortune by building merchant carriers, then selling off their fleet of ships when the market was at its most buoyant. They then invested elsewhere until the shipping market crashed, rebuilding their fleet when prices at the yards were at their lowest.

When William Burrell (1861-1958), *above,* **purchased No. 8 Great Western Terrace in 1901, he instructed his good friend, prominent Edinburgh architect Robert Lorimer, to alter the interiors to accommodate his already sizeable collection of valuable art, furniture, tapestries and stained glass. Many of the works pictured in these *c.*1905 photographs (*right* and *opposite*) were amongst the 1944 bequest by Burrell to the Corporation of Glasgow. Burrell and the city's councillors and officials, however, rarely saw eye to eye, and there was a serious breakdown in their relationship in the latter years of Burrell's life. Similarly, during the planning of Burrell's Hatton Castle home near North Berwick, the great collector had an irrevocable falling out with his architect friend Lorimer.**

6

With the profits from these endeavours (as well as the lucrative exporting of Clyde-built goods), Burrell was able to finance his relentless quest to enlarge his eclectic collections of artefacts and works of art from around the world. His status as a collector was such that in 1901, at the age of 39, Burrell was not only a leading committee member for Glasgow's International Exhibition, but was also the single greatest lender to the fine art section.

Alexander Thomson's Great Western Terrace, arguably his grandest residential work, was prominently sited at the highest point along the Great Western Road turnpike. Begun in 1869, progress on the terrace was so slow that the westerly houses were not completed until after the architect's death in 1875.

9

Despite its success in developing a prestigious residential enclave along the Great Western Road, the Kelvinside Estate Company was never actually a thriving concern. In fact, Matthew Montgomerie and John Park Fleming, and their heir, James B. Fleming, amassed enormous debts between 1839 and 1898 which the estate's trustees were not able to pay off until the middle of the twentieth century.

In 1856, the Kelvinside Estate Company obtained a sizeable loan (£50,000) from the Standard Life Assurance Company. In subsequent years, however, repeated requests for further loans were consistently rebuffed by Standard Life, which, at the time, remained very cautious about residential property speculation. It was not until 1869, by which time the estate had been taken over by James B. Fleming, that Standard Life finally agreed to advance Kelvinside the staggering sum of £109,000.[4] By the time of Fleming's death in 1899, the Kelvinside Estate Company had borrowed some £180,000 from Standard Life.[5]

Exactly how the Standard Life funds were used is not known. At this time, the estate company was no longer building houses itself (having only just finished its showpiece, Windsor Terrace, after nearly twenty years), and Fleming was already in the process of raising revenue by selling numerous large tracts of Kelvinside outright to other developers. No doubt some of the Standard Life money was used for essential infrastructure improvements around the estate, but the scale of these works would hardly account for the formidable sum borrowed.

The Kelvinside Estate Company's infrastructure improvements prompted steady development during the last three decades of the nineteenth century. Once the straightening and levelling of Crossloan (now Cleveden) Road was complete, Fleming commissioned a revised feu plan for the remaining sections of Kelvinside. New streets were laid out and serviced by the estate company, and further parcels of land were sold off to developers. In addition to the large rectangular tract west of Crossloan Road taken by Thomas Russell for his 'Kelvinside Gardens' villa development, another sizeable plot nearer the crown of Balgray Hill was purchased by developer William Young.

Around 1874, architect John Burnet senior was commissioned by Young to erect a sweeping crescent of large self-contained houses on this prominent, south-facing site in the newly laid-out Montgomerie (now Cleveden) Drive. Burnet's Montgomerie (now Cleveden) Crescent was constructed over several years, and it

Large villas began to appear on Balgray Hill, high above the Great Western Road, from the mid-1870s onwards. The impressive towered structure of Hayston (*right*) stood on the gushet facing James B. Fleming's Beaconsfield mansion. Part of a double (*i.e.* semi-detached) villa, Hayston dominated the approach up Crossloan (now Cleveden) Road with its tall, crenelated tower. It was built by shipowner Leonard Gow around 1883. A few years earlier, at the western end of Montgomerie (now Cleveden) Drive, a fine villa called Dariel had been built by James Hislop of the Partick, Hillhead & Maryhill Gas Works (located alongside the Forth and Clyde Canal near Temple). In the middle decades of the twentieth century, Dariel (*above*) was used as an annexe to Homeland, a Salvation Army maternity hospital in Red Hall in Great Western Road. Both Dariel and Red Hall were demolished in the postwar years.

10

11

is likely that the architect's son, John James, having recently returned from studying at the Ecole des Beaux Arts in Paris, assisted in its completion. Soon after this major development was started, others began to feu land on Balgray Hill. At first, wealthy Glasgow businessmen built detached villas for themselves, then, over the following two decades, local builders began to construct speculative semi-detached villas and terraced houses. William and Peter Miller of Partick, for example, built some 43 houses in Kelvinside in the last quarter of the century.[6]

Soon after work started on Montgomerie Crescent, several large villas were built nearby in Crossloan Road. At the top of the hill, at the gushet with the newly constructed North Balgray (now Beaconsfield) Road, James B. Fleming built his own substantial villa around 1875, which he claimed to have named after Lady Beaconsfield, the wife of the former Tory Prime Minister Benjamin Disraeli.[7] Beaconsfield then stood at the periphery of the built-up part of Kelvinside estate. To the west, the lands of Balgray were leased out for farming and mineral extraction. The ancient lands around Gartnavel farm, renamed Flemington around 1878 to dissociate them from the nearby asylum, were not feued until the 1890s. This area later became known as Claythorn.[8]

Development during James B. Fleming's lifetime was concentrated on the lands east of North Balgray Road (which was renamed Beaconsfield Road around the time of Fleming's enlargement of his mansion *c.*1895). By the third quarter of the nineteenth century, however, residential building was advancing westward towards Beaconsfield Road, and the continued extraction and burning of brick-clays, ironstone and other minerals on the lands of Balgray prompted a lengthy legal wrangle between Fleming and his new neighbours.

Residents in Montgomerie Drive and Crescent became very unhappy with the noxious smoke emanating from the mineral works leased by Fleming to local operators. The legal battle began in the late 1870s and persisted through the Sheriff Court in Glasgow and the Court of Session in Edinburgh, eventually reaching the House of Lords (where Fleming ultimately lost his case). Local residents, led by James Hislop of Dariel, claimed that the burning of blaes so close to the new residential quarter of Kelvinside was violating the very same clean and unspoiled environment advertised by the estate company to entice feuars.

One of architect John Burnet's last important works was Montgomerie (now Clevedon) Crescent, built in the mid-1870s at what was then the periphery of development in Kelvinside. It has been claimed that the architect's son, young John J. Burnet, may have had a hand in the construction of this 'unostentatiously sumptuous' terrace (pictured here in 1894).[9] Over the course of the next twenty years, detached villas of varying styles were constructed across from the crescent on the opposite side of Montgomerie (now Clevedon) Drive.

The periphery of Victorian Kelvinside moved westward along the Great Western Road between the late 1870s and the early 1890s. Imposing villas were built on the north side of the turnpike in 'Kelvinside Gardens,' (*right*) and grand terraces on the south. The last of the great villas to be built along the Great Western Road, Red Hall, is pictured here in 1894 on its conspicuous site at the corner of Beaconsfield Road. Red Hall, a rambling Tudor-style mansion, was designed by Thomas L. Watson for Alexander Anderson of the Royal Polytechnic department store. The prominent villa of Glentower, which became the Glasgow Homeopathic Hospital in 1931, can be seen further to the east.

12

13

The short terrace of Devonshire Gardens (*centre*) was among the last developments built at this end of the Great Western Road. Shipowner and art collector William Burrell was the original owner of No. 4. Nearby Marlborough (now Devonshire) Terrace (*right*) was begun in 1883, but only nine of the proposed twenty houses were completed. The views of this terrace and its neighbour Devonshire Gardens were taken in the 1930s, some four decades before their front gardens were truncated as part of the failed bid by the Corporation of Glasgow to reconstruct Great Western Road as a dual carriageway between Anniesland Cross and the city's new motorway at St George's Cross.

14

15

Archival views of the palatial villa Carlston, built by James Boucher, are surprisingly rare. In a late Saracen Foundry catalogue, however, there is an invaluable view of the opulent cast iron conservatory that was constructed on the western side of this large double feu high above the Great Western Road. Carlston has had many owners during the twentieth century, including the flamboyant showman A. E. Pickard. For many years from the 1960s, Carlston was the home of the former pupils' club of St Mungo's Academy. The fine conservatory has long since been demolished.

During the 1870s, a number of substantial detached villas were constructed on the north side of the Great Western Road at the western edge of Kelvinside. By 1892, all the feus between Crossloan (now Cleveden) Road and Beaconsfield Road had been built upon in magnificent style. The most palatial house to be constructed in Thomas Russell's development of 'Kelvinside Gardens' was Carlston, built around 1878 for James Marshall, a founding partner in the famous Saracen Foundry. Marshall's architect was James Boucher, who designed a grand Italianate palazzo with extravagant interiors, a large stable block and a Saracen conservatory.

Across from Kelvinside Gardens were two luxurious terraces, Devonshire Gardens and Marlborough (now Devonshire) Terrace. The latter was begun in 1883 to designs by the prolific James Thomson, architect of the two Belhaven terraces further east in the Great Western Road (as well as numerous terraces in Dowanhill). Marlborough Terrace was intended to be twenty houses long, extending west to the gates of Gartnavel Asylum. Nine houses were built in the first few years, after which construction abruptly stopped. The rest of the site remained vacant until it was acquired by the Hillhead War Memorial Trust in the 1920s to be used as playing fields. Devonshire Gardens, on the other hand, was a more modest scheme of only five terraced houses and was built very quickly around 1892. Among the original residents was the young shipping magnate and art collector William Burrell, who showed himself to be a significant patron of contemporary art by commissioning decorative glass windows from George Walton, a leading exponent of the new Glasgow Style.

As tenements and shops began to be built along Byres Road in the 1870s, development soon followed in the side streets. The original route of University Avenue (*right*, looking north-east toward Gilmorehill) was lined with tenements and terraced houses looking out over the grounds of the Western Infirmary. Prior to the development of the suburban West End, the route of University Avenue was part of the legendary track leading from the pre-Reformation Glasgow Cathedral to the Bishops' holdings at Partick.

16

Boundary Commission photographs from 1912 show University Avenue (*opposite, top*) looking towards Byres Road, with tenements in the foreground occupying the site later cleared for the Boyd Orr building car park (and Ashton Lane leading off to the right). All the buildings on the north side of University Avenue were demolished in the 1970s. At the opposite end of Ashton Lane (*opposite, bottom*) Byres Road has changed far less since 1912, although two shops below the Van Houten Cocoa sign had to make way for the new Grosvenor Picture Theatre around 1920. The other shops were demolished in the 1970s. To the right, the Partick/Glasgow Boundary of 1912 is shown extending into Roxburgh Lane.

W ith the exception of the period of deep economic depression which followed the collapse of the City of Glasgow Bank in 1878, there was steady growth in most parts of the West End of Glasgow during the 1870s and 1880s. Around this period, the first large tenements began to be built along Byres Road, and in many cases small single-storey rows of shops were constructed between tenement developments in order to serve the growing population. From the 1870s, Horslethill farm was built over with terraced houses; progress (albeit slow) was made on the many terraces under construction on the Dowanhill estate; and the first houses were built on the lands of Hyndland (at Kingsborough Gardens). The hiving off of large parts of Kelvinside promoted much new development during these decades, and there was sustained growth in the new Burgh of Hillhead as well. As was the case throughout the history of the West End's early years, development was haphazard, with new building schemes frequently separated from each other by large areas of vacant, undeveloped ground.

The first major development around Byres Road was Ashton Terrace, laid out in Parkville Road from the early 1860s by architect James Thomson. The terrace stood in isolation for several years, looking out over the vacant land and stone quarries of Donaldshill until John Burnet's Western Infirmary was built in the early 1870s. From the late seventies onwards, tenements and terraced houses were built, filling the triangle between Ashton Terrace, University Avenue and Byres Road. Sutherland Street, a new street parallel to Byres Road which split this triangle, was laid out in accordance with a feu plan by John Carrick, long-time City Architect of Glasgow. Carrick had drawn up a feu plan of residential streets for Glasgow Town Council not long before it exchanged its lands of Donaldshill for property at Clayslaps (the site where the university originally wished to build its new teaching hospital).

A century after the fine tenements and terraces between Parkville Road, Sutherland Street and University Avenue were constructed, this area suffered greatly from the devastating urban redevelopment policies of the University of Glasgow, the Western Infirmary and Glasgow Corporation's roads department. In the early 1970s, in order to make room for the proposed Boyd Orr tower and car park, some thirteen houses and two tenements in Ashton Terrace were demolished. With the exception of seven tenements fronting Byres Road, all the buildings within the triangle around Sutherland Street were demolished in the 1970s, both to make way for nurses' houses and to facilitate the realignment of University Avenue. The new line of the road met Highburgh Road at Byres Road, leaving a triangular car park facing the old 'Victoria Cross' at Albion Street (now Dowanside Road). At the same time the original western end of University Avenue became a cul-de-sac called University Place. In early 2000, the university demolished the short-lived nurses houses to make way for a new medical college building on the gushet site of University Place.

19

When local industrialist James B. Mirrlees was invited to lay the memorial stone at Westbourne Free Church (*above*), he took the opportunity to launch a withering attack on the Free Church of Scotland, having recently become disenchanted with the direction the church was taking. When Mirrlees' nearby Redlands mansion suffered a devastating fire a year later, there were many comments about divine retribution.[10]

The second half of the nineteenth century witnessed a feverish period of church-building throughout Glasgow. Not only was the city approaching the pinnacle of its commercial wealth and power, but relentless population growth required the establishment of churches in new residential suburbs such as Hillhead, Dowanhill and Kelvinside. During this time, the Scottish Presbyterian church was undergoing the most fractious period in its history. Divisions in the Established Church led to the formation of many new churches around the country. The most important bodies were the Free Church, formed in the wake of the Great Disruption of 1843, and the United Presbyterian Church, established in 1847 by original dissenters from the Established Church. (In 1900, these two breakaway churches merged to form the United Free Church. The UF Church then reunited with the Established Church in 1929, forming the new Church of Scotland.)

The intense population growth in Glasgow in the nineteenth century also led to an influx of people of a wide variety of faiths. In addition to the three main Presbyterian denominations, there were also churches catering for Baptists, Congregationalists and Anglicans in the West End. The only Roman Catholic churches, however, were to be found in Partick (at St Peter's in Hyndland Street and St Simon's at Partick Cross).

The great wealth in the West End of Glasgow during the latter half of the nineteenth century spawned a wide variety of splendid church buildings designed by the city's leading architects. The majority were in the Gothic style (William Leiper's Dowanhill United Presbyterian; James Miller's Belmont Parish; James Sellars' Hillhead Parish and Belhaven UP Churches), but there were also several important classical churches. The scholarly architect John Honeyman, who had originally trained for the ministry, designed the Westbourne Free Church in 1882. This Italianate neoclassical church was a far cry from Honeyman's Early English

20

Architect Thomas L. Watson built two classical churches in Hillhead in the early 1880s, the monumental Wellington United Presbyterian (*left*) in University Avenue, and the more modest Hillhead Baptist in Cresswell Street (*below*). Watson had also been responsible for Hillhead Baptist's mother church in Adelaide Place a few years earlier.

Gothic design for Lansdowne Church, built in 1862 when the architect was barely thirty years old.

During the second half of the twentieth century, the Church of Scotland remained constitutionally intact, but due to falling membership many congregations merged and churches closed. These mergers generally led to redundant church buildings being converted to secular uses (*e.g.* Dowanhill Church becoming the Cottier Theatre and Belmont Parish Church being taken over by Laurel Bank School). Some church buildings have remained in ecclesiastical use, with other faiths moving in (*e.g.* Belhaven Church becoming St Luke's Greek Orthodox Cathedral, and Westbourne Free Church — later Belhaven-Westbourne Parish Church — becoming Struthers Memorial Church). The only West End churches which were demolished in the postwar period were Church of Scotland buildings in Montague Street, Wilton Street and Queen Margaret Drive.

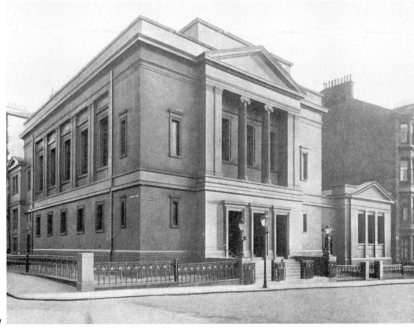

21

Much of the wealth enjoyed by the West End's mercantile elite was generated along the Clyde, in Maryhill and in other manufacturing quarters of the city. Apart from the few builders' workshops and dairies in the back lanes, there was little commerce based in the West End itself. At the end of the nineteenth century, however, this area became the first home of one of the great success stories in Glasgow's modern industrial history. The story of Barr & Stroud is unusual in that, whereas nearly all the other great engineering firms of Victorian Glasgow have long since disappeared, this famous firm of optical equipment makers is still thriving — now under the new name of Pilkington Optronics — after more than 110 years.[11]

In 1888, Paisley-born Archibald Barr, Professor of Engineering at Yorkshire College of Science, teamed up with a colleague, Dr William Stroud, in order to take on a public challenge from the War Office to submit, 'for competitive trial, Range-Finders for Naval Use.'[12] Barr had been a prize-winning student at the University of Glasgow under James Thomson, Regius Professor of Civil Engineering and Mechanics and the country's leading engineering scientist. Barr was also fortunate enough to work on research projects with his mentor's brother, the eminent physicist Sir William Thomson (later Lord Kelvin). Stroud, from Bristol, originally intended to enter the Church, but instead studied chemistry at Oxford and by the age of 35 held the Cavendish Chair of Physics at Yorkshire College.

Although Professors Barr and Stroud failed in their first attempt to win a War Office commission, they formed a partnership in order to continue their research into optical instruments. In 1889, Barr succeeded James Thomson in the chair of engineering at Glasgow, but the partners continued their research and development by post and during Stroud's holidays in Glasgow. Through the early 1890s, Barr & Stroud had increasing success in providing the War Office and Admiralty with artillery instruments which could accurately gauge the distance, direction and rate of motion of moving targets.

Private stables, carriage houses and mews buildings were relatively rare in the West End, with most residents relying on cabs or omnibuses (and subsequently trams, trains and subway services). Some stables were built to service nearby terraces, however, such as those in Ashton Lane (*below*). Small workshops were also built in some lanes; these were often used by building trades or light industries such as cabinetmakers. By the time this photograph was taken in 1933, Barr & Stroud had long since moved out of its premises at the far end of the lane (beyond the motorcars). Several decades later, restaurants, cafés and bars slowly infiltrated Ashton Lane, beginning in 1971 with the famed Ubiquitous Chip (to the right). By the late 1990s the last of these mews buildings had been converted.

23

The newly-established firm of Barr & Stroud's Patents required proper premises, having outgrown the informal works in the attic of Dr Barr's house, Royston, in Dowanhill. In July 1895, Barr established the firm's first formal laboratory, workshop and office in rented space above the new Hillhead subway entrance at 250 Byres Road. The business thrived, receiving orders for their rangefinders from governments around the world. In 1899, having outgrown the premises at 250 Byres Road (and the later annexe at No. 230), Dr Barr leased a three-storey brick workshop at 44 Ashton Lane to hold the additional machinery and increased labour force of some sixty-five men and boys. Within a few years, however, Barr & Stroud made plans to build expansive new premises on open land north of Anniesland Cross, a site which remained the firm's home for ninety years. The company moved to Linthouse in Govan in 1993.

Dr Barr and Dr Stroud were granted over a hundred British patents between 1888 and 1931. In Barr & Stroud's Ashton Lane workshop, the components for their high-quality rangefinders were machined on the ground floor, fitted on the first floor, and then assembled and tested on the second floor (*above*). The steps at the far right of this *c.*1902 view led to the rooftop viewing platform.

24

A Barr & Stroud employee in his TA uniform sets his sights on the unfinished terraces of Kingsborough Gardens in a *c.*1902 publicity photograph for a new rangefinder. The buildings to the right are in Sydenham Road.

The original high-level Great Western Bridge (more popularly known as the Kelvin bridge) was troubled from the very beginning of the turnpike project. First, there were delays due to concerns about the bridge's effect on the flow of water to the mills at South Woodside. Then, after construction began, the engineer was forced to recalculate the span of the arches, having originally misjudged the bridge's length. Also, a tragedy followed when a little girl playing near the construction site was killed by a carter dumping a load of stone from the Hillhead quarry. Finally, the sluggishness of the stonemasons greatly distressed the turnpike trustees as the two-year delay in the bridge's completion put back the road's opening and postponed the collection of much-needed toll revenue.[13]

Once the new stone-arch bridge opened in 1841, the trustees were faced with a loss of revenue owing to carriage drivers and haulage contractors using the local road network to circumvent the tollbars. They also had to contend with local boys vandalising their tollbars and tollhouses, and, in 1858, they instructed the clerk to write to their own tacksman regarding complaints about his 'furious and insolent behaviour' towards travellers on the bridge.[14]

The physical shortcomings of the Great Western Bridge first came to light around 1858. When the pipeline for the city of Glasgow's new water supply from Loch Katrine was being planned, it was determined that the existing bridge over the Kelvin was neither wide nor strong enough to carry the pair of three-foot diameter cast iron pipes. The Loch Katrine Water Commissioners paid for a cast-iron arched extension to the north, which widened the roadway by about fifty per

In April 1890, Glasgow Bailie Thomas Cumming laid the foundation stone for the new road bridge over the Kelvin. In the grandstand are representatives of Glasgow Town Council, Hillhead Burgh Commission and Lanarkshire County Road Trust, the three bodies which underwrote the desperately needed improvements. In this Annan view, James B. Fleming of Kelvinside, chairman of the County Road Trustees, is in the front row, leaning against the grandstand with bowler hat in hand. The Fleming family sits in the front row to his left. Behind the assembled crowd is the temporary timber bridge and Lansdowne Church.

26

cent. This improvement was fortuitous, for it is unlikely that the original structure would have been able to cope with the city's new tram network when it was introduced in 1872.

When the tramway opened, the West End was beginning one of its periods of great population growth. With further traffic of all sorts on the Great Western Road, congestion on the bridge became a serious problem, with carriages, omnibuses, horse carts, contractors and other miscellaneous vehicles and beasts of burden all vying for space with horse-drawn tramcars and, of course, the many pedestrians. As early as 1875, the Hillhead Burgh Commissioners were being called upon to pay half the cost of widening the bridge.[15]

Over the next fifteen years there were constant calls to improve the Kelvin bridge, and regular bickering between Glasgow town councillors and Hillhead Burgh Commissioners over who should pay. In fact, the failure to agree on improvements to the bridge was one of the major factors in the final annexation battle over Hillhead in the late 1880s. Annexationists laid the blame for the bridge problem squarely on the Hillhead Commissioners (who had claimed that they lacked the statutory powers to raise funds to pay for such a project). According to James B. Fleming, the problems with the bridge were not merely questions of congestion and delays, but also public safety. As the local population had increased, said Fleming, it 'soon showed that the Bridge was quite insufficient for the traffic. This became more apparent when the tramway lines were laid, as the over hang of the Car came almost on to the narrow 4-feet footpath on the south side of the Bridge, and made the passage along that footpath dangerous.'[16]

In the end, the burgh found a way to raise funds to cover one third of the cost of a new bridge (with the remainder coming from Glasgow and the Lanarkshire County Road Trustees). Designed by Bell & Miller, the new Great Western Bridge was an elaborate structure of steel, cast iron and granite, with Glasgow's city crest in the spandrels of the arches over the river. The steelwork was provided by Sir William Arrol's works in Dalmarnock (which had only recently completed work on the Forth Bridge). Ironically, the new bridge opened only months after Hillhead was finally absorbed into the city of Glasgow.

James B. Fleming's daughter Elisabeth cut the ceremonial ribbon to open the new bridge on 29 September 1891, and Glasgow Provost John Muir led the procession east toward the city (*above*), while a crowd watched from the west bank and from the temporary timber bridge. Such a walk across the old bridge would have taken one from the Burgh of Hillhead to the City of Glasgow, but by the time the new bridge opened, Hillhead had been annexed by its powerful neighbour. Today, one of the few surviving remnants of Hillhead's brief independent existence is the pair of burgh crests (with the motto *Je Maintiendrai*) cast into the iron parapet of the new bridge. As late as the 1930s, it was said that the foundations of the timber bridge could still be seen in the riverbed.[17]

Prior to 1850, residents of the West End relied on shops in Glasgow or Partick for their provisions. Although a post office had opened in Bank Street in the 1840s, there was little, if any, retail activity until 1853, when the first important new business was established in the suburb, William Farmer & Sons, grocers and provision merchants. William Farmer was well known in Hillhead for several generations, not only for the shop he operated for nearly 50 years, but also because he was a Hillhead Burgh Commissioner and a magistrate. He was also a prominent churchman and elder of Wellington UP Church.

Farmer set up shop at 1 Craiglaw Place (the corner of Oakfield Avenue) on the Great Western Road. His grocery business was very much like that of his later rival, Cooper & Co., but according to one resident, Farmer's was 'purely local and more personal in administration.' Another writer recalled that Farmer 'did a particularly high-class trade, specialising in rice grown in different parts of the East.'[18] As the local population grew, other retailers followed, most of which were independent businesses, although there were branches of large stores from the city too. One such branch was the famous Cooper & Co., by its own account one of 'The Most Progressive and Successful Department Stores in the Country.'[19]

In the early years, shopping in the West End was a simple affair. For the most part, the large houses sent an errand boy with a daily list to the grocer or butcher, and provisions were then delivered. Larger household purchases such as clothing and furniture were the domain of the 'carriage trade,' the special excursions undertaken by the lady of the house to the grand department stores in the city

A delivery boy pauses on the Kelvin bridge in the early morning sunshine *c.*1905. As early as 1877, all the gap sites along the Great Western Road had been built upon. The last vacant site was filled by the tenement between Belmont and Colebrooke Streets (to the right), across from Caledonian Mansions. Before Glasgow Academy and the nearby houses were built, the land between Belmont Street and the Kelvin had been used by the Caledonian Cricket Club. It was also famously the venue for an exhibition staged by Canadian lacrosse players (hence the nearby Lacrosse Terrace). As the area between Belmont Crescent and the Kelvin was 'made ground' from decades of use as a public tip, or 'free coup,' subsidence has always been a problem here. The corner tenement, known as Salisbury Place, was taken down in the 1970s and the site remained empty until a stone-clad block of flats by architects Elder & Cannon was constructed — on substantial piling — in 1996.

28

centre. One early Hillhead resident remembered: 'The ladies from the bigger houses did their shopping in broughams or carriages and pairs, . . . [with] a dignified air of opulence. Shopping was part of the social graces.'[20]

It was not until the 1870s and 1880s that the expanding population in the West End created a significant demand for local shops, and an increasing number of tenement buildings with ground floor shops were built along the Great Western Road, Gibson Street, Byres Road and other main streets. Until the early twentieth century, the Great Western Road remained the most important shopping district in the West End. The demand for retail accommodation along the Great Western Road was such that in 1892, the owner of Alfred Terrace commissioned architects John Burnet, Son & Campbell to draw up plans to build over the communal gardens in front of the terrace in order to provide sixteen new shop units. Due to the restricted and awkward nature of the site, the basements of the terraced houses were converted into back storage rooms (located well above street level).

The first shops to be established in Hillhead were located along the Great Western Road, and this area remained the principal shopping district of the West End until the 1920s and 1930s. This easterly view from Belgrave Terrace taken *c.*1905 shows the mid-morning traffic on the road and pavements. Local billboards advertise a couple of bygone beers, as well as a few product names still common in the early twenty-first century: Nestlé's, Lipton's Tea and Camp Coffee.

29

As the population of the West End grew in the late nineteenth century, the demand for shops increased accordingly. In the early 1890s, the pleasure grounds in front of Alfred Terrace were supplanted by a row of 16 small shop units (*left*). Also noticeable in this mid-1920s view of Great Western Road is the lack of ornamental central tram poles. The elegant 1901-vintage poles had only recently been replaced with more utilitarian kerbside ones. Although traffic here seems light, the central poles had become a safety problem due to the increase in the number of motorcars after the First World War.

30

In the late nineteenth century, new building began to encroach upon the river bank. This view of *c*.1895 shows Kelvin Drive at the far right, Lismore House with its Italianate tower, and, across the Kelvin, the tall red sandstone tenements of Kirklee Quadrant. In the 1890s, the Corporation of of Glasgow purchased 'Montgomerie's Woods,' comprising some 80 acres of steep slopes plus the Garrioch haugh on the north bank of the Kelvin. In 1900, land near the new Kirklee Bridge was also acquired and both areas were added to the city's Botanic Gardens, with the Kirklee lands being laid out as an arboretum.

Upon the death of Matthew Montgomerie in 1868, the lands around his former residence of old Kelvinside House were among the first of several large parcels of land to be sold by his nephew and heir, James B. Fleming. When John Ewing Walker purchased these lands on the north bank of the Kelvin in 1869, he immediately laid them out for feuing. To facilitate access to North Kelvinside, Walker funded the building of a bridge in 1870. Called Queen Margaret Bridge, this iron lattice-girder structure stood on tall sandstone piers and connected the newly-built Hamilton Drive with a massive Grecian retaining wall on the north bank, designed by architect Alexander 'Greek' Thomson.

The retaining wall incorporated a formidable flight of sixty stone steps up to the new Kelvinside Crescent (now Kelvinside Terrace South) where the first tenements were built in the early 1870s. Around the same time, just to the west, the first row of terraced houses were being built in Kelvin Drive. Within five years, other streets to the north, such as Montgomerie (now Clouston) Street and Kelbourne Street were being built. By the 1880s, the hill of Sheepmount was dotted with small villas situated in Kelvinside Drive and, to a lesser extent, Cambridge (now Fergus) Drive. Kelvinside House survived for a number of years until it was demolished to make way for Derby (now Botanic) Crescent.

It was not until the late 1870s and 1880s that developers began to exploit the picturesque views along the River Kelvin. This *c*.1905 view, taken from John E. Walker's Queen Margaret Bridge, looks across to Kelvin Drive, which was built just in front of the site of the old Kelvinside House of 1750. Twenty years later, this wide stretch of the Kelvin behind Jackson's Dam was spanned by the new Queen Margaret Bridge.

31

32

Around the same time that Walker purchased North Kelvinside, the ill-fated City of Glasgow Bank began to develop the lands it had been accumulating between Northpark and the Kelvin bridge. The gentle slope falling to the east down to the river's old haugh had been filled up to the level of the new turnpike by the 1860s, and by 1870 work was progressing on the early buildings at Belmont Crescent. The bank had also purchased the old country estate of Northwoodside on the opposite side of the river (which once had belonged to cotton-miller William Gillespie). The Italianate Northwoodside mansion was destroyed around 1870 when the bank constructed its stone-arch Belmont Bridge over the Kelvin.

The North Kelvinside estates belonging to Walker and the City of Glasgow Bank grew steadily through the last quarter of the nineteenth century, though neither area really prospered. It was left to the bank's successor to complete the development after the great crash in 1878, and thus the higher land above Wilton Street was not built upon until the end of the century. Walker's land was developed haphazardly, with areas fronting the Kelvin being built over quickly, but upland areas nearer to the industrial burgh of Maryhill proving slow to be feued. Even the prestigious Kirklee Bridge, built in 1900-1901, only led to a few new tenements being built, and large areas remained vacant over the next one hundred years.

Prior to the erection of estate bridges by John Ewing Walker and the City of Glasgow Bank in 1870, there was no vehicular river crossing between Woodside and Kelvindale. Around 1900, Glasgow Corporation joined forces with the North Kelvinside Feuing Company and the Caledonian Railway to construct the extravagant Kirklee Bridge (*above*) 'to facilitate the means of communication' to the nearby railway station.[21] As far back as the 1840s, Montgomerie & Fleming had intended to construct a bridge here to promote the feuing of the two parts of their estate.

33

The first Queen Margaret Bridge was built by John Ewing Walker to attract feuars to his lands in North Kelvinside. Although 'Walker's Bridge,' as it was informally known, was made redundant by a new Queen Margaret Bridge in the late 1920s (from which this easterly view was taken), it remained in use until 1970 when extensions to the BBC in Hamilton Drive were built over the access road. The roadbed and most of the stone piers were dismantled, but much stonework can still be seen along the banks of the river.

The first sports club in the West End was the Hillhead Bowling Club, established in 1849. The site of the club's first green was a former potato field in Bank Street rented from James Gibson of Hillhead. In 1860 the Hillhead Bowling Club moved to the corner of Bute Gardens and Great George Street (later the site of the university's Hetherington building). It moved again in 1882, this time to Hamilton Drive and a location between Walker's Bridge and Queen Margaret College's medical building (*right*). The terraced grounds included a bowling green close to Hamilton Drive and a lower area set out as tennis courts (which could be flooded for curling in the winter). Overlooking the bowling club premises (*below*) is Alexander 'Greek' Thomson's Northpark Terrace, built in the late 1860s on the site of Provost John Hamilton's Northpark House of *c*.1800.

34

As communications between the various West End neighbourhoods began to improve, closer social networks developed, and recreational clubs began to be established as early as 1849 when the Hillhead Bowling Club was formed. By the 1880s, there were numerous bowling and other sports clubs on both sides of the Kelvin. The Glasgow Skating Club (which included curling) was located first at Byres Road before moving to Hughenden and eventually to Bingham's pond at Gartnavel. The Kelvinside Tennis Club built courts in Beaconsfield Road (now the site of a private hospital) around 1888. Cricket was played at Garrioch Road, Belmont Street and Napiershall Street (as well as at the famous West of Scotland Cricket Club in Peel Street, Partick, the sole surviving

Bowling Green and Tennis Court, Kelvinside.

35

36

cricket pitch at the start of the twenty-first century). In the late 1860s, the Arlington Bath Club was established, one of Britains earliest swimming clubs.[22] Soon afterwards, the Western Baths Club opened in Cranworth Street.

In the latter decades of the nineteenth century, Glasgow's robust economy led to the creation of a new middle class. Although the city's mercantile elite resided in the largest properties in the West End, an increasing number of houses were built to suit the professional classes and other 'white-collar' workers. Glasgow post office directories reveal a cross-section of professions, with lawyers, doctors, teachers and architects represented, along with countless bankers, accountants and insurance brokers. Far more numerous, however, were the small merchants and members of the second tier of Glasgow's commercial world: the managers, senior clerks and foremen in the city's great industries and businesses. Towards the end of the century, far fewer new villas and terraces were built for the very wealthy, and instead modest houses and large flats were constructed in North Kelvinside, western Hillhead and Hyndland.

William Lang Edgar of No. 9 Lyndhurst Gardens was typical of the new West End professional man of the late Victorian era. In the 1890s, he formed a partnership with William Fullerton in a firm of photographers and 'fine art publishers' at 167 St George's Road. By 1903, however, Fullerton is also listed in post office directories as owning 'luncheon and tea rooms' at 20 Saltmarket. Within two years, the partnership of Fullerton and Edgar had been disbanded, with the former establishing himself as a commercial photographer, as well as keeping the Saltmarket restaurant and the fine art publishing business. William Edgar, however, apparently gave up photography and joined his erstwhile partner in the restaurant trade as manager of the Hydro Tea Rooms, first in St Vincent Street and later in Candleriggs.[23]

The Edgar family were typical members of the new West End middle class which emerged in the late nineteenth century. William Lang Edgar, a master draper who later became a photographer and restaurateur, is pictured in an 1895 family portrait taken in the family's sitting room at No. 9 Lyndhurst Gardens, North Kelvinside. The handwritten sign on the piano behind reads: 'Molly and I and the Baby.' Around 1906, the family moved to larger premises in No. 4 Doune Quadrant, where 'the Baby,' later Mrs Henrietta Peacock Edgar Hutchison, grew up and ultimately resided until her death in 1987.[24]

The suburban district of North Kelvinside was by and large completed by the early part of twentieth century, around the same time that picture postcards became a national phenomenon. From *c.*1905, the West End was the subject of hundreds of different postcard views. An unusually large number were taken in the new residential streets north of the Kelvin and published by both national and local concerns. The viewpoint at the end of Hamilton Park Avenue was a popular vantage point for photographers, particularly as it overlooked North Woodside flint mill, Doune Quadrant, Doune Gardens, Kelvin-Stevenson Church and Belmont Bridge over the River Kelvin (*right*).

37

38

The buildings originally known as Wilton Crescent, on the south side of Wilton Gardens (*centre*), were the first properties to be built in North Kelvinside. Constructed in the mid-1850s as part of the unsuccessful 'Queen's Park' development near Queen's Cross in New City Road, the terraced houses of Wilton Crescent were eventually surrounded by tall tenements in Wilton Street. The tall slate roof of the Wilton Church of Scotland is visible in the distance behind the communal gardens in Wilton Street. By the beginning of the twentieth century, large numbers of tenements for the middle-classes had been constructed in Cambridge (now Fergus) Drive (*right*), Oxford (now Oban) Drive and throughout North Kelvinside.

39

Wilton Church of Scotland.

40

North Kelvinside's rapid population growth required new churches. Around 1906 an Established Church was built at the corner of Wilton Street and Yarrow Gardens (*left*). In Queen Margaret Drive, the Kelvinside United Presbyterian Church (*below*) was built in Collegiate Gothic style by architect John Bennie Wilson only a few years before the 1900 merger between the UP and Free Churches. Three decades later, this then United Free Church joined a reunited Church of Scotland. After the last war, falling numbers forced many congregations to merge and churches soon became redundant (the Wilton Street Church, for example, was replaced in 1988 by a block of flats). The former Kelvinside UP Church was ultimately demolished in 1987 due to subsidence.

41

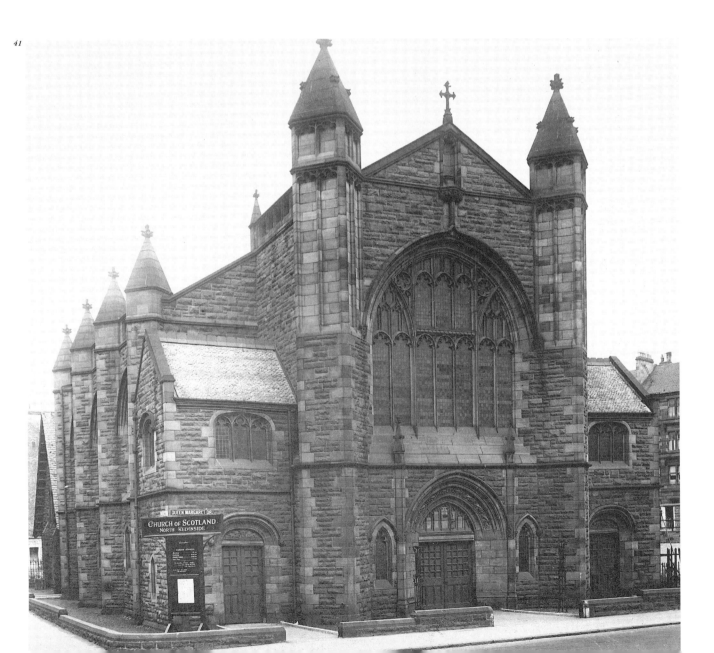

The 1901 International Exhibition was far more exotic than its 1888 predecessor, featuring buildings from Russia and Japan, and incorporating popular features such as the Indian street musicians and Venetian gondolas on the Kelvin. More familiar domestic events, such as the bandstand concerts and fire brigade demonstrations, also drew large crowds. The university sports grounds were frequently used for motorcar trials, cycle races and other sporting events, such as this charity cup-tie between Third Lanark and Queen's Park.

42

43

Many sporting events held during the 1901 exhibition were recorded by the official photographers T. & R. Annan, including these three views published in the weekly magazine, *The Exhibition Illustrated*. An unfortunate incident during a cycle race (*centre*) is watched by a large crowd in the grandstand below Professors Square. The starting line of the '220 yards flat race' (*right*) was photographed against the backdrop of the tenements and terraces of old University Avenue and Sutherland Street.

44

Glasgow was a latecomer to the prestigious world of international exhibitions.[25] In the wake of the famed 1851 exhibition in Paxton's Crystal Palace, notable expositions were held in several European capitals and many major American cities. Glasgow held its first international exhibition in the West End Park in 1888, with further exhibitions there in 1901 and 1911. These shows were highly successful, with all three making handsome profits and becoming firmly established as major events in the city's cultural history. The exhibitions were temporary in nature, although a few physical remnants can still be seen in Kelvingrove Park. The most important legacy was, of course, the construction of the 1901 Kelvingrove Art Gallery & Museum with the proceeds from the 1888 exhibition.

As international exhibitions, the first two extravaganzas were designed not only to showcase products from Glasgow, but to feature items from all corners of the empire and around the world. These shows were outward-looking and exuded Glasgow's (and Britain's) prosperity, very much in the spirit of the late Victorian era. The 1911 exhibition, on the other hand, was of an entirely different nature, being a Scottish Exhibition of Natural History, Art and Industry intended to raise funds to establish a Chair in Scottish History and Literature at the University of Glasgow.

Glasgow's international exhibitions of 1888 and 1901 were events of royal patronage, and most of the vice-presidents, honorary members of the association and members of the executive council were peers of the realm and miscellaneous titled gentry. The management committees, however, consisted of Glasgow's mercantile elite, with West End names like Blackie, Burrell, Fleming, Mirrlees and Russell very much in evidence. West End architects and artists were also important figures. Hillhead resident James Miller was architect of the 1901 exhibition, and West End men such as John Keppie, John J. Burnet and Fra Newbery were also prominent committee members.

'In consideration,' states the 1901 *Official Guide*, 'of the fact that so many Scottish emigrants, during the past century, found homes in the Dominion, and that prosperity reigns among the kinsfolk in that country of almost inexhaustible natural resources, the Canadian exhibits at the Pavilion and in the Industrial Hall will be viewed with peculiar interest by Scottish visitors.'[26] Among the many impressive Canadian exhibits, the guide made particular comment about the 'large model of the dome of the Library at Ottawa, decorated with corn, oats, barley, wheat, rye and buckwheat, as well as prairie and cultivated grasses and fodder plants' (*above, behind motorcars and canoes*).

The 1911 Scottish Exhibition of Natural History, Art and Industry in Kelvingrove Park was never intended to rival the more extravagant international exhibitions of 1888 and 1901. Though it was on a much smaller scale than its predecessors, attendance was very high, with 9.4m visitors (as opposed to 11.5m in 1901). By 1911, the Scottish economy was showing signs of decline, however, and the nation was feeling more introverted. For the previous few years the Liberals had held on to power by promoting plans for Home Rule. Perhaps in sympathy with the recent death of Kelvinside-born Liberal Prime Minister Sir Henry Campbell-Bannerman, the Scottish electorate showed strong support for Asquith's party (which was returned to government in 1910).[27]

With the city's new art gallery and museum occupying the Clayslaps lands of Kelvingrove Park, and new bowling greens taking up land alongside it, the 1911 exhibition was restricted to a site entirely east of the line of Kelvin Way. Unlike the two earlier exhibitions, the 1911 masterplan produced by architect R. J. Walker (who had worked under Miller in 1901, producing the Canadian Pavilion) did not contain a massive main hall.[28] The largest structure was the Palace of Industry which stood on the site of the present tennis courts near Sauchiehall Street. There were several small exhibition and concert halls, the most notable being the Palace of History. There was a certain irony that the main exhibition of Scottish history was held on the site of the oldest building in the area, Patrick Colquhoun's Kelvingrove House (demolished for the 1901 exhibition). The Palace of History was modelled on the Stewart kings' Falkland Palace and incorporated John Carrick's 1876 extension to Kelvingrove House Museum.

Although the main exhibitions were concerned with romantic notions of Scottish culture and history, there was still an international flavour in the shape of Laplanders in an 'Arctic Village,' citizens of the 'West African Colonies' and a Japanese tea room. As at the 1888 and 1901 exhibitions, amusements and demonstrations were an important feature of the 1911 programme. At the northern end of the park, near Eldon Street, there was a rifle range, aquarium, mountain slide and so-called 'Joy House,' as well as the popular Mountain Scenic Railway, a mile-long roller coaster. The most dramatically situated amusement was the aerial railway,

A crowd assembles on the Prince of Wales Bridge during the 1911 Scottish Exhibition in Kelvingrove Park to watch the daily pageant of model ships on the Kelvin (featuring a Spanish galleass, 'The type of ship of the Spanish Armada which lies at the bottom of Tobermory Bay'[30]). Also on display was a model of the Clyde-built *Lusitania* and an ancient coracle, the only full-size vessel in the pageant (seen to the left in this picture postcard view).

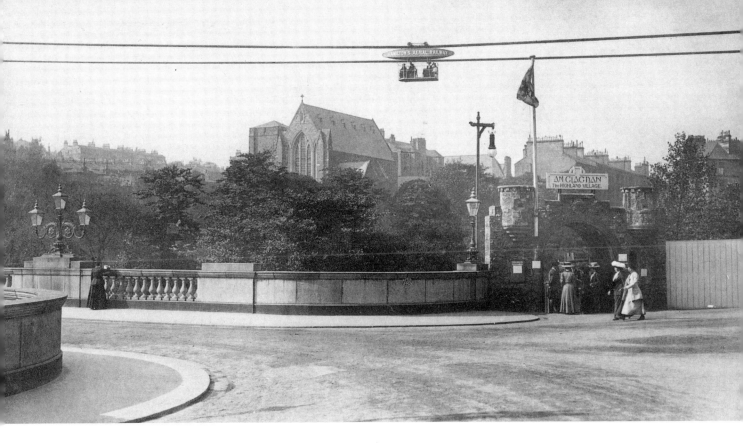

which consisted of cable cars resembling small dirigibles that carried passengers between Woodlands Hill and Gilmorehill. Down below on the Kelvin, there were no Venetian gondolas as in 1901, but instead a flotilla of model historic vessels was on display.

The university's new Chair of Scottish History and Literature was founded with the profits from the 1911 exhibition, though there was a certain amount of debate about the appropriateness of this particular method of raising the necessary funds. David Murray, a prominent Glasgow lawyer, historian, member of the University Court, and a major benefactor of the university library, had doubted that profits could be earned, as it was claimed during the planning stages, through the historical exhibits alone. 'Everybody knew that the money would be raised by the sideshows,' claimed Murray, 'they had simply put the University on the same footing as one of these sideshows — such as water-chutes, flip-flap, cinematograph and the skittle alley, the tea-room, the drinking bar, the smoking parlour, and the other adjuncts of a variety entertainment.'[29]

The Highland village, or *An Clachan* (*left*), was a highlight of the 1911 exhibition. The village of but-and-ben cottages and ancient blackhouses (constructed of canvas and plaster) was populated by Gaelic-speaking pipers and cotton spinners, assembled to depict the primitive traditions of the Highlanders. There was a post office and Gaelic bookshop selling *An Clachan* picture postcards, an inn serving non-alcoholic beverages, and a village store where traditional craft products were sold.[31] *An Clachan* was located in a hollow on the east bank of the Kelvin, below the aerial railway (*above*). A small inscribed stone on the site serves as a rare memorial to the park's three great exhibitions.

The Sunday procession along the Great Western Road was a weekly highlight for many West End residents, one of whom recalled the scene of the 1890s: 'Before the days of motor cars, . . . the stretch of this gracious promenade from Byres Road to Bingham's Pond was used on the Sabbath by the fortunate folks who lived in the West End as a church parade, between noon and lunch time. The "best" people paraded in the middle of the road, while the ordinary folks used the blaes-covered sidewalk.'[35] So important was this tradition that it featured in *Quiz*, *The Bailie* and many other local periodicals. Interestingly, it was also captured by the latest medium of the age, the cinema camera. In 1915, James Hart, manager of the Hillhead Salon, filmed the procession (*right*) to entice curious locals into his picture house. He repeated the stunt in 1922 when he moved to the new Grosvenor Picture Theatre.

49

GLASGOW SUFFRAGETTES ATTEMPT TO BLOW UP KIBBLE PALACE.

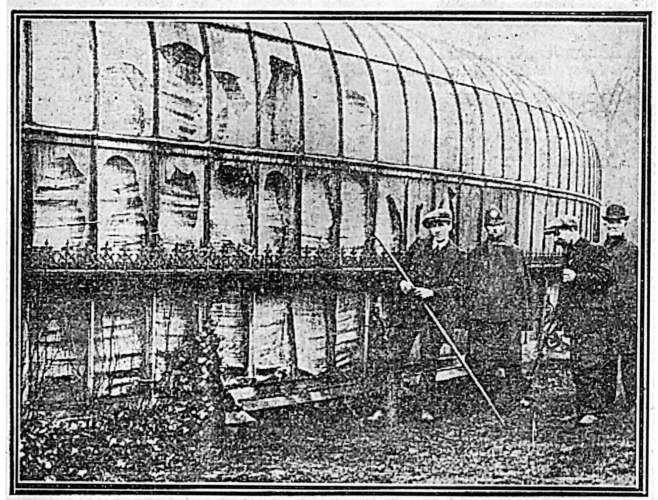

A dastardly attempt was made by Suffragettes, early on Saturday morning, to blow up Kibble Palace, in the Botanic Gardens, Glasgow, by means of bombs. Had it not been for the vigilance of the night attendant, there is no saying what terrible damage might have resulted. As it was, 27 panes of glass were shattered, as shown in our picture.

50

Despite its reputation as a quiet residential district, the West End of Glasgow has witnessed many noteworthy public events over the years. Some of these events, such as the Sunday promenades along the Great Western Road, were regular features during the golden years of the West End; other public gatherings were infrequent but not uncommon, such as royal visits or parades of soldiers from Maryhill barracks. One notable incident was the minor earthquake which hit Glasgow on 14 December 1910. There was 'considerable excitement and puzzled alarm,' particularly in the West End, where 'many householders stated that their walls seemed to rock, that their windows rattled, and that furniture was displaced and ornaments smashed.'[32]

The most unusual event to occur during the West End's golden years was the so-called 'Bomb Outrage' in the Botanic Gardens on 24 January 1914. 'Awakened from their slumbers in the early hours of Saturday morning by the loud noise of an explosion,' reported the *Daily Record & Mail*, 'residents in Hillhead, Kelvinside, and Maryhill thought something serious had occurred at the Dawsholm Gasworks. For a time there was considerable alarm, but inquiries brought out the fact that a dastardly attempt had been made to blow up the Kibble Palace in the Botanic Gardens by means of bombs.'[33]

The newspaper claimed that 'evidence clearly indicates that this was the work of militant Suffragettes ... [who] would have been successful but for the presence of mind and prompt action of the night attendant, Mr David Watters.' The paper reported that 'one bomb exploded and seriously damaged the large winter gardens, and shattered twenty-seven large panes of glass.' Watters had seen a burning light in the dark undergrowth near the Palace, and finding it to be a fuse, extinguished it. As he took the device to the workshop, a second bomb, which he had not noticed, exploded. A search the next day found no specific evidence with which to incriminate the Suffragettes, with the exception of 'a lady's black silk veil,' some footprints which 'clearly indicate the high heels of ladies shoes, and pieces of cake and an empty champagne bottle.'[34]

Royal visits to the West End were rare in the early years of the suburb's development. Queen Victoria did not care for Glasgow, returning only once after her initial 1849 visit. On the other hand, her son and heir, the Prince of Wales, visited the West End several times prior to his assuming the throne in 1901. As Prince he laid the foundation stone of the new university buildings in 1868, and twenty years later officially opened the city's first International Exhibition. Later visits to Glasgow usually included trips to Gilmorehill. This photograph shows King Edward and Queen Alexandra parading down Gibson Street by the Hillhead Congregational Church in 1903.

Opening Day at the Western Lawn Tennis Club, 1924.

VII.

The Interwar Years

The heavy toll suffered by the Scottish population during the First World War was no less devastating for the wealthy families of Glasgow's West End than it was for the city's middle or working classes. On one single day at Gallipoli, 28 June 1915, no fewer than 12 former pupils of Kelvinside Academy and 15 from Glasgow Academy were killed. Eight of the former Glasgow Academy pupils photographed with their fellow Cameronians (*right*) were killed on that tragic day.

8th Battalion The Cameronians (Scottish Rifles)
WAR STATION.   DECEMBER 1914.
OLD GLASGOW ACADEMY BOYS.

A. C. BRUCE, O.P.,
Naval and Military Photographer

B Annfield,
Newhaven, LEITH

Lieut. H. M'Cowan.   Lieut. W. N. Sloan.   2nd Lieut. W. Maclay.   2nd Lieut. T. Stout.   Lieut. E. Maclay.   Capt. Chas. J. C. Mowat.
Lieut. A. D. Templeton.   Capt. W. C. Church.   Capt. A. B. Sloan, R.A.M.C.   Capt. J. W. H. Pattison.   Capt. E. T. Young.

2

For much of the United Kingdom, the First World War marked the end of an era. Not only did it wreak incalculable devastation upon all sections of British society in terms of loss of life, but it also exacerbated the country's weakening position in the world economy. For Glasgow and industrial Clydeside, the slow decline prior to 1914 was temporarily halted by the demands of wartime production. From 1919, however, the reality that the industrial heartland of the west of Scotland would never again be a dominant force in the world marketplace began to sink in. The ensuing unrest led to strikes, culminating in the famous events of 31 January 1919 when a riot erupted in George Square (due more to inept crowd control by the police than to any sinister Bolshevik plot). The next day, however, a worried London government drafted in troops and tanks to quell the anticipated uprising, though it was soon apparent that such a heavy hand was hardly needed. By 2 February, the labour leaders' 'rank and file were venting their fervour, revolutionary or otherwise, at football matches.'[1]

More than 2,000 former pupils from the area's three major schools served in the 1914-1918 war. Of the 540 men from Kelvinside Academy who saw active service, some 131 were killed.[3] A total of 179 men from Hillhead High School also died in action, whilst out of the 1,375 former Glasgow Academy students who served, 327 gave their lives.[4] After the war's end, all three schools formed War Memorial Trusts to commemorate their war dead. The two academies used their trusts to strengthen the financial future of their schools in addition to establishing memorial playing fields (as did Hillhead's trust). Glasgow Academy commissioned architect Alexander N. Paterson to design a war memorial at the corner of their property on Great Western Road. Rector Edwin Temple is seen in the centre of this view at the 1924 unveiling, which was undertaken by former pupil Sir Robert Mackenzie (standing to the rector's left).

3

4

On a cold Armistice Day in 1924, a crowd of West End families (*left*) gathered to witness the dedication of the Glasgow Academy war memorial at the corner of Great Western Road and Colebrooke Street. The academy's own OTC, in full kilt uniform, are seen standing at attention with their backs to the traffic in Great Western Road (*below*). The memorial was unveiled by Sir Robert Mackenzie, an erstwhile academy boy and chairman of the War Memorial Trust. Mackenzie was not only a former Scottish rugby international and president of the Scottish Rugby Union, but was also president of the Society of Accountants and Actuaries in Glasgow, a member of the Glasgow Stock Exchange and a leader of the volunteer and territorial forces during the war.[5]

Throughout Scotland, profound social changes followed the end of the war. The economic depression of the 1920s led to renewed emigration, with some 400,000 Scots (more than 8% of the population) starting new lives abroad.[2] The mercantile elite of Glasgow's West End saw the demise of their privileged way of life. The country's economic decline, so heavily felt in Clydeside, led to the closure of many of the businesses which had permitted the construction of substantial villas and terraces throughout Glasgow. In the 1920s and 1930s, many large houses in the West End ceased to be manageable as family homes, and were frequently sold for institutional use or conversion to flats.

5

6

During the interwar years, Byres Road gradually overtook Great Western Road as the main shopping precinct of Glasgow's West End. Cooper & Co. and William Farmer's were still the dominant grocery and provision merchants in the area, although they stood only a few streets away from each other in Great Western Road. By its own declaration, Cooper's was 'The Best Known Name in Scotland.'[6] Henry B. Morton recalled that, early in the century, Cooper's was like a 'large family grocers with the addition of a household emporium reached upstairs by an ornate central staircase from the patterned terracotta ground floor with its several long counters from which cash was swished in little round clip-on boxes along overhead wires in a direct line to the cashier's cubicle.'[7] Cooper & Co. was founded in 1871 in Howard Street, and within ten years there were branches not only around Glasgow, but in London and throughout Britain. Always a progressive firm, Cooper's had a field telegraph installed between the first three stores in Howard Street, Great Western Road, and Sauchiehall Street, and the latter was one of the first shops in Britain to be lit with electricity. Cooper's was also one the first shops in Glasgow to use motorcars for delivery purposes.[8]

Across Great Western Road from Cooper's landmark tower stood the popular bakery and restaurant of Walter Hubbard. Founded in 1848, Hubbard's had a string of shops around Glasgow. Although Hubbard had established a baker's shop in Great Western Road in 1872, at that time the Glasgow fashion of tea rooms had yet to reach the West End. As Marion Gilchrist, a student at Queen Margaret College in the 1890s, later recalled, 'No meals of any kind could be got in the West End, except a cookie or scone or cake and a glass of milk at Hubbard's counter.'[9]

Cooper & Co.'s grocery and department store, a long-time West End institution, was appropriately situated in a flamboyant landmark building along Great Western Road. According to an 1897 visitors' guide to Glasgow, 'few other cities can boast as artistically finished and massive business premises as those of Cooper & Co., at the corner of Bank Street. In the evenings when lighted with electric [sic] these grocery and provision stores have a splendid appearance and are in good harmony with the surroundings.'[10] The regular displays in Cooper's windows were also designed with appropriate panache (above). By the 1950s, however, Cooper's star had waned, and in 1955 the chain became part of the FineFare supermarket group.

7

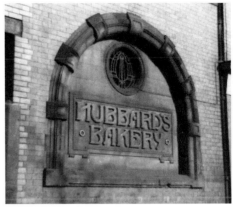

THE Restaurant of the West End

BELMONT HOUSE

508 GREAT WESTERN ROAD

BREAKFASTS
LUNCHEONS
HIGH TEAS

WALTER HUBBARD LIMITED
Bakers of Quality Goods
GLASGOW

8

11

9

Around 1906 Hubbard's erected a handsome brick and sandstone bakery and office overlooking the Kelvin (*left*, built on the site of Hillhead's last surviving dairy). This local landmark, which had a central tower and fine ornamental carving (detail, *above*), later became a bonded warehouse prior to its demolition *c.*1989. Hubbard's fine Art Deco shop and restaurant in Great Western Road (*below*) was built in 1930 and clad in faience (glazed terracotta). In the 1950s, Hubbard's became part of the massive City Bakeries empire. The building survives today as a nightclub and public house, though the elegant shopfront was destroyed long ago.

10

In 1920, architects Duff & Cairns drew up
proposals for a new picture house on the
corner of Bank and Great George Streets. The
front elevation in Bank Street (*right*) was to
be an exotic Spanish baroque fantasy in glazed
terracotta, not unlike many other fanciful
'palaces of dreams' that were built during the
boom years of cinema in Glasgow. This
scheme, like many other cinema projects
proposed for the residential streets of the West
End during the interwar years, never came to
fruition.

12

The area between the River Kelvin and Bank Street was among the first
parts of suburban Hillhead to be developed in the 1840s, and it has always
been the most architecturally eclectic. Early buildings varied from Gothic
cottages on the river bank, to late Georgian terraces (Great Kelvin Terrace in
Bank Street) and tenements such as Bloomfield Place, built between King (now
Gibson) and Great George Streets. On the other side of Great George Street
stood a matching pair of chaste Georgian villas, built in 1836 for James Gibson of
Hillhead. It is likely that mason Robert Cruikshank constructed the small villas
with stone from the quarry near Byres Road he was then leasing from Gibson.[11]

Through the nineteenth century and until the First World War, the Hillhead
lands east of Bank Street continued to be developed in piecemeal fashion. John
Ewing Walker built his Royal Horse Bazaar in Smith (Otago) Street in 1872, and
had the same architects, Thomson & Turnbull, design rather plain tenements on
adjacent land. In the mid-1880s, Peter Hepburn's furniture works, Kelvin House,
were built high above the river opposite the foot of Glasgow Street. Twenty years
later, by which time most sites had been covered with tenements, Walter Hubbard
built his bakery and office next to Walker's old stables.

Further changes to the area were proposed after the end of the First World War.
In the early 1920s, several new 'motion picture houses,' the great architectural
fantasy of the age, were planned for the salubrious West End. Most such cinema
schemes met with strong objections from local residents. At one point, the great
Glasgow showman A. E. Pickard wanted to build a picture house in Great Western
Road opposite Cooper & Co., but his efforts failed and Hubbard's new restaurant
was built on the site.[12] In 1920, a scheme submitted to the Dean of Guild Court
proposed a picture house with an exotic terracotta facade fronting Bank Street.
This cinema project (which was eventually abandoned) would have required the
demolition of the two Gibson villas (Parkview at No. 2 Great George Street and
Bloomfield Cottage at No. 4).

For a time, Parkview, on the corner of Great George and Otago Streets, was the family home of local furniture-maker Peter Hepburn. His son Charles established the highly successful Red Hackle brand of whisky, and went on to become one of Glasgow's greatest philanthropists of the twentieth century. Charles Hepburn and his partner Herbert Ross began their whisky operations in 1919 in a small office in Peter Hepburn's old premises in Kelvin House. The partners invested their war gratuities amounting to £300, and some forty years later Hepburn sold the business for a remarkable £2m. Upon his retirement in 1959, he recalled how the early years were a struggle to survive. 'Then came our first real break,' he told the *Bulletin*, 'when the Prince of Wales, in a night club in Vienna with Mrs. Simpson . . . ordered the Red Hackle. After that nobody would drink anything else on the Continent.'[13]

Hepburn was an important collector of art and antiques, arms and armour, and also antiquarian books (300 of which are now in the University Library's Special Collection). His interest in fine art led to him amassing 'one of the best private collections in the country. It includes works by Rembrandt, Reynolds, Raeburn and Ramsey.'[14] During his lifetime, Hepburn became a generous benefactor not only of his old school, Hillhead, but also the University of Glasgow, where he received the honorary degree of Doctor of Laws in 1964.

Among Hepburn's notable philanthropic gifts were the stained glass window by Gordon Webster in the university's Randolph Hall (displaying the coats of arms of past rectors dating back to 1690), an antique Persian carpet for Glasgow Cathedral and an extension to the Hughenden grandstand for Hillhead High School War Memorial Trust. He also paid for underground heating cables for the Scottish Rugby Union pitch at Murrayfield in Edinburgh.[15] Hepburn's lasting legacy to his home area, however, was his patronage of the invaluable local history book, *A Hillhead Album*, produced two years after his death by another long-time resident of Hillhead, Henry B. Morton.

14

A 1933 view behind Kelvin House (later known as the Red Hackle building) in Otago Street showing the stables which once housed Corporation tramway horses. Long after the death of Charles Hepburn, the first floor still retained the mock-medieval fittings installed to show off the whisky magnate's collection of antique arms and armour.

13

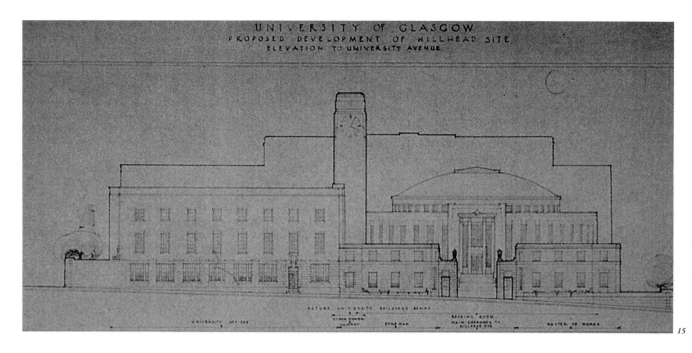

15

Fifty years of steady expansion across Gilmorehill and Donaldshill prompted the University of Glasgow to look towards Hillhead for room for further expansion in the early twentieth century. The first move across University Avenue came in 1917, when the Psychology Department took over New Hillhead House, a detached villa situated in a large garden between Hillhead Street and Ann Street (now Southpark Avenue). Hillhead House was built *c.*1850 by Andrew Dalglish, a third-generation muslin manufacturer and calico printer. The house was later owned by John Wilson, MP for Govan, and was eventually donated to the university by the family of Walter MacLellan of Rhu.

In 1936, architects Hughes and Waugh provided the university's New Buildings Committee with plans for a new library, lecture rooms, and art gallery, along with additional space for 'Future Extensions.' In addition to the unusual circular Reading Room, the site was to be defined by a tall campanile alongside the main entrance. Due to the outbreak of war in 1939, only the Reading Room was built, and revised postwar masterplans discarded Hughes and Waugh's clock tower and adjacent buildings.

The Reading Room was designed to house some 565 of the 3,000 undergraduates then attending the University of Glasgow. Although the Second World War and its aftermath led to a decline in the number of students, by the early 1950s matriculations were reaching unprecedented levels, prompting the university to draw up a masterplan for further expansion in Hillhead. Although the Reading Room was meant to have been the centrepiece of the proposed interwar redevelopment (*above*), postwar masterplans left it in splendid isolation in its ornamental gardens. The simple elegance of the Reading Room has long been praised, and, in 1950, architects Hughes and Waugh were awarded the Scottish Area Bronze Medal of the Royal Institute of British Architects for 'the best building erected in Scotland during the period 1936-1950.'[16]

16

17

TEXT BOOKS,

NOTE BOOKS.

FOUNTAIN
PENS.

COLOUR CRAYONS.
From 6d. par box.

ALEX. STENHOUSE,
University and Students' Bookseller,
COLLEGE GATE, GLASGOW.

20

To meet the needs of a growing student
population, a new Men's Union building
opened in University Avenue in 1931,
supplanting a row of shops dating from 1870
(vignette, *above*). The Queen Margaret Union
(for women) then took over the former men's
building by John J. Burnet (now called the
McIntyre building) near the Main Gate.

18

19

The most important alteration to the
Gilmorehill campus in the interwar period
was the enclosure of the western quadrangle
by Sir John J. Burnet's chapel (*top*).
Originally planned in 1914, construction did
not begin for nearly ten years. The building
ultimately became the university's War
Memorial Chapel, containing the names of
755 alumni who died during the 1914-1918
war (with 432 further casualties added after
1945). In 1933, not long before he reluctantly
became King George VI, the Duke of York
visited Gilmorehill and was photographed
(*centre*) with the Duchess (the future Queen
Mother), Rector Compton Mackenzie (left)
and Principal Sir Robert Rait (right). By the
end of the 1930s, war loomed again, and the
university took all the necessary precautions
— including inviting students to return early
from their holidays to help protect the
landmark buildings from enemy attack (*left*).

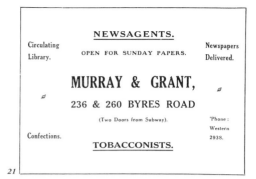

21

22

Among the many small shops which opened in Byres Road during the interwar years was Murray's newsagents (*above*), located in the ground floor of The Curlers public house. Henderson's Cab and Funeral Office (*below, left*) stood at the south end of the row of single-storey shops above the Hillhead subway station. This photograph was taken a few years after Henderson's moved from the other side of Ashton Lane, having been supplanted by the Grosvenor Picture Theatre. After the last war, a Cooper's supermarket was built on the Henderson's site.

Byres Road changed slowly but steadily in the early decades of the twentieth century as it began to supplant Great Western Road as the West End's main shopping district. Its buildings were a combination of traditional tenements (with ground floor shops) and single-storey rows of shops. In addition to the typical dairies, bakers, grocers, dry goods sellers, ironmongers and butchers, there were also stables in various backcourts (accessible through pends). These backcourts often housed cab operators, blacksmiths and other equine trades. There were three major stable premises on the east side of Byres Road between Ashton Road and Elliot (now Cresswell) Street; one was replaced by the Grosvenor Picture Theatre in 1921, another nearby (between Ashton Lane and the subway) became a supermarket in the early 1960s, and the third was built over by Woolworth's in 1958.

23

24

The Grosvenor Picture Theatre,
BYRES ROAD, HILLHEAD (adjoining Subway).

"THE THEATRE SUPERB."

Continuous Programme of the World's Best Films, from 6 to 10.30 daily.
Saturdays, 2 to 10.30.

HALF PRICE MATINÉES—TUESDAYS at 2 o'clock.

PRICES—Stalls 1/-, Balcony 1 6.   Box Seats (bookable in advance) 2/4.

CAFÉ and AMERICAN SODA FOUNTAIN	THE GROSVENOR ORCHESTRA
ON FIRST FLOOR.	of picked Musicians, directed by Manuel L. Luna, renders delightful musical accompaniments at every performance.
Popular Prices. Quick Service.	
Luxurious WAITING ROOM	Organist: H. C. TONKING (Royal Albert Hall, London).
For STALLS Patrons.	

THE GROSVENOR GAZETTE (published monthly) obtainable from the Attendants, or will be posted free on receipt of name and address.

General Manager,   GEORGE HARCOURT.

25

During the interwar period, the single-storey shops began to disappear. In 1920, Glasgow Dean of Guild Court granted permission for the construction of a new picture house by the architects Gardner and Glen, to be built on the site of Henderson's Cab and Funeral Office a few doors south of the corner of Byres Road and Ashton Lane. The Grosvenor Picture Theatre opened in May 1921, its narrow terracotta facade in Byres Road deceptively obscuring the bulk of the picture house (seating 1,350) which stood on the site of Henderson's stables behind. In her speech at the opening ceremony, the Lady Provost Mrs Paxton stated that

> nothing was more fitted to raise the taste of the rising generation than a well-conducted cinema, where great care was taken that the pictures should be of such a nature as to minister to the educational and social aspirations of the patrons. One heard a good deal about the evil effect of what were popularly called the "movies," but criticism could only be levelled at places of entertainment where the management left much to be desired.[17]

The Grosvenor was such a success that in 1929 its café and 'American Soda Fountain' on the first floor was converted to a waiting room. During the 1970s reconstruction, this space became the balcony section of a new public house.[18]

With its unusual terracotta facade and deep projecting canopy, the Grosvenor Picture Theatre was a Byres Road landmark for more than 50 years. Upon its opening the *Glasgow Herald* described the interior as 'large and commodious,' adding that the building was 'tastefully decorated.'[19] Despite the many changes to Glasgow's cinema habits in the postwar period, the Grosvenor remained open. Under new ownership in the late 1970s, the old picture house underwent a major reconstruction, as a result of which the entrance was moved to the rear lane, the balcony was blocked off and twin screens were put in the stalls. The part of the building fronting Byres Road was redeveloped into a public house behind a dull brick facade.

26

Ross's Electric Bakery at 251 Byres Road was one of many shopfronts which was modernised during the interwar period, though few were accomplished so tastefully. Like most Byres Road shops, the premises were used for many different purposes after the last war, eventually becoming the home of a firm of opticians.

27

During the early decades of the twentieth century, Glasgow's famous Edwardian tea rooms gave way to the fashion for cocoa rooms, no doubt in the wake of the popular Van Houten's Cocoa Houses at the 1888 and 1901 exhibitions. By the 1930s, however, it was the milk bar which had become the vogue. The leading name in Glasgow milk bars in the interwar years was Ross's Dairies. Ross's was a forward-looking firm very much in the Glasgow tradition, discovering a new market and exploiting it to its maximum potential. In an age when the Scottish Milk Marketing Board was heavily promoting the drinking of milk for health reasons, Ross's Dairies keenly advertised the benefits of its 'Certified Milk' which was 'Best for Babies and Everyone.'[20] Ross's empire in Glasgow and the surrounding district extended to more than 50 branches, including small dairy shops, milk bars and bakeries. In the West End, Ross's established its 'Clarence Drive Creamery,' a striking Art Deco complex near Broomhill Cross.

Although the firm enjoyed its peak period in the 1930s, Ross's shops had already been a local institution for many years. Henry B. Morton recalled his boyhood home in Great George Street near Byres Road shortly before the First World War: 'The one shop here was Ross's Dairy from which a great clattering of milk cans with long wire handles emanated every morning.'[21]

A typical branch of Ross's came to Byres Road in the early 1930s in the form of

28

Ross's Dairies was a progressive firm in many ways, most notably in its use of Art Deco and other modern styling for its shops, milk bars, and manufacturing plant. The company's landmark creamery building (*left*) was built near the gushet of Crow Road and Clarence Drive in 1938. Paradoxically, as late as the 1950s, the firm still relied on traditional horse-drawn milk wagons (albeit with pneumatic tyres!) for making deliveries in streets such as Hamilton Drive in Hillhead (*below*).

a so-called 'Electric Bakery.' The company's premises were clean, fresh and very modern — thus calling further attention to themselves in a dreary age of economic depression. The shop in Byres Road was very distinctive with its decorative tiles, neon-lit sign and ubiquitous reminders that 'If It's Ross's, It's Right.' In 1938, Ross's Dairy sponsored one of the featured milk bars at the Empire Exhibition in Bellahouston Park.

For Good Fruit

Choice Fruits and Flowers at moderate prices. :: ::

Vegetables, Salads, etc., fresh daily. :: :: :: ::

Potatoes a speciality. ::

The finest Dunbar and East Country Varieties only sold.

Bags and Half-Bags at wholesale prices. :: ::

GEORGE TODD

High-Class Fruiterer and Florist

253, 255, and 262 BYRES ROAD
:: :: HILLHEAD :: ::

Tele- { 262 Byres Road   253 Byres Road   255 Byres Road
phones { Western 47   Western 5615   Western 5616

The Hub of the West End

30

The popular fruiterer and florist George Todd began his business at 253 Byres Road, expanding into No. 255 not long after this photograph was taken in 1926. He also had a florist's shop across the street by the Hillhead subway station. After the last war, Todd's Byres Road shops were taken over by florist Carole Wilson, whose 1950s shopfront at Nos. 253-255 survived until the mid-1990s when it was rebuilt by a national chain of off-licenses.

Throughout the twentieth century, West End residents enjoyed a wide variety of shops in Byres Road. Some, like Ross's Dairy, were branches of city-wide chains. Others, like George Todd's Fruiterer and Florist, began in Byres Road and success there led to eventual expansion throughout Glasgow. After the Second World War, national and international chains such as Woolworth's moved into Byres Road. In the first half of the century, however, the character of Byres Road was distinctively local. As the district's principal shopping area, Byres Road came to be the West End's high street.

One of the most fondly remembered shops from the early twentieth century was the toy shop operated by the Bell family. Located near the corner of Elliot (now Cresswell) Street, 'Miss Bell's' was an institution for generations of local children. Henry B. Morton remembered the shop as 'a veritable magic cave.'[22] Alison Blood, in her 1929 memoir, *Kelvinside Days*, recalled her youthful awe:

> What a vista opened before us when we entered that stationer's-cum-fancy-goods-cum-toy-shop door! There was simply nothing that you could want that was not to be had there. On the left-hand side was a three-tier stand with the more expensive toys, tea-sets, dolls, trains, all tastefully set out, and on the floor such super toys as rocking-horses and tricycles.[23]

Like many old family businesses in Byres Road, however, the Bell's toy shop closed after the last war.

The attractive shops of Mr and Mrs George Todd were also well remembered by West End residents. It was recalled that George Todd 'employed a man full-time, to dress the windows of all his shops. People would always stop and look in the fruit shop window in Byres Road — it was among the finest window-displays in the city.'[24] Maurice Lindsay remembered 'the comfortably rounded Mr and Mrs Todd who would annually add their contribution to the Christmas scene with a gift of tangerines to all their regulars.'[25] Another recalled George Todd 'wearing a panama hat, cream linen jacket and smoking what he called "cheroots".' He was often heard to say, 'Byres Road didn't make me — I made Byres Road!'[26]

31

32

33

34

Long known simply as 'Miss Bell's,' this self-styled 'Children's House' was a local favourite for more than fifty years. During the interwar period, when a new generation of the Bell family took over the business, the traditional tenement shopfront from *c.*1875 (*top*) was updated to a design more in keeping with the style of the late 1920s (*left*). Bell's toy shop was eventually incorporated into the premises of the Clydesdale Bank next door.

'This palatial addition to the palaces of amusement in Glasgow,' declared *Scottish Country Life* in February 1922, 'is to be erected at the corner of Byres Road and Observatory Road, Hillhead. The building has been designed on a lavish scale — the "last word" in comfort, and will contain lounge, lunch, and tea rooms open to the public. A feature will be a new invention for the projection of colour films.'[31] Due to protracted legal battles brought on by protesting neighbours, and the subsequent liquidation of the developers, the cinema never came to be built.

35

In the 1920s, there was stiff competition among picture-house operators in Glasgow. In neighbourhoods like the West End, developers also had to contend with strong opposition from local residents. The first picture house in the West End was the Hillhead Picture Salon in Vinicombe Street. Opened in 1913, the Salon was the first purpose-built picture house west of the city centre. After the hiatus of the 1914-1918 war, an increasing number of new cinemas were proposed around the city. Within five years of the armistice, petitions for four West End picture houses (one in Clarence Drive, one in Bank Street and two in Byres Road) were submitted to the Glasgow Dean of Guild Court. Of these, only the Grosvenor Picture Theatre was actually built. The other Byres Road scheme became entangled in lengthy legal proceedings and the site was subsequently used for housing and shops.

The proposed Botanic Gardens Picture House was designed by Glasgow cinema architect Charles McNair (who later drew up plans for the Ascot at Anniesland). When the scheme was announced in 1922, it was promoted by the developers as the city's 'latest and most up to date cinema.'[27] Proposed for the corner of Byres and Observatory Roads, the massive new building was intended to replace an old row of single-storey shops. In 1923, the developers received their lining (*i.e.* building warrant) from the Dean of Guild Court. The authority had rejected the neighbours' objections that the proposed picture house contravened the original feu disposition, and that 'the buildings would be injurious to the amenity of the district.'[28]

The nearest neighbour to the proposed development, Dr R. O. Adamson of 15 Grosvenor Crescent, refused to let the matter lie, and appealed to the Court of Session. He claimed that the original 1868 feu charter (and later deed conditions) not only prohibited the erection of any buildings other than 'tenements of dwelling houses of three rooms and a kitchen,' but also that no buildings 'should be erected which would, by reason of any trade or occupation carried on therein, be hurtful, nauseous, or noxious or occasion disturbance to the houses or inhabitants in any part of that estate.'[29] The Court of Session rejected one part of the appeal and was uncertain about another, and thus sent the matter back to the Dean of Guild Court for review. Undeterred, Dr Adamson and his neighbours battled on for another seven years before The Botanic Gardens Picture House Ltd. went into liquidation.[30]

After the failure of the cinema project, a local contracting firm called Mackinlay & Co. acquired and redeveloped the entire corner site. In an unusually bold move, considering the economic climate of the time, Mackinlay & Co. built a handsomely appointed block of private flats to be called Grosvenor Mansions.

36

The row of shops on the corner of Byres and Observatory Roads (*left*) was built *c.*1884. The best-known names were Andrew Sadler's upholsterers and antique dealers in the double shop on the corner, and Weir's the photographer, a few doors down. Weir's moved to a new studio between the Wylie & Lochhead garage and No. 1 Grosvenor Terrace after this row was demolished *c.*1930.

37

38

One of the old shops to be displaced by the proposed picture house was that of Mackinlay & Co., plumbers and electricians. In the end the firm acquired the site themselves and built the splendid red sandstone building called Grosvenor Mansions (*above*). It was the first new tenement block to be built in the West End following the First World War (and one of the last to be clad in natural stone for some fifty years). Not surprisingly, Mackinlay & Co. took the prominent corner shop unit, which later became a branch of the Royal Bank of Scotland.

39 A *c.*1925 picture postcard view from the tower of St Bride's Church looking north-west over the recently opened Western Lawn Tennis Club, with the unfinished Montague Terrace alongside in Hyndland Road. Beyond Hughenden Terrace at the left are the playing fields of the Hillhead High School War Memorial Trust. Between the little white farmhouse of North Balgray (visible just above the Hughenden fields) and the Dawsholm Gas Works in the distance is the southern slope of Balgray Hill, where Mactaggart & Mickel's development of 'New Kelvinside' was built a few years later. The low white roofs immediately above the tennis courts belonged to the greenhouses of Malcolm Campbell, the prominent produce merchant who lived in the adjacent Hughenden House.

Patterns of residential building in Glasgow went through great changes after the First World War. Different market forces, shortages of materials and skilled labour, and new social priorities led to a revolution in the provision of housing, both in the public and private sectors. During the 1920s and 1930s, there was little new construction in the greater West End other than the modest houses and flats developed by Mactaggart & Mickel and other private housebuilders on the old estate lands of Kelvinside, Baronald and Kelvindale. Across Glasgow, most new building was undertaken by the Corporation in the wake of 1919 legislation which permitted massive state spending on public housing.

In the west of Glasgow, there was great activity at the early Corporation schemes in Anniesland (red sandstone tenements) and Knightswood (a garden suburb of cottages). On the other hand, few of the gap sites on the old Victorian estates of Hillhead and Downhill were built upon in the 1920s or 1930s. In fact, many prime sites (*e.g.* between Prince Albert Road and Crown Road North) remained vacant until they were used for Corporation housing after the Second World War. Other sites around Kirklee and Bellshaugh Roads were cultivated as allotment gardens in the 1930s and 1940s. The lands at Kirklee had long been intended for feuing, but had lost much of their appeal since the 1890s when the Glasgow Central Railway severed access to the Kelvin.

During the reign of King Edward VII, the western extremity of Kelvinside's development extended to Claythorn, where the lands of Flemington farm were feued for large villas. Nearby were two of the largest parcels of undeveloped land in the West End at that time, North Balgray farm and the lands of Hughenden. A small area behind North Balgray farm had been leased by Kelvinside Academy since the turn of the century as a sports ground, and the lands at Hughenden had been laid out for feuing since the early 1870s, but had only been partly built upon. In the early 1920s, North Balgray farm and the lands of Hughenden were acquired by the memorial trusts of Kelvinside Academy and Hillhead High School respectively. The ancient North Balgray farmhouse (long known as Semple's farm, after its last tenant), survived in Beaconsfield Road until the 1930s.

Prior to the outbreak of war in 1914, Glasgow's private housebuilding industry had been in the doldrums for many years. Many West End gap sites dating from the relatively buoyant period remained vacant well into the interwar period (and some remain so up to the present day). Many speculative housing ventures failed in the early years of the twentieth century due to a general building recession exacerbated by Lloyd George's 'People's Budget' of 1909. The Liberal Chancellor's new Increment Duty not only squeezed builders' profits, but also limited their ability to raise funds to undertake new speculative schemes.[32] Building projects which had struggled on after 1909 certainly stopped dead when war was declared in 1914. There are many unfinished terraces throughout the West End, discernible by the 'gap-toothed' ashlar blocks of their truncated gable ends. Some projects, of course, failed for other reasons — usually builders' insolvency or ground problems. Marlborough Terrace, for example, was begun in 1883 and nine houses were built shortly thereafter. Construction then stopped and the other eleven properties were never built. In 1924, the undeveloped lands were laid out as playing fields.

At Montague Terrace in Hyndland Road (behind Devonshire Gardens), construction of the Grecian-style houses began *c.*1883 and half the terrace was built in the space of only two years. As the terrace progressed south along Hyndland Road, however, it began to encroach upon the site of the old South Balgray stone quarry. Although the developers had planned to build across to the site of the new Hyndland railway station, the cost of preparing the ground of the old quarry was apparently far in excess of the expected market value of the finished houses. This low-lying site lay empty for some forty years until the Western Lawn Tennis Club acquired it in the early 1920s and constructed new courts along with a small clubhouse pavilion.

This 1936 view looking north-east across Great Western Road serves as a valuable record of Dowanhill and eastern Kelvinside before the many changes of the postwar era. Many of the detached villas in 'Dowanhill Gardens' (foreground) were demolished in subsequent decades, including four houses in Victoria Circus below the old observatory and immediately west of the Notre Dame convent complex (centre right). The observatory itself was replaced after the last war by the new Notre Dame High School. Another structure in this view which has since disappeared is the Botanic Gardens bandstand (next to the flagpole, just right of centre).

40

41

Mactaggart & Mickel became the leading housebuilders in Glasgow during the interwar period with speculative estates such as 'New Kelvinside' in the West End and King's Park on the city's South Side. In order to boost sales of private homes during the poor economic conditions in the 1920s, new legislation permitted the Corporation to promote these private schemes through cheap loans. Proprietors would pay a deposit of about 20%, with the Corporation providing a 25-30 year loan at reasonable rates.

The prospectus for 'New Kelvinside' was effusive about 'what is possibly the most ideal site in this most exceptionally desirable district.' It boasted that the location was 'a particularly healthy one, and the magnificent outlook and feeling for fresh, healthy atmosphere make it difficult to believe that the scheme is within twenty minutes of the centre of the City.'[42] The brick and pebbledash houses owed more to English than Scottish building traditions, yet Mactaggart & Mickel decorated them with stained glass made by the local firm of James P. MacPhie of St George's Cross (probably the same studio which had provided the decorative glass in Mactaggart's tenements in Hyndland some twenty years earlier).

Decimus Burton's 1840 feu plan for the Kelvinside Estate Company laid out the high ground of the west side of Balgray Hill with sweeping concentric roads, liberally populated with detached villas surrounded by thick plantings of trees.[33] With the exception of James B. Fleming's mansion of Beaconsfield (built *c*.1875), there was no residential building on the original Kelvinside lands west of Beaconsfield Road until after the First World War. Beyond Fleming's house, the traditional local pursuits of farming, mineral extraction and brick-making were the primary activities for many years.

In the latter decades of the nineteenth century, the Kelvinside Brick Works stood at the highest point of Crossloan (now Cleveden) Road, just above the steep brae down to the bascule bridge over the Forth and Clyde Canal. Brick-clay and coal were excavated all around these western lands of Kelvinside, and a tramway was constructed to carry material from the hollow near Great Western Road up to the brickworks. Although the leases for these industries brought valuable income to the Kelvinside Estate Company, James B. Fleming had to contend with a lengthy legal battle with his feuars over the noxious smells coming from the burning of heaps of blaes. It was reckoned that there were about 260,000 tons of this mining waste around the lands of Balgray in the 1870s, some of it very close to the houses in Montgomerie (now Cleveden) Crescent.[34]

Even after he lost his right to burn the blaes, Fleming appears to have taken an odd pride in these slag heaps. He wrote in his 1894 book, *Kelvinside*, that

> there still remains a large "Bing" of Blaes which was put out by Messrs. Addie when working the Ironstone on Kelvinside, and which has accordingly been dubbed by the local children at Beaconsfield as "Ben Addie." The dining-room at Beaconsfield is 175 feet above the ordnance datum, and the top of Ben Addie is about 275 feet, and from it can be seen nine Counties in Scotland — Lanark, Renfrew, Ayr, Bute, Argyle [*sic*], Dumbarton, Stirling, Perth and Midlothian.[35]

Mineral extraction continued to be undertaken on the lands of Balgray until the early twentieth century.

In 1908, the trustees of James B. Fleming had a new feuing plan drawn up by prominent Glasgow civil engineers Babtie, Shaw & Morton.[36] This basically rectilinear plan (with most main streets running parallel to Great Western Road) was never implemented, possibly due to the turmoil in the housebuilding market in the years prior to the First World War. In the 1920s, Glasgow's traditional system of privately-owned or rented housing was turned on its head. The middle-class rent strife of the war years and the virtual collapse of the private speculative housebuilding industry after the armistice were among the factors that led to the

Winchester Road, Kelvindale, Glasgow

42

Cleveden Road, Kelvindale, Glasgow.

Housing Act of 1919. This legislation enabled local authorities like Glasgow Corporation to assume responsibility for providing the vast numbers of new houses needed in the 1920s and 1930s. Prior to 1914, the Corporation had provided a mere 1% of all city housing (through the work of the City Improvement Trust, which had been in existence since the 1860s).[37]

In the 1920s, Glasgow and other Scottish cities underwent a revolution in the provision of residential buildings. A Royal Commission deemed that the traditional tenement form was outdated and, due to the high density of residents, prone to deteriorate into slum conditions. Early in the 1920s, Glasgow Corporation adopted the English 'garden suburb' planning policies which encouraged low-density developments of cottages (detached, semi-detached or in short terraces), each with its own garden. Tenements, however, were not wholly rejected by the Corporation. In fact, a two-tier system was created in interwar Glasgow, with garden cottages at sites such as Knightswood populated by 'skilled and white-collar tenants, and tenements, new and old, housing the less well-off.'[38] Some interwar Corporation tenements were well-built and thus particularly desirable, such as the red sandstone-faced three-storey blocks at Anniesland Cross.

One of the men who promoted the benefits of the garden suburb was builder and housing reformer Sir John Mactaggart. In the early years of the twentieth century, Mactaggart formed a partnership with architect Andrew Mickel and together they constructed a large number of traditional tenements in and around Glasgow (including many of the early buildings in Hyndland).[39] Mactaggart & Mickel prospered in the interwar period not only through their own speculative building, but also by constructing garden suburb estates for the Corporation of Glasgow.[40] In 1923, the Fleming trustees (with the permission of the Kelvinside Estate Company's bondholder, Standard Life Assurance) sold the last large parcel of undeveloped Kelvinside land — some 114 acres — to Messrs Mactaggart & Mickel for a price of £33,000.[41]

Much of the building material used in the construction of the new houses in Mactaggart & Mickel's 'New Kelvinside' was shipped by railway to the yards near Hyndland station, and taken from there by horse and cart up Balgray Hill. The horses were quartered overnight at North Balgray farm at the foot of Beaconsfield Road. By the time the new estates were complete, Crossloan Road had become Cleveden Road (by decree of Glasgow's postmaster, so as to avoid further confusion with Govan's Crossloan Road). Before long, New Kelvinside became known as Kelvindale, taking the name of the scheme begun a year earlier on the old lands of Baronald between Cleveden Road and the Kelvindale Paper Works.

44

The Collins family's sprawling Kelvindale Paper Works (*above*, centre) included railways, reservoirs, a prominent chimney and the stately mansion of Kelvindale House (seen in the foreground of this *c.*1947 view). Branches of the Collins family (probably unrelated to the Glasgow publishers of the same name) built mansions in Crossloan (now Cleveden) Road called West Balgray and Highfield. In 1900, Edward Collins, one of the last members of the family to control this historic firm, shot himself in the head at Highfield, having just returned from his country house after months of illness and depression.[44] Some time after the Collins family left, the wooded estate of West Balgray became a horseriding establishment, though it had once been shortlisted as a possible site for the proposed new Royal Hospital for Sick Children and it was once destined to be the site of a new homeopathic hospital. In the 1960s the site was cleared for a new high school.

From the mid-1920s, both sides of Balgray Hill began to be developed with modest middle-class houses. Those streets east of Cleveden Road were the first to be built and consisted of a mixture of building types. Some had red sandstone facades, others were harled, and a number were constructed of aggregate-faced concrete blocks. Within a year of the first houses being occupied, residents of Kelvindale had formed a local association to maintain and enhance the amenity of the new district. This fledgling residents' group, later renamed the Kelvindale and Kelvinside Association, is said to have been the first such voluntary organisation to be formed in Glasgow.

Two centuries prior to Kelvindale becoming a residential district, the area was known as the home of several important industrial sites, including one of the earliest paper mills in Scotland. In the late seventeenth century, the Huguenot refugee Nicholas Deschamps introduced papermaking to Glasgow (at Woodside), and within a few decades other paper mills were established further up the river. In 1736, Glasgow printer James Duncan purchased the ancient Balgray grain mill in Kelvindale and over the next ten years established not only a paper mill, but also built an oil mill and two snuff mills on the site. By 1746, Duncan was employing 16 men at Balgray.[43]

In the mid nineteenth century, the Balgray paper mill was taken over by the Collins family who, over several generations, developed the Kelvindale Paper Works, one of Scotland's most important papermaking sites and one of the longest-surviving traditional industries along the River Kelvin. Just upstream from the Kelvindale works, there were several other grain, snuff and paper mills, as well as a printworks and related industries, all of which relied on the power of the Kelvin. Another important early industry, located upstream from Kelvindale, was William Stirling's linen and calico works (Scotland's oldest) at Dawsholm.

45

Not long after the new district of Kelvindale was built, a St George's Cooperative shop opened nearby. This photograph of the buildings, situated on the corner of Kelvindale Road and Balcarres Avenue, was taken in February 1931. The small white building at the right is the Balgray farmhouse (not to be confused with the older North and South Balgray farms near Great Western Road). The site of the old Balgray steading was later cleared and used for a temporary primary school after the last war. It eventually became a playing field. The Kelvindale Paper Works (*centre*), Glasgow's oldest surviving paper mill, closed in 1975 after more than two centuries of operation at Balgray.

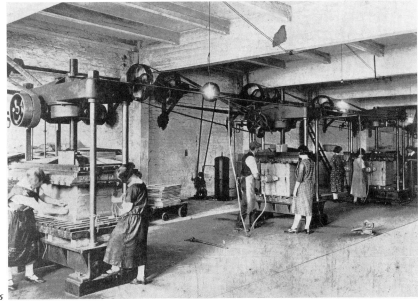

46

47

William Stirling established linen and calico printing at Dawsholm in 1750. He was succeeded by William Robb, a bleacher and calico printer from Meadowside in Partick (who also leased a printfield at Gilmorehill). After Robb went bankrupt in 1792, Dawsholm was acquired by Richard Gillespie, son of William Gillespie (of Anderston and South Woodside). Many more firms took over the site during the nineteenth century until Glasgow Corporation acquired the area for a new gasworks in 1871. Twenty years later, the two gasometers were badly damaged by a bomb explosion, thought at the time to have been yet another 'Fenian outrage.'[45] This 1955 view shows the 1790 Kelvin Aqueduct of the Forth and Clyde Canal in the foreground, with Dawsholm Park on the horizon to the right. The original line of Skaethorn Road runs parallel to the canal.

St John's Renfield Church in Beaconsfield Road (*right*) was built between 1929 and 1931 to accommodate two merged congregations from old Glasgow churches. The new single church moved to Hyndland first (as Hyndland UF), and then relocated to the Kelvindale area in the late 1920s to become a parish church for the recently reunited Church of Scotland. The robust design of St John's Renfield, a modern church built with traditional materials (*opposite*), deftly links Victorian Kelvinside with its interwar neighbour, Kelvindale. The church hall (*below*) was completed first and used for services from 1929.

48

Since the early 1860s, one of the defining features of Great Western Road has been its string of impressive stone-built churches. Five major church buildings were constructed along the old turnpike from St George's Cross to Anniesland, and all but one (Woodside Church at Montague Street, Woodlands) still survive. Three of the first four churches (St Mary's Cathedral, Lansdowne Church, and Kelvinside Free Church) have dramatic spires which punctuate the views along Great Western Road. St John's Renfield, the last major church built in the West End, was given prominence by being sited on a hill above the old turnpike. Its construction in the late 1920s followed a design competition involving some twenty-eight architectural firms. The submission by James Taylor Thomson, proposing a lofty stone structure standing high above the natural hollow of North Balgray farm, was selected because it 'fitted admirably to the site.'[46]

49

51

St John's Renfield Church was one of the last traditional stone buildings to be constructed in the West End. Among the impressionable visitors present during its construction were Sunday school children who often played on the scaffold after early services in the newly-completed church hall. The view behind young Will Scott (*above*) looks in a westerly direction over Leicester Avenue and the Balgray playing fields.

Like many nineteenth-century churches in the centre of Glasgow, the congregations of St John's and Renfield were forced to close their city buildings and follow parishioners westward to the suburbs. In the 1920s, the merged congregation of St John's Renfield moved to new premises in the West End. Despite having sold their valuable city centre sites, the parishioners still had to raise almost a third of the final cost of £39,000 for the construction of the new Kelvindale building. The minister during the time of the merger and the relocation to the West End was Dr G. H. C. Macgregor. In order to attract new members to the congregation, Dr Macgregor 'visited every family in West Kelvinside [*sic*] and Kelvindale schemes and everywhere had a wonderful welcome.'[47]

Dr Macgregor was supported in his promotion of the new church by Col. William D. Scott, Chairman of the Buildings Committee. Scott, owner of the Dundashill Bakery, was Food Officer for Glasgow during the last war and had been the 'Captain of the Glasgow 5th' for 46 years.[48] In a remarkable series of photographs taken during construction of the church, Col. Scott and his young son Will are seen clambering on the sarking, rafters and scaffold of the massive building. A number of views show masons and other craftsmen at work on the site as the new building begins to take shape above Balgray.

St John's Renfield was constructed by mason John Train, and in the lofty nave there is fine joinery work by Wylie & Lochhead and a stained glass window by Douglas Strachan. In the aftermath of the Great War and the subsequent economic depression of the 1920s, traditional building techniques went into steep decline. The few major building projects which were undertaken in the interwar period increasingly relied on modern construction techniques. St John's Renfield, however, was built of coursed squared rubble sandstone with polished dressings. The roof was constructed with a timber truss and covered in slate. The architect declined to incorporate a traditional spire, instead favouring a delicate timber and lead flèche over the crossing.

52

53

By the time St John's Renfield was nearing completion in 1931, the Corporation of Glasgow had extended Great Western Road out to the new housing estate at Knightswood. There, on the highest part of the new boulevard west of Anniesland, stood the crow-stepped tower of St Margaret's, the most westerly landmark church in Glasgow. A rare Glasgow work by the firm of Sir Robert Lorimer, St Margaret's church was completed after the architect's death in 1929.

In March 1941, on the second devastating night of the Clydeside blitz, Kelvindale was one of the many isolated parts of western Glasgow that suffered extensive damage from stray Luftwaffe land mines (Dowanhill, North Kelvinside and Hyndland — where 36 died in Dudley Drive and Airlie Street — were also badly affected).[49] All the windows of St John's Renfield (with the exception of the decorative glass) were blown out in the blast of the mine which hit Kelvindale. During the raid, several houses were destroyed or badly damaged in Leicester Avenue and Chelmsford Drive and nine people were killed.

The congregation's building convenor, Col. W. D. Scott (*below*, centre), and his son Will, are pictured in the upper reaches of the new St John's Renfield church during the final stages of construction in the summer of 1930. The wooded eminence of Balgray Hill, where the Collins family had houses at Highfield and West Balgray House, is visible behind the group in the trusses (*above*).

54

The second Queen Margaret Bridge, designed by Glasgow City Engineer Thomas Somers, was the last major road crossing to be built over the River Kelvin. Unlike the old stone, cast iron and steel bridges in the West End, this new bridge was constructed with a reinforced concrete arch. This technology permitted it to have the longest span over the Kelvin at over 135 feet (41m). With its polished Peterhead red granite parapet and red sandstone cladding from Corncockle in Dumfriesshire, Queen Margaret Bridge soars above the millpond behind Jackson's Dam. Two rare construction views show the timber centering being built across the Kelvin (*right*) and the new junction with Kelvin Drive nearing completion on the north bank of the river, *c*.1929 (*centre*).

55

56

Bomb damage in North Kelvinside in March 1941 provided a postwar gap site overlooking the wide expanse of Queen Margaret Bridge. The Glasgow Tree-Lovers Society later established a little neighbourhood park (*right*), which remained for several years before the site was developed for lock-up garages. The villa of Northbank, in Wilton Street (demolished in the 1970s), stands on the hill in the distance on the left.

57

58

In the 1920s, the last of the great bridges across the River Kelvin was built as part of a new tramway which had been authorised by Parliament shortly before the outbreak of war in 1914. Construction did not start until 1926, and the new Queen Margaret Bridge (just upstream from its 1870 namesake) did not open until 1929. The extreme width of the new bridge and approach road from Byres Road (built to accommodate trams) forced the reconstruction of the front gates of the Botanic Gardens as well as the side garden of No. 1 Grosvenor Terrace. Upon completion, a motorbus trial showed a lack of passenger interest in the proposed tram route, and thus the rails were never laid on the bridge.

One of the major changes to affect the West End during the interwar years was the conversion of many large villas and terraced houses into institutional and commercial facilities. A large number of hotels opened in the West End during the period, especially around the time of the 1938 Empire Exhibition in Bellahouston Park. One of the most prominently sited new establishments in the area was the Grosvenor Hotel, originally Nos. 1 & 2 Grosvenor Terrace. The 1929 picture above shows the entrance to Grosvenor Terrace being reconstructed to accommodate the widening of Byres Road for a new tram route.

The Glasgow Homeopathic Hospital has been a thriving institution since the establishment of the first premises at 5 Lynedoch Crescent in 1914. After a decade-long search, large new premises were opened at Glentower, No. 1000 Great Western Road, in 1931 (*right*). Soon thereafter, however, this 30-bed hospital proved to be insufficient for the numbers of patients seeking treatment, and an appeal was launched to erect new purpose-built premises. Lands were acquired at Julian Avenue in Kirklee, though the outbreak of war in 1939 and the creation of the National Health Service in 1947 halted the scheme. When the Glasgow Homeopathic Hospital joined the NHS, the appeal fund of £75,000 was not transferred to the Secretary of State 'along with the buildings and equipment,' but was held separately under certain conditions according to special clauses in the NHS legislation.[57] More than 50 years later, this original endowment was used towards the construction of the new purpose-built premises which were opened in 1999 in the grounds of Gartnavel Asylum.

61

GLASGOW HOMŒOPATHIC HOSPITAL

TWENTY-SEVENTH

ANNUAL REPORT

FOR YEAR ENDING 30TH JUNE, 1936

Hospital—
1000 Great Western Road
(West of Hyndland Road),
Glasgow, W.2.
Telephone—Western 382.

Dispensary—
5 Lynedoch Crescent,
Glasgow, C.3.
Telephone—Douglas 4490.

Secretary and Treasurer—
R. GORDON LAING, C.A., 53 Bothwell Street, Glasgow, C.2.
Telephone—Central 3766 (2 lines).

60

Homeopathic medicine, the practice of using drugs 'to excite physical resistance, to restore balance and enable the system to defeat in a natural manner the germs of disease,'[50] has a history in Glasgow dating back to 1880 when a dispensary first opened in St Vincent Street. The success of subsequent dispensaries in Berkeley Street and at No. 5 Lynedoch Crescent paved the way for the eventual establishment of Scotland's first homeopathic hospital. The new hospital opened at the Lynedoch premises in 1914. After the interruption of war, it enjoyed a period of 'uninterrupted progress,' with the numbers of patients increasing from some 3,000 in 1920 to well over 12,600 in 1926.[51]

It soon became apparent that new premises were required and in 1921 a committee was formed to seek a site for a new hospital. Over the next eight years the committee searched for an appropriate location west of Charing Cross. The first building to be considered was Redlands House, the former mansion of James B. Mirrlees in Great Western Road (and in recent years a hostel for teacher training students from Jordanhill College). The committee, however, 'found it unsuitable as a replacement for the hospital in Lynedoch.'[52] Redlands was later converted into the new home of the Glasgow Private Women's Hospital (a role it served until 1978).

In 1922, the search committee inspected several houses around Park Circus as well as Arnewood in Cleveden Road. The following year, its members finally decided on West Balgray House, the former home of papermaker Edward Collins. West Balgray was situated in Crossloan Road in a large mature garden across from the former Fleming mansion of Beaconsfield. Some fifteen years previously, the directors of the Royal Hospital for Sick Children had considered this elevated and airy site for their own new building (eventually built by Sir John J. Burnet at Yorkhill). Coincidentally, when West Balgray was obtained for a new homeopathic hospital, it was Burnet's firm that drew up the plans to redevelop the site, including converting the existing mansion house into a nurses' block.

For the rest of the decade, funds were raised to pay for the construction of the new homeopathic premises at West Balgray (during which time the property was leased out for rental income). It was finally decided, however, that the Burnet plans were far too costly, and the directors sold West Balgray in order to assess whether 'more Favourable premises could be obtained.'[53] After two years of negotiating, the directors sold the site to the Glasgow Educational Authority in early 1929. The search for new West End locations continued apace, with the committee inspecting four large properties in close proximity along Great Western Road. They considered Red Hall on the corner of Beaconsfield Road (which they found 'would not adapt without considerable expense'[54]), Westbourne House on the corner of Hyndland Road, Windsor House (also deemed unsuitable), and Glentower (No. 1000 Great Western Road). The subcommittee favoured the latter, but was deterred from choosing because of concerns over the restrictive feu conditions.

Concerns over the cost of converting Glentower or similar properties led the committee to decide in August 1929 to 'look for vacant ground and abolish the idea of converting an old house into Hospital premises.'[55] Various sites around the West End were considered, including lands in Dowanhill, Hamilton Crescent and Semple's farm at North Balgray. After two months, however, the committee again changed its mind, deciding that the cost of a new-build hospital would be too expensive after all (estimated at £35,000 for a Dowanhill site, including equipping a new building) and returned to the idea of converting Glentower. After some months of haggling over the price, the committee purchased the house in January 1930 for the sum of £4,500. Soon thereafter, architects Sir John J. Burnet, Dick & Son were commissioned to convert the old mansion.[56] In October, the new 30-bed Glasgow Homeopathic Hospital was formally opened by its patron, the Earl of Home.

DID YOU SEE?

at the Empire Exhibition, Scotland, 1938, in the Scottish Pavilion (North) the model of the proposed HOMŒOPATHIC HOSPITAL FOR SCOTLAND. . . . . A photograph of this is reproduced on the opposite page. . . . .

WILL YOU HELP?

to build this Hospital by completing and forwarding to Lord Inverclyde, our Honorary Treasurer, the form printed on page 56 . . . .

63

During the 1930s, the appeal for new premises raised a third of the estimated cost of £225,000 required for the building of a new homeopathic hospital. The proposed hospital, designed by James Taylor (architect at 'New Kelvinside'), was to be situated on a large parcel of open land in Julian Avenue at Kirklee, just east of Redlands Women's Hospital and behind Redlands and Lowther Terraces. The model (*below*) of the new buildings was displayed at the Empire Exhibition at Bellahouston Park in 1938.

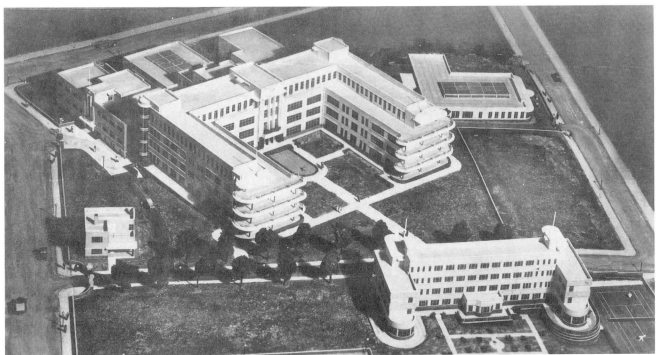

James Watt Engineering Building, c.1958.

VIII.

The Postwar Years

Bute Gardens (*above*), laid out in the late 1880s near Lilybank House, was an L-shaped street of terraced houses located between Hillhead and Great George Streets. In Hillhead Street (across from the top of Gibson Street), adjacent to the terrace, a lofty range of five-storey tenements called Bute Mansions was completed around 1892. Although the terraced houses were demolished in the mid-1960s to suit the university's expansion plans, all but one tenement still survive as university offices and residences. This view, taken by the City Assessor's department in September 1925, looks north from Hillhead Street (leading off to the right) along the south-facing flank of Bute Gardens (which, in the mid-1960s, would become the site of the new University Library). Bute Mansions can just be seen behind the trees to the right.

Prior to the First World War, there had been 80 years of steady residential development in the West End of Glasgow. In the years between the wars, on the other hand, there was relatively little change to the area's physical appearance. The most dramatic (and tragic) event occurred on the night of 13 March 1941, when stray German land mines intended for Clydebank caused extensive building damage and great loss of life in and around western Glasgow. Another major effect of the last war was the removal of vast amounts of Glasgow's ornamental cast ironwork during the massive scrap metal drives. Cast iron was being salvaged at such a rate throughout Glasgow from 1943 that the contractors undertaking the removal works refused at one point to continue the operations, owing to the lack of storage space.[1]

More incremental were the socio-economic changes that affected the West End, as the last remaining families of the old mercantile elite began to sell or convert their large Victorian and Edwardian houses after 1918. The 1920s and 1930s saw an increasing number of Glasgow institutions moving into the large houses along Great Western Road and elsewhere in the greater West End. Houses around Park Circus and Woodside were increasingly converted to professional or medical offices. Conversion to hotel use was also common. Changing economic conditions in the aftermath of the 1939-1945 war contributed to a steady but dramatic shift in the demographics of the West End, as small flats were created within the palatial Victorian and Edwardian houses. Bedsit flats, or 'Houses in Multiple Occupancy,' often had several bedrooms carved out of subdivided public rooms.

As smaller properties became available in Hillhead, Dowanhill and Kelvinside, the local student population increased. Many large houses, especially those set in large gardens or double feus in Kelvinside and Dowanhill, succumbed to redevelopment pressure. Some had been requisitioned during the last war and abandoned thereafter. Many others were simply demolished to make way for rather nondescript blocks of flats or, as in the case of Richmond, the cast-iron fronted villa in Dowanhill, a large telephone exchange.[2] The greatest impact on the West End's historic fabric, however, resulted from the University of Glasgow's redevelopment programme of the 1960s and 1970s when hundreds of houses and flats were demolished in Hillhead.

3

In the midst of the physical upheaval in the West End during the postwar period, the passing of the older generation also signalled a decline in the awareness of the area's history. In order to capture this history, long-time Hillhead resident Henry B. Morton compiled one the great works of Scottish local historiography, *A Hillhead Album*, published in 1973 by the Charles A. Hepburn Trust. In addition to his achievement in assembling a wealth of images, recollections and anecdotes of old Hillhead, Morton also compiled an informal portfolio of snapshots taken around the area in the late 1960s and early 1970s. Morton cycled or walked with his dog 'Girlie' on summer evenings, recording Hillhead in the midst of this period of great change.

4

5

Among the most compelling snapshots taken by Henry B. Morton are the views recording the redevelopment of his beloved Hillhead. Morton, however, chose not to publish these bleak views in *A Hillhead Album*. During the 1960s, he photographed the gradual demolition around Bute Gardens as it was cleared for the new University Library and Hunterian Art Gallery. A lorry (*top*, photographed in 1966) is piled high with rubble in the centre of the site of Bute Gardens (seen from a similar vantage point in the picture opposite). Demolition progressed from Hillhead Street around the corner towards the new Adam Smith building (*centre*). A few years later, Girlie (*left*) inspects the rear of the University Library as the shadow of Adam Smith looms over the future site of the Hetherington building.

6

The University of Glasgow's postwar rebuilding programme peaked in the late 1960s, when the Adam Smith building and the University Library were completed (the Hunterian Art Gallery came later). The handsome terraces of Bute Gardens were demolished to make way for these towering concrete structures. Surprisingly, old Lilybank House survived despite the encroachment of the Adam Smith social sciences building (*above*, centre). In this *c.*1966 view, the latter is well underway whilst the foundations for the massive Library/Hunterian complex are being excavated in the boulder clay. At the far end of University Gardens (left) the first postwar departmental building, Modern Languages, can be seen. Behind that is the western end of Lilybank Gardens, awaiting demolition.

The University of Glasgow had begun to make preliminary incursions north of University Avenue prior to the end of the First World War, when the Psychology Department took over New Hillhead House (later the site of the round Reading Room) in 1917. Major interwar buildings nearby included the new Men's Union in University Avenue and the 1939 observatory in University Gardens. The round Reading Room of 1939 was meant to be the centrepiece of a classic academic quadrangle alongside Wellington Church, but the scheme died with the war. In the years following the end of hostilities, the university became increasingly constricted within its old Gilmorehill/Donaldshill campus. During its quincentennial year of 1951, the university celebrated its impressive past whilst simultaneously launching its agenda for future expansion. By the early 1950s, the last of the large departmental buildings, Hughes and Waugh's Chemistry building and Basil Spence's new Natural Philosophy block, were nearing completion.

In 1947, the university acquired Garscube, the ancient wooded estate of the Campbells of Succoth, which formed Glasgow's north-westerly boundary with Bearsden. The Veterinary Department was soon transferred to Garscube, and for a time the feasibility of creating an altogether new campus there was seriously considered.[3] During the Jubilee year, the university planned to capitalise on postwar government changes which facilitated capital spending on new buildings. Edinburgh architect and planner Sir Frank Mears was commissioned to produce a masterplan for a new Hillhead campus, an area which was anticipated to encompass the rectangle between Byres Road, Great George Street, Bank Street and University Avenue.

Mears' plan envisioned a linked series of rectangular blocks set in quadrangles which roughly followed the old Hillhead gridiron, but which paid little heed to the contours of the drumlin.[4] The final Mears scheme of 1951 called for the phased demolition of every building within the remit area with the exception of Wellington Church and the university's three buildings of recent interwar vintage. The subsequent masterplan, substantially revised by architects Wilson & Womersley in 1963, was far less radical in its treatment of the older buildings in Hillhead (pardoning Laurel Bank School, University Gardens and half of the twin Oakfield Terraces). The topography of Hillhead, however, was still to be overpowered by large linking slab blocks in Great George Street, Bute Gardens, Lilybank Gardens and Byres Road. By the time the rebuilding programme got underway in earnest in the late 1960s, elements of both masterplans had been taken up, but on the whole the end result was much more haphazard.

Rebuilding started slowly in the late 1950s. The first postwar buildings in Hillhead were Modern Languages (built on a gap site at the end of University Gardens) and the Stevenson sports building in Oakfield Avenue, both of which were finished c.1959-1960. Prior to the second half of the 1960s, little had changed in Hillhead. From 1965, however, over a period of five years, sites were cleared for seven major multi-storey buildings in a confined area north of University Avenue. Few of these massive blocks respected any aspect of the existing context except perhaps the street grid and the fine views.

The construction of so many large university buildings required extensive and rapid demolition of numerous properties south of Great George Street, starting with the easterly Oakfield Terrace at the end of the 1950s. Another early casualty was Florentine Terrace, a row of modest houses that stood opposite Wellington Church in Ann Street (now Southpark Avenue) and behind the round Reading Room. No. 6, the end house in this short terrace, was best remembered as the home of Charles Rennie Mackintosh and Margaret Macdonald during their last eight years in Glasgow.

In this 1965 view taken from Hillhead Street, the remaining houses in the western flank of Bute Gardens are shown temporarily propped, as foundations for the new University Library and Hunterian Art Gallery rise in front of the nearly completed Adam Smith building. The site of the condemned buildings in Bute Gardens was latterly cleared, but it remained undeveloped until the early 1980s when the famed Glasgow architects Gillespie, Kidd & Coia designed the yellow brick Hetherington building on the corner of Great George Street.

7

Between 1906 and 1914, the house at the end of Florentine Terrace, No. 6, (at the far left of this 1963 picture) was the home of Charles Rennie Mackintosh and Margaret Macdonald, the only property ever owned by the couple. Mackintosh made some alterations to the exterior, the most notable of which was the addition of new windows to the south-facing gable wall overlooking the gardens of New Hillhead House. The south gable of Florentine Terrace can be seen in the 1937 view by T. & R. Annan below, taken from the university tower. The gable of No. 6 is at the centre, between New Hillhead House and Wellington Church. The new Hillhead High School is also visible in this view, behind the church.

Florentine Terrace was built *c.*1865 in Ann Street (now Southpark Avenue), immediately behind New Hillhead House (now the site of the round Reading Room). The house at the end of the terrace, No. 6, contained what were probably the most significant domestic interiors in the rich architectural history of the West End. From 1906 to 1914, this house was the last Glasgow home of Charles Rennie Mackintosh and Margaret Macdonald. When they moved to Florentine Terrace from Mains Street in Blythswood, the architect was at the height of his powers. The couple made dramatic alterations to the modest terraced house, most notably by removing walls to enlarge the major east-facing rooms, and strategically adding new windows to the south-facing gable wall. They also installed their own designs for fireplaces, bookshelves and light fixtures, all part of a grand composition that included their own wall and floor coverings, stencils, and, of course, their distinctive furniture designs.

For one reason or another, Mackintosh's architectural career in Glasgow went into steep decline not long after he moved to Hillhead. In 1914, he and Margaret were wintering in East Anglia when war was declared. They moved to London for the duration of the war, finally settling in France in 1923. In 1920, having let the house in Hillhead, the Mackintoshes sold the building and furniture to their friend William Davidson, the patron of the architect's celebrated villa of Windyhill at Kilmacolm.

William Davidson spent the last twenty-five years of his life in Florentine Terrace, amidst a growing collection of Mackintosh and Macdonald furniture and fittings. Five years after Mackintosh's death from cancer in 1928, Davidson commemorated his friend in an important Memorial Exhibition, the first major retrospective of the great man's career. After William Davidson's death in 1945, the university acquired not only the collection of Mackintosh furniture, but also the house in Florentine Terrace. When the juggernaut of the university's postwar redevelopment programme approached Southpark Avenue, Florentine Terrace — despite its valuable interiors — stood no chance of survival. Prior to demolition, however, the Mackintosh interiors were removed for later reconstruction in the new Hunterian Art Gallery. Though there was some criticism of the propriety of the new museum setting for the Mackintosh fittings, in view of the fact that at the time of the demolition there was scant regard for the architect's work, with hindsight it is miraculous that the Florentine Terrace interiors were preserved at all.

The Mackintoshes left Glasgow and Florentine Terrace (*above*) in 1914, moving first to England and then to France. Friend and patron William Davidson bought the house and furnishings in 1920 and lived there until his death in 1945. The property was then acquired by the University of Glasgow, which used it as a professorial residence for many years. The most notable tenant was Professor of Botany John Walton, son of 'Glasgow Boy' E. A. Walton and nephew of the artist George Walton (who had been a friend of the Mackintoshes).[5]

The 1963 masterplan by architects Wilson & Womersley (*right*) for the University of Glasgow's redevelopment of Hillhead was a somewhat scaled-down version of the original 1951 plan by Sir Frank Mears, which had proposed the redevelopment of the entire area between University Avenue and Great George Street (with provision for later extensions north to Great Western Road!). In either case, there were to be only a small number of nineteenth-century buildings left standing.

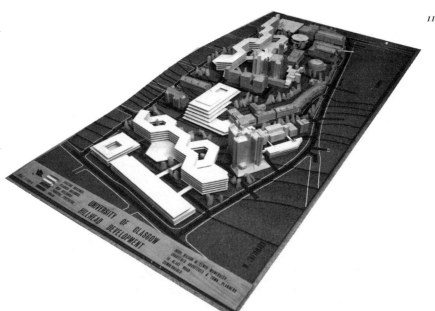

11

A spectacular aerial view (*opposite*) *c.*1967 shows a pause in the University of Glasgow's reconstruction of Hillhead. The Adam Smith building and new library, both nearing completion, can be seen surrounding the *c.*1836 Lilybank House (centre left), whilst work on the Queen Margaret Union is just getting underway beneath a crane at the end of University Gardens. In the foreground, the terraces and tenements between Ashton Terrace and the Western Infirmary still stand; they were to be removed a few years later for the realignment of the intersection of Byres Road and Highburgh Road. Tenements and terraces in Lilybank Gardens (lower left) were also soon to be demolished.

The boom period of the university's redevelopment of Hillhead was over by the early 1970s. Although more demolitions were still to come in Ashton Road, the major redevelopment strategy, dating back in part to the Hughes and Waugh plan of 1936, had virtually come to an end. In the 1970s, the only significant structure built by the university in Hillhead was the ponderous Boyd Orr building (*c.*1972), erected astride Ashton Terrace and Lilybank Gardens. Over the next ten years, there were only two additions to the Hillhead campus, the brick-faced Geology building (sympathetically hugging the curve of Lilybank Gardens), and the Hetherington building in Bute Gardens. Complementing the postwar expansion of the university came improvements to the facilities of its teaching premises at the Western Infirmary. After the arrival of the National Health Service in 1947, the Western expanded comprehensively, not only on its historic Donaldshill site, but also along the realigned University Avenue (where nurses' residences were built on a reconstructed gushet opposite the truncated Ashton Terrace).

By and large, the university's postwar expansion in Hillhead was complete by the early 1980s, though gap sites and unfulfilled plans were still numerous. Through the 1980s and 1990s, the sloping site on the corner of Great George Street and Lilybank Gardens was left as a tarmac car park after tenements were demolished in the early 1970s. Although the university continued to acquire property in the old terraces and villas of Hillhead in the last quarter of the twentieth century, there was scant demolition (relative to the 1960s), with most properties being reused as departmental or administrative offices.

There is some random architectural merit in the university's postwar redevelopment, but little positive contribution was made to the overall built environment of the West End, when compared to the grand buildings by Scott, Burnet, Miller, and Hughes and Waugh dating from 1866 to 1939. There is a feeling of physical oppression near the massive concrete postwar buildings which seem to sit very uneasily on Hillhead's tight Georgian grid. Fortunately, the university's inability to fully implement either the 1951 Mears scheme or the revised plan of 1963 saved old Hillhead from comprehensive destruction.

The Boyd Orr building was the last of the massive concrete blocks to be built by the university in the postwar period. The towering copper-roofed slab required the demolition of the easterly half of Ashton Terrace and a good part of Lilybank Gardens. Named after the Nobel Prize-winning nutritionist and one-time Chancellor of the University, the building dominates University Avenue.

Student numbers continued to rise steadily as the end of the twentieth century approached, though not at the heady rate of the 1960s and 1970s, when the campus population rose by a third. During the 1960s alone, there were some 30 appointments to newly created departmental chairs. As student numbers increased during the last two decades of the twentieth century, the university adopted a policy of developing its lands outside of the West End, most notably at the Garscube Estate, thus easing the pressure on Hillhead, Gilmorehill and Donaldshill. In the mid-1990s, extensive student residences were constructed on the site of a former glassworks, picturesquely situated on the Forth and Clyde Canal at Ruchill. The Westerlands playing fields near Anniesland were sold to private house developers in the late 1990s, and, around the same time, there was a gradual shift of activities from the congested Western Infirmary site to the more spacious lands at Gartnavel.

By the end of the twentieth century, after the long-standing threat of university redevelopment had evaporated, Hillhead became a more stabilised neighbourhood. There had been, in fact, other residential property demolished during the postwar era, but these losses were generally due to the poor ground conditions caused by old mineral works. Although student accommodation had long been the predominant housing type in Hillhead, changing market forces in the 1990s led to many multiple occupancy properties being converted back to family-sized flats.

13

14

One area of Hillhead that was particularly devastated by the University of Glasgow's postwar expansion was Lilybank Gardens, a curving crescent built *c.*1882-1890 in the lower policies of Lilybank House, just east of Byres Road. This development was originally intended to link through to the lands of Sauchfield House, another early Hillhead villa which was demolished *c.*1883 to make way for University Gardens. The two developments, however, were never joined, and today these streets are still closed off along the old estate boundary between the Mathematics and Boyd Orr buildings.

In the late 1960s and early 1970s, the south and west buildings in Lilybank Gardens were demolished as part of the university's masterplan. Despite the scale of the clearances of fine terraced houses and tenement blocks, there was only limited reconstruction in the area after the looming Boyd Orr tower was finished in 1972. The brick-clad Geology building (*c.*1980) was built at the south-west corner of the old gardens, sitting more happily on its site than many of the university's other postwar developments in the area. By the 1980s, the statutory protection of much of Hillhead's historic architecture had led to a sympathetic conversion of the surviving easterly half of Lilybank Gardens to departmental use. At the turn of the twenty-first century, there was still uncertainty over the future of the large gap site at the corner of Lilybank Gardens and Great George Street. A design for a new business studies complex by architect Terry Farrell was in the midst of development in the late 1990s when the project was abruptly shelved.

17

The intrepid chronicler of Hillhead, Henry B. Morton, photographed with his dog 'Girlie' in Professors Square, *c.*1971.

15

16

Lilybank Gardens was a handsome crescent of terraced houses and tenements, housing a variety of Hillhead's professional families. Of the two terraces seen from Great George Street (*opposite, above*), only the easterly side (to the left) survived the university's postwar redevelopment. The southern end of Lilybank Gardens (*opposite, below*) was replaced by the Boyd Orr and Geology buildings. Around 1970, Henry B. Morton photographed Lilybank Gardens (*left, above*) as it was being partially cleared for the Boyd Orr building. Morton's later view of the Boyd Orr (*left*) was taken from the path of the newly realigned University Avenue near the corner of the erstwhile Sutherland Street, where new nurses houses were soon to be built.

18

This *c.*1968 view looking up Byres Road from the corner of Highburgh Road changed dramatically within a few years when University Avenue was realigned, forcing the demolition of the tenements to the right (immediately below the corner of Ashton Road). This pedestrian crossing still exists, but now leads from Tennent's public house to a car park in front of the truncated Ashton Terrace.

The twentieth century brought many changes to Byres Road, the ancient parish road from Partick to Kirklee, which had become the main spine of Glasgow's West End by the latter part of the century. Although the postwar changes were relatively minor when compared to the comprehensive redevelopment in other parts of Hillhead, the small alterations to the face of Byres Road in the second half of the century cumulatively diminished the integrity of the area's Victorian townscape. Postwar modernisation of shopfronts has led to the loss of many original Victorian examples, as well as some fine Art Deco shops from the interwar period. The lifting of the tramlines in the 1960s not only removed an important feature of the streetscape, but also signalled a symbolic and permanent change from the era of rail transport to that of the car and bus.

Other postwar transport alterations which affected Byres Road included the realignment of University Avenue and the reconstruction of the Hillhead subway station site. With the cessation of tram services around 1960 and the subsequent increase in vehicular traffic, the Corporation of Glasgow prepared road improvement proposals on a grand scale. The masterplan involved a network of expressways and motorways spread throughout the greater Strathclyde region. Aside from the construction of the M8 motorway through Charing and St George's Crosses to the east, and the improvements to the Anniesland Cross junction, the West End was relatively unscathed by the 1960s road-building programme. Minor changes were made along Great Western Road (mostly involving the closure of side streets and terrace driveways), but these amounted to only a fraction of the original expressway plans mooted for the historic boulevard. The full scheme had featured a dual carriageway from Anniesland to St George's Cross, complete with a dozen pedestrian overpasses.

The most radical change to the heart of the West End during the era of suburban road improvements was the creation of a new intersection at the corner of Byres

19

Road and Highburgh Road. In order to shift the main east-west route across
Byres Road from the old Victoria Cross (at the corner of Dowanside and Ashton
Roads), the Corporation demolished three tenements on the east side of Byres
Road across from Tennent's public house. In conjunction with the university's
site clearance for the new Boyd Orr building, the path of University Avenue was
shifted north near the truncated Ashton Terrace in order to meet Byres Road at
Highburgh Road.

20

In the late 1970s, Glasgow's 80-year-old
subway network was overhauled, with the
construction of new stations and station
entrances. As part of the Hillhead station
redevelopment, several old shops in Byres
Road were demolished. One popular
business, the Grosvenor Café (*above*, awning
at centre), moved into Ashton Lane across
from the Ubiquitous Chip. Cooper's
supermarket (built on the site once occupied
by Henderson's stables, illustrated on page
148), with its unusual portico, stands on the
corner. All the 1890s shops alongside The
Curlers public house (*left*, left of centre) were
demolished to provide a new station entrance
and two large shop units.

In 1970, only a few years before celebrating its centenary, the old Hillhead Burgh Hall was demolished to make way for a new public library. Across Byres Road from the demolition scene stands Grosvenor Mansions, an interwar tenement block, and the former Hillhead Parish Church in Observatory Road (then called Belmont Hillhead Parish Church). Henry B. Morton recorded this dramatic view of the demolition, but left the image out of his masterpiece, *A Hillhead Album*. A large collection of Morton's Hillhead material is preserved in the Glasgow University Archives.

21

I n the 1960s and 1970s, two important landmarks at the top end of Byres Road were demolished. The greatest loss in the area was the destruction of Hillhead Burgh Hall in 1970. Although it had been the seat of burghal power for a mere two decades before Hillhead was annexed by Glasgow in 1891, the hall remained a popular local venue for another 80 years. It was used for a wide variety of functions throughout the twentieth century, including dancing classes, religious lectures, school prize-giving ceremonies and a variety of public meetings. Despite being a hub of the area's social life, the Burgh Hall was thought to be ill-suited for conversion to the one facility sorely needed by the local community — a public library.

West End residents had been demanding a public library for many years, and the Corporation of Glasgow first sought an appropriate site in Hillhead as early as 1907.[6] The Burgh Hall was deemed to be too difficult to convert, and structural problems eventually prompted the Corporation to demolish the venerable Clarke & Bell building. The implementation of plans for a new Hillhead Library on the site of the hall did not proceed without some difficulty, however. There was a public outcry when the Corporation mooted plans for a retail development which excluded library provision, and official denials were followed by an acknowledgement that a new library would probably form part of a larger, commercial development on this site.[7]

Alongside the venerable Western Baths Club in Cranworth Street stood a late 1880s villa called Cranworth House (*right*). Built as a private house, it was subsequently used as a function suite for dances and receptions. In 1965 the building became the office of the first Radio Scotland, a short-lived pirate station, then lay derelict for several years before its demolition in 1973. At that time, the Arnold Clark garage in Vinicombe Street coveted the site as a car park, and a property developer failed in an attempt to build a small block of flats. Eventually, the Corporation acquired the site and created a small rose garden. By the early 1990s, the garden had become dilapidated and the site was sold to the Baths Club, which built a large sports hall on the site.

22

In the end, a purpose-built public library was the only building to be constructed on the site of the Burgh Hall. A large open space was left to the rear 'in view of long-term plans to divert the main traffic route from Byres Road' into a parallel feeder road along the line of Ashton and Cresswell Lanes, and 'this resulted in a considerable curtailment of the area available for the library, and accounts for the somewhat peculiar shape of the building at the rear.'[8] (Fortunately, these ancillary road improvements were never implemented.) When it was completed in 1972, the concrete-clad Hillhead Library was the first in the city to be fully air-conditioned and to have audio facilities, an automated loan recording system and a purpose-built community hall.

Another long-time fixture in Byres Road which disappeared in the 1970s was the Wylie & Lochhead garage between Grosvenor Terrace Lane and Grosvenor Mansions on the corner of Observatory Road. When Wylie & Lochhead built their new motorcar garage in the mid-1920s, this site was the last undeveloped plot in the entire length of Byres Road, recalled by Henry B. Morton as being 'a small field with a low wall broken by one or two tradesmen's huts.'[9] Architect Charles McNair designed an elegantly utilitarian building with an unusual serrated roofline. The garage, like its rivals in Vinicombe Street and Julian Avenue, primarily provided storage space for cars belonging to local residents. In the postwar period, however, regulations governing on-street parking were relaxed and these large garages soon fell into decline. In 1971, the Wylie & Lochhead organisation (then owned by House of Fraser) sold the Byres Road site to Reo Stakis' Ravenstone Securities company, which built a large mixed-use development on the site, including a supermarket surmounted by a car park and 24 maisonettes.

24

One local landmark which escaped the demolitions of the postwar era was the Salon cinema (*above*). The Salon was abruptly closed in 1992 and a protracted wrangle over the site led to seven years of uncertainty before it was ultimately converted into a restaurant. *Below*: Wylie & Lochhead's Byres Road garage, photographed in the 1960s.

23

25

When the Grosvenor Hotel caught fire in the midst of a firemen's strike in 1978, all hope of limiting the damage was lost when it proved impossible to get the Navy's green goddesses close enough to the terrace. Only a few years before, the original carriage drives off Great Western Road had been closed as part of reconstruction works for the ill-fated Great Western Road Expressway plan.

Several devastating fires struck the West End of Glasgow during the postwar years. In the late 1960s, James Miller's fine railway stations at Kelvinbridge and the Botanic Gardens were destroyed by fires that occurred only sixteen months apart. A decade later, the most dramatic fire to be seen in the West End took place directly across from the old Botanic Gardens station site. The 1978 Grosvenor Hotel fire was not only a spectacular conflagration, but the subsequent replication of the original facade was also a milestone in the development of building conservation in Glasgow.

The Grosvenor Hotel was established in Nos. 1 & 2 Grosvenor Terrace in the 1930s. During the early 1970s, prominent Glasgow hotelier Reo Stakis took it over and began acquiring adjacent properties. Within a few years, Stakis had extended the hotel across the nine easterly houses of the terrace. Disaster struck, however, on the night of 7 and 8 January 1978, when in the midst of a protracted firemen's strike in Glasgow a devastating fire broke out in the hotel kitchen, eventually engulfing the easterly half of the terrace. The Navy and Royal Marine firefighters had difficulty coping with the blaze, and the situation was exacerbated by a fire at Templeton's carpet factory on the same night.

The hotel was virtually gutted by the fire, though the ashlar facade stood more or less intact. Conservationists urged retention of the facade and construction of new building behind, though others claimed it would be too expensive to either save or reconstruct the original stonework. A compromise of sorts was reached, with John T. Rochead's original facade being reconstructed in pre-cast panels of glass-reinforced concrete (GRC) in order to produce a virtually seamless match with the remaining half of the terrace.

Replicating the facade of the Grosvenor Hotel was one of the most ambitious applications of GRC technology at the time. Materials such as pre-cast or *in situ* concrete were not practical options for copying the highly detailed classical stonework. According to architects T. M. Miller & Partners, only GRC permitted the fineness of detail and the lightness of panel which permitted the complicated assembly procedures on this restricted site.[10]

26

The Grosvenor Hotel fire of January 1978 destroyed the premises of Glasgow hotel magnate Reo Stakis (*left*). The decision to demolish rather than retain the original stone facade (*centre*) was a notable *cause célèbre* in the postwar architectural history of the West End, due to the building's significance in the townscape. In the end, the replication of the historic facade in a modern material was considered to be an acceptable compromise.

27

28

After the demolition of the original hotel stonework, casts of the salvaged details were used to produce some 1,800 glass-reinforced concrete panels. These lightweight panels were fixed onto a concrete frame with 'screwed adjusters' used to ensure 'exact alignment.'[11] The complete rebuilding of the Grosvenor Hotel permitted the creation of a modern layout to the latest standards and a large rear extension facing the back lane. The reconstructed facade, along with the neighbouring nine houses to the west, were painted to present a uniform appearance across the front of the terrace.

For seventy years, the gloriously rambling and exquisitely detailed mansion of Red Hall formed the western gateway to Kelvinside at the corner of Great Western and Beaconsfield Roads. Red Hall was built *c.*1892 by architect Thomas L. Watson for Alexander Anderson, son of the founder of 'the greatest store in Glasgow,' the Royal Polytechnic in Argyle Street.[13] From 1936, Red Hall was known as Homeland, a Salvation Army maternity hospital and home for 32 unmarried mothers.[14] Unfortunately, after the Salvation Army closed Homeland in the early 1960s, the building rapidly deteriorated. The splendid oak panelling, leaded windows, marble fireplaces and great hall (complete with minstrel gallery) all fell victim to vandals before Red Hall was finally demolished in 1968. The prominent corner site lay undeveloped until yellow brick flats were built in the 1980s.

29

30

In January 1970, fire claimed one of the West End's best-loved buildings, the old Botanic Gardens station (*centre*). At the time of the fire, the building housed the popular Silver Slipper Café, a plumbing contractor and the Sergeant Pepper's nightclub. Further west along Great Western Road (*right*), another local landmark, Charles McNair's massive Ascot cinema, is seen peeking out from behind a tram in this 1954 view. From the 1960s to the 1980s, Mactaggart & Mickel built numerous blocks of flats on the north side of Great Western Road (to the right), and, in the late 1990s, the University of Glasgow's Westerlands playing fields (behind the Ascot) were also developed for housing. The *c.*1925 Westerlands pavilion is visible at the far right.

31

The closing years of the twentieth century saw steady but relentless change along Great Western Road. In 1960, the last trams travelled along the boulevard from St George's Cross out to the city's western frontier. A few years later, two of the most picturesque railway stations in urban Scotland were destroyed by fire. Old gap sites of demolished villas were soon redeveloped with brick-clad blocks of flats, and numerous interwar institutions moved out of their palatial villas and terraced houses.

For many years, the West End also faced the lingering threat of having the old Great Western Road turnpike upgraded into a fully fledged expressway linking the city centre with the 'Trossachs Motorway' in a new, state-of-the-art road network. A public local enquiry was held in 1970, the star witness being Lionel Balliol Brett, Lord Esher, the eminent architect and town planner. Esher's contribution eloquently stated the conservationist's maxim that protecting our architectural heritage is not mere nostalgia, but rather a practical matter of preserving the valuable investments of previous generations. Maintaining these investments permits the use of current resources for other essential purposes. Any other approach, to use the jargon of the present day, is basically unsustainable.

For a variety of reasons, the expressway scheme never came to fruition. Still, there were minor alterations to side streets and the complete reconstruction of the old communal drives of the terraces. In the 1990s, after many years of neglect and decay, cast iron railings were reinstated in several terraces along Great Western Road under the auspices of the Glasgow West Conservation Trust. All the while, the grand houses and the arboreal canopy over the old turnpike continued to mature. Ultimately, at the start of the twenty-first century, Great Western Road still survives, and is still recognisable as what the irrepressible James B. Fleming once called, 'by far the handsomest thoroughfare in Glasgow, and indeed as handsome as is to be found in any commercial City.'[12]

Bingham's pond was built at Gartnavel in the early 1880s on the site of old brick and coal pits. Popular skating and boating activities were run by three generations of the Bingham family, with tea rooms established in the *c*.1885 clubhouse (*above*, pictured in 1955). Glasgow Corporation tried to acquire the site in 1956, but it was sold for redevelopment. Various schemes were mooted in the late 1960s, and eventually the easterly third of the pond was filled in to allow Reo Stakis to build a five-storey hotel. The remainder of the site was donated to the Corporation for use as a public park.

References

I. Early History

1   'Notes on Glasgow,' n.284, 335
2   Blaeu (1654)
3   Mitchell and Guthrie Smith (1878), *passim*
4   *Ibid.*, 249
5   Devine (1975), 134
6   *Ibid.*, 132
7   *Ibid.*, 157
8   Mitchell and Guthrie Smith, *op. cit.*, 146
9   Oakley (1980), 5
10 Mitchell and Guthrie Smith, *op. cit.*, 147
11 Glasgow Institute of Fine Arts (1894), 112
12 Black, William G. 'David Dale's House,' in *The Regality Club* (1912), v.4, 93
13 Gordon (1866), v.1, 455
14 Eyre-Todd (1934), v.3, 100
15 Gordon, *op. cit.*, 456
16 Mitchell, John Oswald. 'Balshagray,' in *The Regality Club* (1893), v.2, 114
17 Pagan (1847), 54
18 Glasgow Institute of Fine Arts, *op. cit.*, 115
19 Glasgow Institute of Fine Arts, *op. cit.*, 118
20 *Feuing Plan of Hillhead and Northpark*
21 *General Plans of the Lands of Hillhead*
22 Gibson Sequestration papers, 1826-27
23 Ross, David. 'Monument with a rich history of its own,' *The Herald*, 7/10/1998
24 Mitchell and Guthrie Smith, *op. cit.*, 197
25 Anderson (1942), 111
26 *Glasgow Mechanics Magazine*, 26/5/1824, 339
27 Mitchell and Guthrie Smith, *op. cit.*, 197-8
28 *Ibid.*, 199
29 Blaeu, *op. cit.*
30 Mitchell, John Oswald. 'Wellfield House,' in *The Regality Club* (1899), v.3, 9
31 Kelly (1996), 49
32 Fleming (1923), 106
33 Mitchell and Guthrie Smith, *op. cit.*, 195
34 *Plan for laying out the North Park Estate*
35 Fleming (1923), 105

II. The New Suburb

1   Anniesland and St George's Turnpike Road Act, 1836 (6 & 7 Wm. IV c.xxxviii)
2   Sederunt Book of the Trustees on the New Anniesland or Great Western Road, 12
3   *Ibid.*, 4
4   *Ibid.*, 17
5   *Ibid.*, 215
6   *Ibid.*, 74
7   *Ibid.*, 86
8   *Ibid.*, 332
9   *Glasgow Herald*, 30/11/1835
10 *Local and Municipal Souvenir of Glasgow*, 31
11 *Glasgow Herald*, 13/2/1873
12 Tang dissertation (1995), Fig. DH.01
13 Great Western Road Sederunt Book, 343
14 Glasgow University Archives holds papers of the Dowanhill Estate Co. [GUA UGD 92]
15 Worsdall (1981), 36
16 Thanks to Geoffrey Jarvis, a former resident at Benvue, for his 1974 ms research on the life of George Smith
17 Thanks to Sam Small for his Register of Sasines research for the Dowanhill estate
18 *Glasgow Herald*, 19/7/1830
19 *Vid.* Simpson dissertation (1970); Reed (1993); Tang (1995)
20 *Glasgow Herald*, 4/4/1850
21 *Building Chronicle*, 1/6/1855
22 Tang, *op. cit.*, 103
23 *The Bailie*, 12/11/1884
24 *Glasgow Contemporaries* (1901), 215
25 Williamson, *et al.* (1990), 320
26 *Glasgow Herald*, 18/3/1908
27 *Ibid.*
28 *Ibid.*, 26/3/1908
29 *Ibid.*
30 *Daily Record*, 26/3/1908
31 Frank Worsdall's transcription of the *Herald's* account of the Belmont tragedy (21/9/1870, 30-31/12/1870 & 2/1/1871) is held in the National Monument Record of Scotland, RCAHMS, Edinburgh
32 *Glasgow Herald*, 2/1/1871
33 Glasgow Academy (1946), 62
34 Municipal Extension Bills 1870-72, 277
35 Hillhead Burgh Minutes, 13/5/1870
36 Simpson (1970), 184
37 Municipal Extension Bills 1870-72, 209
38 Hillhead & Kelvinside (Annexation to Glasgow) Bill, v.3, Evidence of James Muirhead, 182
39 Glasgow Boundaries Commission, Report, v.1, 45
40 Hillhead & Kelvinside Bill, v.1, Proof of J. B. Fleming, 305
41 Hillhead & Kelvinside Bill, v.3, Evidence of James Morrison, 533
42 Glasgow Boundaries Extension, Report, 644
43 Hillhead & Kelvinside Bill, v.3, Evidence of James B. Russell, 211
44 Glasgow Boundaries Extension, Report, 644
45 Hillhead & Kelvinside Bill, v.3, Evidence of Robert Bruce, 239
46 Hillhead & Kelvinside Bill, v.3, Evidence of William R. W. Smith, 144
47 Simpson (1970), 154
48 Hillhead & Kelvinside Bill, v.3, Evidence of James Caldwell MP, 582

III. Early Institutions

1   Bell and Paton (1896), 346
2   Royal Botanical Institution Minute Book, 6/9/1832
3   *Ibid.*, 25/4/1837
4   *Ibid.*, 3/12/1838
5   *Ibid.*, 8/1/1839
6   *Ibid.*, 6/9/1839
7   GWR Sederunt Book, 3/6/1840
8   Aird (1894), 164
9   Bell and Paton, *op. cit.*, 346
10 Glasgow Boundaries Commission, Report, v.1, Evidence of James Carrick, 158-9
11 *Comparative Statement of Rating and Resume of New Work, 1894-95*. Glasgow: Glasgow Corporation, 24
12 *History of Glasgow by Writers of Eminence* (1872), 657
13 Coutts (1909), 388
14 Tweed (1872), 48
15 Williamson *et al.*, *op. cit.*, 358
16 Andrews and Smith (1993), 7
17 MacDonald (1910), 307-8
18 *The Philosophy of Insanity* (1947), 103
19 *Ibid.*, 98
20 Andrews and Smith, *op. cit.*, 35
21 *Ibid.*, 35-6
22 *Ibid.*, 9
23 MacDonald, *op. cit.*, 325
24 Bell and Paton, *op. cit.*, 335
25 *Ibid.*, 336
26 *Tweed's Guide* (1872), 42
27 MacDonald, *op. cit.*, 325-6
28 *Tweed's Guide*, 42
29 Tang, *op. cit.*, Fig. KG.14
30 *Tweed's Guide*, 43-4
31 *Municipal Glasgow*, *op. cit.*, 37
32 Mitchell and Guthrie Smith, *op. cit.*, 147
33 *Municipal Glasgow* (1914), 37-8
34 Kinchin and Kinchin (1990), 44-5
35 *Building Industries*, v.9, 15/2/1899, 163
36 *The Glasgow Herald*, 16/2/1899
37 'Kelvingrove House - Proposed removal' [petition], *c.* 2/1899 [GCA D-TC14/1/30]
38 Black, *op. cit.*, 110
39 'Glasgow Scraps,' v.13, 34

IV. Education

1   Robertson (1994), 11
2   *Glasgow Mercury*, 6/1/1789
3   Mitchell and Guthrie Smith, *op. cit.*, 121
4   *Ibid.*
5   Letter, R. Hunter to Sir Donald MacAlister
6   Pagan, *op. cit.*, 124
7   Mackie (1954), 281
8   Stamp and McKinstry (1994), 29
9   *The Glasgow Herald*, 9/10/1868
10 Napier (1873), 273
11 *Glasgow Herald*,13/10/1870
12 *North British Daily Mail*, 8/5/1866
13 MacLeod (1997), 2
14 *Scots Pictorial*, 23/5/1914, iii
15 MacLeod, *op. cit.*, 37
16 *Ibid.*, 40
17 *Ibid.*, 59
18 *Scots Pictorial*, 23/5/1914, vi
19 *Westbourne School for Girls* (1977), 38
20 Fleming (1894), 20
21 *Westbourne School for Girls*, *op cit.*, 61
22 MacLeod, *op. cit.*, 203
23 *Scots Pictorial*, 23/5/1914, vi
24 *Westbourne School for Girls*, *op cit.*, 60
25 Mackay (1978), 9
26 Fleming (1894), 6
27 Mackay, *op. cit.*, 49
28 Gomme and Walker (1987),153
29 Low (1928), 13-14
30 *Hillhead High School* (1935), 42; *Hillhead High School* (1962), 67
31 *Hillhead High School* (1935), 42
32 *Hillhead High School* (1962), 67
33 Roxburgh, James M. *The School Board of Glasgow 1873-1919*. London: University of London Press, 1971, 137
34 *Laurel Bank School 1903-1953*, 6
35 *Ibid.*, 10
36 *Ibid.*, 104
37 *Ibid.*
38 *Ibid.*, 101, 10
39 *Ibid.*, 17
40 *Laurel Bank School Magazine* (1915), 2
41 *Laurel Bank School 1903-1953*, 17
42 *Ibid.*, 21
43 *Vid.* McAlpine (1997), Geyer-Kordesch and Ferguson (1994)
44 *Pass it On* (1935), 2
45 McAlpine, *op. cit.*, 191
46 *Pass it On* (1935), 4
47 *Ibid.*, 10
48 *Ibid.*, 5
49 *Ibid.*
50 Mackie, *op cit.*, 305

V. Transport

1   Simpson (1972), 146
2   Fleming (1894), 4
3   Simpson (1970), 239
4   Simpson (1972), 150
5   Gordon (1872), 1243

6   *Glasgow Herald*, 20/1/1870
7   Cormack (1962), 4
8   Oakley (1962), 49
9   Bell (1932), 27
10 The Scottish Tram and Transport Society have published numerous works useful for local history research. *Vid.* Bibliography.
11 Gildard, Thomas. '"Greek" Thomson,' *Proceedings of the Philosophical Society of Glasgow*, v.19, 1887-8, 203-4
12 *People's Journal*, December 1915
13 Patton (1994), 10
14 Simpson (1972), 158
15 Fleming (1894), 23
16 'Glasgow Central Railway,' in *Engineering*, v.53, 641
17 Formans & McCall album, *passim*
18 Kellett (1964), 234-6
19 *Ibid.*, 233; Tang, *op. cit.*, 97 *et seq.*
20 Smith and Anderson (1993), 79-80
21 'Glasgow Central Railway,' in *Engineering*, v.54, 104
22 *The Builder*, 9/7/1898, 26
23 *Glasgow Herald*, 18/11/1881
24 Johnston and Hume (1979), 108
25 *Glasgow Herald*, 18/11/1881
26 Smith and Anderson, *op. cit.*, 95
27 'Glasgow Central Railway,' in *Engineering*, v.54, 9-10; v.53, 643
28 Proprietors of Kelvinside Estate - Petition, 3
29 Hamilton and Horan dissertation (1996), 11
30 Johnston and Hume, *op. cit.*, 115
31 Smith and Anderson, *op. cit.*, 101
32 Johnston and Hume, *op. cit.*, 110
32 Corporation of Glasgow - Petition, 12
33 Johnston and Hume, *op. cit.*, 127
35 *Ibid.*, 128
36 Wright and MacLean (1997), 175
37 *Gang Warily: The Jubilee of the Royal Scottish Automobile Club 1899-1949*. Glasgow: The Club, 1949, 22

VI. The Golden Years

1   *Vid.* Dow (1985); Slaven and Checkland (1990), v.2, 182-3
2   McFadzean (1979), 164
3   *Ibid.*, 238
4   Moss (2000), 76
5   Simpson (1970), 103
6   *Ibid.*, 107

7   Fleming (1894), 21
8   *Vid.* Claythorn Commmunity Council (1990)
9   Gomme and Walker, *op. cit.*, 160
10 Dow, *op. cit.*, 27
11 For the definitive history of Barr & Stroud, *vid.* Moss and Russell (1988)
12 *Ibid.*, 13
13 GWR Sederunt Book, vols. 1 & 2 *passim*
14 Simpson (1970), 239
15 Hillhead Burgh Minutes, 12/8/1875
16 Fleming (1894), 4
17 Cowans (1951), 154
18 Morton (1973), n.p.
19 *Glasgow & Lanarkshire Illustrated, op. cit.*, n.p.
20 Morton, *op. cit.*, n.p.
21 Richmond, Sir David. *Notes on Municipal Work*. Glasgow: Glasgow Corp., 1899, 146
22 Williamson *et al.*, *op. cit.*, 280
23 *Post Office Glasgow Directory*, 1899-1900 to 1904-5
24 Thanks to Calum Crawford for details of Mrs Hutchison's family history
25 *Vid.* Kinchin and Kinchin, *op. cit.*; Hunter (1990)
26 *Glasgow International Exhibition, 1901 Official Guide*, 29-30
27 Kinchin and Kinchin, *op. cit.*, 96
28 *Ibid.*, 190
29 *The Curious Diversity* (1970), 66
30 Kinchin and Kinchin, *op. cit.*, 105
31 *Ibid.*, 122
32 *Glasgow Herald*, 15/12/1910
33 *Daily Record and Mail*, 26/1/1914
34 *Ibid.*
35 Morton, *op. cit.*, n.p.

VII. The Interwar Years

1   Ferguson, W. *Scotland: 1689 to the Present.* Edinburgh: Oliver & Boyd, 1978, 361
2   *Ibid.*, 363
3   Mackay, *op. cit.*, 91
4   *Hillhead High School* (1962), 23; MacLeod, *op. cit.*, 80
5   MacLeod, *op. cit.*, 96
6   *Glasgow & Lanarkshire Illustrated* (c.1904), n.p.
7   Morton, *op. cit.*, n.p.
8   Oakley (1975), 181

9   *Pass it On, op. cit.*, 10
10 *Guide to Glasgow by the Corporation Tramways* (1897), 35-6
11 Cruikshank (1879), 80, 93-4
12 Personal communication with Bruce Peter, author of *100 Years of Glasgow's Amazing Cinemas* (1996)
13 *Glasgow Bulletin*, 28/2/1959
14 *Glasgow Herald*, 17/7/1971
15 *Ibid.*
16 *The University of Glasgow through Five Centuries* (1951), 75
17 *Glasgow Herald*, 4/5/1921
18 Personal communication with Bruce Peter
19 *Glasgow Herald*, 4/5/1921
20 *Laurel Bank Magazine*, 1945, n.p.
21 Morton, *op. cit.*, n.p.
22 *Ibid.*
23 Blood (1929), 19
24 Robertson and Pateman (1987), 10
25 Lindsay, Maurice. *Thank you for having me: A personal memoir.* London: Hale, 1983, 17
26 Robertson and Pateman, *op. cit.*, 10
27 Glasgow Corporation City Assessor photograph [GCA D-CA8/502]
28 *Glasgow Herald*, 2/2/1923
29 *Ibid.*, 7/3/1924
30 Doak dissertation (1979), 71
31 *Scottish Country Life*, February 1922, 42
32 Slaven and Checkland, *op. cit.*, 152
33 Burton (1840). *Vid.* Reed *op. cit.*
34 Simpson (1970), 31
35 Fleming (1894), 21
36 Babtie Shaw & Morton (1908)
37 Horsey (1990), 12
38 *Ibid.*, 21
39 Laird (1997), 23
40 Glendinning and Waters (1999), *passim*
41 Kelvinside Feu Contract, 19/7/1923
42 *Ideal Homes at Kelvinside* (c.1928), 3
43 'Notes on Glasgow,' n.287, 1842
44 Slaven and Checkland, *op. cit.*, 193
45 Oakley (1980), 175
46 St John's Renfield Church, Minute Book, 10/10/1927
47 *St John's Renfield Church 1819-1969*, 26
48 *Ibid.*, 21
49 Laird, *op. cit.*, 73
50 *What Homeopathy is doing in the National Health Service in Scotland*, 13
51 *Homeopathy*, December 1932, 486
52 Glasgow Homeopathic Hospital, Committee Minutes, v.1, 8/2/1922
53 *Ibid.*, 22/2/1927
54 *Ibid.*, v.2, 3/4/1929
55 *Ibid.*, 12/8/1929
56 *Ibid.*, 15/1/1930, 3/3/1930
57 *What Homeopathy is doing . . .* , 10

VIII. The Postwar Years

1   *Glasgow Herald*, 30/7, 7/8 and 17/9/1942
2   Worsdall (1981), 36
3   Brown and Moss (1996), 57
4   Mears (1951)
5   *Vid.* Robertson (1998)
6   *Hillhead Library Opening Day* [brochure], 1975, n.p.
7   *Glasgow Herald*, 11/2/1964 *et seq.*
8   *Hillhead Library Opening Day, op. cit.*
9   Morton, *op. cit.*, n.p.
10 *Building*, 26/3/1982
11 *Ibid.*
12 Fleming (1894), 1
13 Oakley (1980), 178
14 *The Deliverer*, July 1936

vii

A parade of old and new tramcars was recorded in Hyndland Road in the mid-1950s, a few years before Glasgow's much-loved tram system was discontinued.

Bibliography

Primary Sources

Corporation of Glasgow - Petition against the Glasgow Central Railway Bill 1888. [University of Glasgow Special Collections Mu-28-f.8]

Formans & McCall album, National Monument Record of Scotland Photograph Album No. 19.

Gibson Sequestration papers, Court of Session. [National Archives of Scotland CS44 Box 630, 1826-27]

Glasgow Boundaries Commission. Report, 1888. [Glasgow City Archives A3/1/106]

Glasgow Boundaries Extension. Royal Commission. Report. 1888. [GCA C3/1/1]

Glasgow Corporation City Assessor photographs. [GCA D-CA/8]

Glasgow Homeopathic Hospital Annual Reports. [Glasgow Collection, Mitchell Library]

Glasgow Homeopathic Hospital, Minute Books. [Greater Glasgow Health Board 4/1/1-2]

'Glasgow Scraps,' William Young scrapbooks. [Glasgow Collection, Mitchell Library]

Hillhead & Kelvinside (Annexation to Glasgow) Bill 1886-87, vols. 1 & 3. [GCA A3/1/94, 99]

Hillhead Burgh Minutes. [GCA H-HIL]

Hillhead Chartulary. [GCA TD162/81, 82]

Kelvinside Feu Contract containing Feu Disposition, 19/7/1923. [Private collection]

Letter from Robert Hunter to Principal Sir Donald MacAlister, 31/1/1920. [Glasgow University Archives PH/PR 1198 Lge]

Municipal Extension Bills 1870-72. Glasgow Corporation Notes. (Bound volume of papers.) [GCA A3/1/12]

'Notes on Glasgow Collected by David Murray.' [UoG Sp Coll MS Murray nos. 284-291]

Proprietors of Kelvinside Estate - Petition against the Glasgow & Suburban Subway Bill 1888. [UoG Sp Coll Mu-28-f.8]

Royal Botanical Institution of Glasgow, Minute Books. [GCA D-TC11/1/1-14]

St John's Renfield Church, Minute Book.

Sederunt Book of the Trustees on the New Anniesland or Great Western Road. [GCA F8.3]

Secondary Sources

Aird, Andrew. *Glimpses of Old Glasgow.* Glasgow: Aird & Coghill, 1894.

Anderson, James R. *The Provosts of Glasgow 1609-1833.* Glasgow: J. Hedderwick, 1942.

Andrews, J. and I. Smith, eds. *Let There be Light Again: A History of Gartnavel Royal Hospital.* Glasgow: Gartnavel Royal Hospital, 1993.

Bell, John Joy. *I Remember.* Edinburgh: Porpoise Press, 1932.

Bell, Sir James and James Paton. *Glasgow: Its Municipal Organisation and Administration.* Glasgow: James MacLehose, 1896.

Blood, Alison F. *Kelvinside Days.* Glasgow: John Smith & Son, 1929.

Boyce, David. *Bridges of the Kelvin.* Glasgow: Glasgow City Libraries, 1996.

Brown, A. L. and Michael Moss. *The University of Glasgow 1451-1996.* Edinburgh: Edinburgh University Press, 1996.

Claythorn Community Council. *The Claythorn Story.* Glasgow: Reprogint, 1990.

Cormack, Ian L. *Glasgow Tramways 1872-1962.* London: Light Railway Transport League, 1962.

_____. *A Century of Glasgow Tramways.* Glasgow: Scottish Tramway Museum Society, 1972.

Coutts, James. *A History of the University of Glasgow from its foundation in 1451 to 1909.* Glasgow: James MacLehose, 1909.

Cowans, James. *From Glasgow's Treasure Chest.* Glasgow: Craig & Wilson, 1951.

Cruikshank, James. *Sketch of the Incorporation of Masons and the Glasgow Lodge of St John.* Glasgow: W. M. Ferguson, 1879.

Curtis, Eric W. *Kibble's Palace.* Glendaruel: Argyll Publishing, 1999.

Devine, Tom. *The Tobacco Lords.* Edinburgh: Donald, 1975.

Dicks, Brian. 'Choice and Constraint: Further perspectives on socio-residential segregation in nineteenth-century Glasgow with particular reference to its West End,' in George Gordon, ed., *Perspectives of the Scottish City.* Aberdeen: Aberdeen University Press, 1985.

Doak, A. M. and A. M. Young. *Glasgow at a Glance.* London: Robert Hale, 1965.

Dow, Derek A. *Redlands House.* Glasgow: Scottish Ambulance Service, 1985.

Dow, Derek A., and Michael Moss. *Glasgow's Gain: The Anderston Story.* Carnforth, Lancs.: The Parthenon Publishing Group, 1986.

Eyre-Todd, George. *History of Glasgow, v.3.* Glasgow: Jackson, Wylie and Co., 1934.

Fleming, J. Arnold. *Scottish Pottery.* Glasgow: MacLehose, Jackson, 1923.

Fleming, James Brown Montgomerie. *Kelvinside.* Glasgow: Maclure MacDonald & Co., 1894.

Geyer-Kordesch, Johanna and Rona Ferguson. *Blue Stockings, Black Gowns, White Coats.* Glasgow: University of Glasgow, 1994.

Glasgow Academy. Glasgow: Blackie & Son, 1946.

Glasgow and Lanarkshire Illustrated. c.1904.

Glasgow Contemporaries at the Dawn of the XXth Century. Glasgow: Photo-Biographical Publishing Co., 1901.

'Glasgow Central Railway,' in *Engineering,* vols. 53 & 54, 1892, *passim.*

Glasgow International Exhibition, 1901. Official Guide. Glasgow: Charles P. Watson, 1901.

Glendinning, Miles and Diane Waters, eds. *Home Builders: Mactaggart & Mickel and the Scottish Housebuilding Industry.* Edinburgh: RCAHMS, 1999.

Gomme, Andor and David Walker. *Architecture of Glasgow.* London: Lund Humphries with John Smith & Son, 1987 (2nd revised edition).

Gordon, J. F. S., ed. *Glasgow Ancient and Modern.* Glasgow: J. Tweed, 1866.

Gow, James. *The Provosts of Glasgow from 1609 to 1832.* Glasgow: J. Hedderwick, 1942.

Grieves, Robert. *Scotland's Motoring Century.* Paisley: XS Publications, 1999.

Hillhead High School 1885-1935 Jubilee. Glasgow: Hillhead High School, 1935.

Hillhead High School 1885-1961. Glasgow: HHS Pavilions Improvement Fund, 1962.

History of Glasgow by Writers of Eminence, Glasgow: J. Tweed, 1872.

Horsey, Miles. *Tenements and Towers: Glasgow Working Class Housing 1840-1990.* Edinburgh: HMSO, 1990.

Hume, John R. *Industrial Archaeology of Glasgow.* Glasgow: Blackie & Son, 1974.

Hunter, Stanley. *Kelvingrove and the 1888 Exhibition.* Glasgow: Exhibition Study Group, 1990.

Ideal Homes at Kelvinside. Glasgow: Mactaggart & Mickel Ltd, c.1928.

Johnston, C. and J. R. Hume. *Glasgow Stations.* Newton Abbot: David & Charles, 1979.

Kellett, John R. 'Urban Transport History form Legal Records . . . .' in *Journal of Transport History,* v.6, n.4 (1964).

Kelly, Henry E. 'The North Woodside & Garrioch Mills . . . .' *Scottish Pottery, 18th Historical Review.* Glasgow: Lomondside Press, 1996.

Kinchin, Perilla and Juliet Kinchin. *Glasgow's Great Exhibitions.* Wendlebury, Oxon: White Cockade, 1990.

Kinchin, Perilla. *Tea and Taste: The Glasgow Tea Rooms 1875-1975.* London: White Cockade, 1991.

Laird, Ann. *Hyndland: Edwardian Glasgow Tenement Suburb.* Glasgow: Ann Laird Books, 1997.

Laurel Bank School 1903-1953. Glasgow: John Smith & Son, 1953.

Local and Municipal Souvenir of Glasgow, 1837-1897. Glasgow: D. Adam & Co., 1897.

Low, D. M. *Kelvinside Academy 1878-1928.* Glasgow: William Hodge & Co., 1928.

Mann, W. M. *The Baths: The Story of the Western Baths, Hillhead from 1876 to 1990.* Glasgow: The Western Baths Club, 1990.

Marks, Richard. *Burrell: A Portrait of a Collector.* Glasgow: Richard Drew Publishing, 1983.

McAlpine, Joan C. *The Lady of Claremont House: Isabella Elder.* Glendaruel: Argyll Publishing, 1997.

MacDonald, Hugh. *Rambles around Glasgow.* Glasgow: John Smith & Son, 1910 (new ed.).

McFadzean, Ronald. *The Life and Work of Alexander Thomson.* London: Routledge & Kegan Paul, 1979.

MacGregor, George. *The History of Glasgow.* Glasgow: Thomas D. Morrison, 1881.

Mackay, Colin H. *Kelvinside Academy.* Glasgow: Kelvinside Academy, 1978.

McKean, Charles, *et al. Central Glasgow: An Illustrated Architectural Guide.* Edinburgh: RIAS, 1990.

Mackie, J. D. *The University of Glasgow 1451-1951.* Glasgow: Jackson, Son & Co., 1954.

MacLeod, Iain. *Glasgow Academy: 150 Years.* Glasgow: Glasgow Academicals War Memorial Trust, 1997.

Memoirs and Portraits of One Hundred Glasgow Men. Glasgow: James MacLehose, 1886.

Memorial Catalogue of the Old Glasgow Exhibition. Glasgow: Glasgow Institute of Fine Arts, 1894.

Ministry of Transport & Civil Aviation. *Report of the Derailment of a Tramcar . . . .* London: HMSO, 1956.

Mitchell, John Oswald and John Guthrie Smith. *The Old Country Houses of the Old Glasgow Gentry.* Glasgow: James MacLehose, 1878.

Moore, John. *The Maps of Glasgow.* Glasgow: Glasgow University Library Studies, 1996.

Morris, Margaret. 'The Observatories of the University of Glasgow,' notes from a lecture given at University of Glasgow, 24/11/98.

Morton, Henry Brougham. *A Hillhead Album.* Glasgow: The Hepburn Trust, 1973.

Moss, Michael. *Standard Life 1825 - 2000.* Edinburgh: Mainstream Publishing, 2000.

_____., and Iain Russell. *Range and Vision: The First Hundred Years of Barr & Stroud.* Edinburgh: Mainstream Publishing, 1988.

Municipal Glasgow. *Its Evolution and Enterprises.* Glasgow: Glasgow Corporation, 1914.

Napier, James. *Notes and Reminiscences Relating to Partick.* Glasgow: Hugh Hopkins, 1873.

Oakley, Charles A. *The Last Tram.* Glasgow: Corporation Transportation Dept., 1962.

_____. *Our Illustrious Forbears.* Glasgow: Blackie & Son, 1980.

_____. *The Second City.* Glasgow: Blackie & Son, 1975 (3rd ed.).

Pagan, James. *Sketch of the History of Glasgow.* Glasgow: Robert Stuart, 1847.

Pass it On: The Magazine of the Women's Educational Union, Queen Margaret College Special Number, v.15 n.1, 1935.

Patton, Brian. *Another Nostalgic Look at Glasgow Trams since 1950.* Peterborough: Silver Link, 1994.

Peter, Bruce. *100 Years of Glasgow's Amazing Cinemas.* Edinburgh: Polygon, 1996.

Post Office Glasgow Directory. Glasgow: William Mackenzie 1899-1900 to 1901-02; Glasgow: Aird & Coghill, 1902-3 to 1904-5.

Prebble, John. *The Darien Disaster.* London: Secker & Warburg, 1968.

Reed, Peter, ed. *Glasgow: The Forming of the City.* Edinburgh: Edinburgh University Press, 1993.

Robertson, Andrew Ogilvie. 'The Provenance of Gilmorehill,' *Avenue,* n.16, June 1994.

Robertson, John and Rachel Pateman. *Byres Road.* Glasgow: The Glasgow File, 1987.

Robertson, Pamela. *The Mackintosh House.* Glasgow: Hunterian Art Gallery, 1998.

Robson, James. *Hillhead Bowling Club 1849-1949.* Glasgow: G. C. Fairservice, 1949.

St John's Renfield Church 1819-1969, Glasgow: St John's Renfield Church, c.1969.

Sherry, Christopher. *The Glasgow Botanic Gardens: Its Conservatories, Greenhouses, etc.* Glasgow: David Bryce & Son, 1902.

Simpson, M. A. 'Urban Transport and the Development of Glasgow's West End, 1830-1914,' in *Journal of Transport History,* 2nd series, (1972), v.1, n.3.

Sinclair, Sir John, ed. *The Statistical Account of Scotland 1791-1799, Lanarkshire & Renfrewshire,* v.8. Wakefield: EP Publishing, 1973.

Slaven, Anthony and Sydney G. Checkland. *Dictionary of Scottish Business Biography.* Aberdeen: Aberdeen University Press, (2 vols.) 1986 & 1990.

Sloan, Audrey. *James Miller 1860-1947.* Edinburgh: RIAS, 1993.

Smith, W. A. C. and Paul Anderson. *An Illustrated History of Glasgow Railways.* Caernarfon, Gwynedd: Irwell Press, 1993.

Stamp, Gavin and Sam McKinstry, eds., *'Greek' Thomson.* Edinburgh: Edinburgh University Press, 1994.

Stewart, Ian G. McM. *Glasgow by Tram.* Glasgow: Scottish Tram and Transport Society, 1977.

_____. *More Glasgow by Tram.* Glasgow: STTS, 1978.

_____. *The Glasgow Tramcar.* Glasgow: STTS, 1994 (2nd ed.).

The Philosophy of Insanity, By a Late Inmate of the Glasgow Royal Asylum for Lunatics at Gartnavel. London: Fireside Press, 1947.

The Regality Club. Glasgow: James MacLehose, 4 vols, 1889 - 1912.

The University of Glasgow through Five Centuries. Glasgow: University of Glasgow, 1951.

Thomson, Alexander. *Random Notes and Rambling Recollections of Dry Dock, the Dock or Kelvin Dock all now known by the more modern name of Maryhill 1750-1894.* Glasgow: Kerr & Richardson, 1895.

Tweed's Guide to Glasgow. Glasgow: J.Tweed, 1872.

Wellington 1884-1984. Glasgow: The Congregation of Wellington Church, 1985.

Westbourne School for Girls: The First Hundred Years 1877-1977. Glasgow: Westbourne School for Girls, 1977.

What Homeopathy is doing in the National Health Service in Scotland. Glasgow: Bone & Hulley, 1953.

Williamson, Elizabeth, *et al. The Buildings of Scotland: Glasgow.* London: Penguin, 1990.

Worsdall, Frank. *The City that Disappeared: Glasgow's Demolished Architecture.* Glasgow: Molendinar Press, 1981.

Wright, J. and I. Maclean. *Circles under the Clyde: A History of the Glasgow Underground.* Harrow Weald: Capital Transport Publishing, 1997.

Dissertations

Doak, Christopher. 'Klondyke of the Kinema World: A Tale of Picture Houses in Glasgow and their design.' DipArch dissertation, Glasgow School of Art, 1979.

Hamilton, Thomas J. and Stephen J. Horan. 'A Measured Drawing Study of Caledonian Mansions, Glasgow.' DipArch dissertation, Mackintosh School of Architecture, 1996.

Simpson, Michael A. 'Middle Class Housing and the Growth of Suburban Communities in the West End of Glasgow 1830-1914.' BLitt dissertation, University of Glasgow, 1970.

Tang, Tommy. 'Victorian Suburbanisation of Glasgow 1830s-1910s.' DPhil dissertation, University of Strathclyde, 1995.

Maps & Plans

Babtie Shaw & Morton. *Kelvinside Estate Proposed Feuing Arrangement* (1908). [GCA TD153/29]

Blaeu, Joan. *Theatrum orbis terrarum, sive atlas novus,* v.5. Amsterdam: J. & W. Blaeu, 1654. [UoG Sp Coll Mu2-x.16]

Burton, Decimus. *Plan of Queenstown, Kelvinside* (1840). W. H. Hill Collection, Library of the Faculty of Procurators in Glasgow.

_____. *Plan for laying out the North Park Estate* (1841). [GCA TD66/5/26a]

Forrest, William. *The County of Lanark from an actual survey* (1816). [UoG Sp Coll Mu2-d.22]

Martin, William. *Map of Glasgow* (1842). [GCA DTC 13 23c-J]

Mears, Sir Frank. *University of Glasgow: Proposed Redevelopment* (1951). [GCA D-TC 6/526]

Smith, David. *General Plans of the Lands of Hillhead, Surveyed in the Years 1823 & 1825.* [GCA TD162/111]

Feuing Plan of Hillhead and Northpark (1855). [GCA TD414/1]

House of Lords Plan and Book of Reference. Anniesland and St. George's Turnpike Road Act,1836. 6 & 7 Wm. IV c.cxxxviii. [The Parliamentary Archive]

Ordnance Survey. *Lanarkshire VI NW.* First edition (surveyed 1858), Second ed. (surveyed 1893-4), Third ed. (surveyed 1909).

Post Offfice Glasgow Directory maps 1848-1914. Glasgow Collection, Mitchell Library.

Sketch Feuing Plan of part of the Lands of Kelvinside (1873). W. H. Hill Collection, Library of the Faculty of Procurators in Glasgow.

viii

Some West End landmarks not only contribute to the dramatic skyline but also provide spectacular vantage points for the intrepid photographer. This 1920s view from the tower of Cooper & Co. looks east along Great Western Road. The tenement to the left succumbed to the area's infamous ground problems in the 1970s.

Index

Oakfield Terrace (east), behind the Men's Union in University Avenue, was the first Hillhead building to be demolished for the university's postwar redevelopment.

Northbank (c.1872) at the western end of Wilton Street was demolished to make way for Corporation flats in the 1970s.

When the Forth and Clyde Canal was closed in the 1960s, the old bascule bridge in Cleveden Road was replaced by a culvert. A new canal bridge was built when the canal was reopened in 2000.

xii

Acknowledgements

The author wishes to acknowledge the courtesy of the following institutions and individuals in the reproduction of images in this book:

Glasgow University Archives: **I.** 1, 9, 10; **II.** 25; **III.** 11, 24, 29; **IV.** 2, 28, 29, 30, 31; **V.** 3, 4, 15, 25, 27; **VI.** 23, 24, 51; **VII.** 11, 15, 16, 17, 18, 19, 22; **VIII.** 1, 3, 4, 5, 6, 7, 9, 10, 11, 12, 15, 16, 17, 19, 20, 21, 22, 23, 24, 30, *ix, xi, xii. Glasgow City Archives:* **I.** 14; **II.** 16, 17, 24, 28; **IV.** 6, 14; **V.** 2, 22, 29, 30, 31 32, 33; **VI.** 7, 13, 14, 22; **VII.** 10, 12, 13, 23, 27, 28, 31, 32, 33, 36, 37, 38, 44, 45, 46, 57; **VIII.** 2, 13, 14, 28; *x. Mitchell Library, Glasgow City Libraries & Archives:* **I.** 11, 13, 15; **II.** 2, 3, 7, 15, 19, 20, 29, 30; **III.** 9, 10, 25, 26; **IV.** 4, 8, 13, 17, 27; **VI.** 9, 15, 17, 18, 19, 34, 38, 42, 43, 44; **VII.** 7, 29, 35, 60, 63. *Collection of the author:* **I.** 5; **II.** 6, 27; **III.** 5, 7; **IV.** 7; **V.** 5; **VI.** 29, 31, 35, 37, 47, 48; **VII.** 39, 41, 42, 43. *Glasgow Conservation Trust West:* **I.** 2, 6; **II.** 11, 21, 23, 26; **III.** 27, 28; **V.** 8, 9; **VI.** 10, 11, 12, 16, 25, 26; **VII.** 58. *Laurel Park School:* **IV.** 20, 21, 22, 23, 24, 25, 26; **VII.** 8 14, 20, 21, 25, 26, 30, 34, 59. *Crown Copyright: RCAHMS:* **II.** 1, 14, 18; **III.** 13, 23; **IV.** 11, 19; **V.** 16, 17, 18; **VII.** 9, 48; **VIII.** 29. *Greater Glasgow Health Board:* **III.** 14, 15, 17, 18, 19, 20, 21; **VI.** 1, 2, 3, 4; **VII.** 61. *Copyright: Glasgow Museums: iii;* **I.** 4, 8; **II.** 4; **III.** 1, 22; **VI.** 6, 8, 45; **VII.** 47; **VIII.** 32. *Glasgow University Library, Department of Special Collections: iv, v, vi;* **I.** 7; **II.** 5, 13, 22; **VI.** 5. *Daily Record/Sunday Mail:* **I.** 3; **III.** 12; **VI.** 49; **VII.** 40, 55, 56; **VIII.** 26, 27. *Glasgow Academy:* **IV.** 1, 9, 10; **VII.** 2, 3, 4, 5. *Glasgow Botanic Gardens Archives:* **III.** 2, 3, 4, 6, 8; **VI.** 30. *St John's Renfield Church:* **VII.** 49, 50, 51, 52, 53, 54. *Dr Ian L. Evans:* **II.** 12; **VI.** 20, 27, 28, 33. *British Railways Board:* **V.** 19, 20, 21, 23. *Robert Grieves:* **V.** 12, 13; *vii. Stanley K. Hunter:* **V.** 6; **VI.** 32, 46. *Stenlake Publishing:* **V.** 10; **VI.** 39, 40. *Brian Deans:* **V.** 1, 7. *Willie Brown: ii;* **VI.** 41. *Geoffrey Jarvis:* **II.** 8, 9. *Royal Faculty of Procurators in Glasgow:* **IV.** 3, 5. *W.A.C. Smith:* **V.** 26, 28. *Scottish Film & Television Archive:* **VI.** 50; **VII.** 24. *Andy Stewart:* **VII.** 6; *viii. T. & R. Annan:* **V.** 11; **VIII.** 8. *Maisie Cessford:* **IV.** 16. *Calum Crawford:* **VI.** 36. *Andy Fairgrieve: i. Glasgow Homeopathic Hospital:* **VII.** 62. *Betty Henderson:* **IV.** 12. *Hillhead Baptist Church:* **VI.** 21. *Hillhead High School:* **IV.** 18. *David Hume:* **V.** 24. *Hyndland Parish Church:* **III.** 16. *Kelvinside Academy (Colin H. Mackay):* **IV.** 15. *Robert Mack and A. D. Packer:* **V.** 14. *Herbert R. M. Ross:* **VI.** 12. *Scottish National Portrait Gallery (from a private Scottish collection):* **I.** 12. *Michael G. H. Smith:* **VIII.** 18. *A. C. Stirling:* **VIII.** 25. *Maureen Waddell:* **VII.** 1. *R.J.S. Wiseman:* **VIII.** 31. Ordnance Survey maps illustrated on the front and back endpapers are reproduced by permission of the Trustees of the National Library of Scotland.

The generous and gracious support of the following parties must also be recognised:

Leslie Richmond, George Gardiner and colleagues in the Glasgow University Archives; Alan McAdams of the Royal Faculty of Procurators in Glasgow; Andrew Jackson, Irene O'Brien and staff of Glasgow City Archives; Staff at the History & Glasgow Room, Mitchell Library; Veronica Steele of the RCAHMS; Winnie Tyrrell of Glasgow Museums; Janet McBain and Alan Docherty of the Scottish Film & Television Archive; Louise Bustard of Glasgow Botanic Gardens; Douglas Annan of T. & R. Annan; Elizabeth Surber, Sally Richardson and Hilary Thomley of Laurel Park School; Iain MacLeod of Glasgow Academy; Betty Henderson of Westbourne School for Girls; Ken Cunningham of Hillhead High School; John Broadfoot of Kelvinside Academy; Maya Dykes of St John's Renfield Church; Graham Sinclair of Hillhead Baptist Church; Willie Brown of Wellington Church; Rev. John Christie of Hyndland Parish Church; Colin McMillan of the *Daily Record/Sunday Mail;* Iain Drysdale of Mactaggart & Mickel Ltd.; Maisie Cessford; Calum Crawford; Eric Curtis; Brian Deans; Dr Ian L. Evans; Thomas Hamilton; Stanley Hunter; John R. Hume; Christine Jamieson; Geoffrey Jarvis; Mr & Mrs Jim Maguire; Michael Moss; Iain Paterson; Mr & Mrs D. Reid; Herbert R. M. Ross; Sam Small; Bill Spalding; Ian G. McM. Stewart; and last, but not least, Maureen C. Waddell MBE.

Special thanks are owed to:

Colleagues and Trustees at Glasgow Conservation Trust West.
West End Lectures speakers and supporters.
Ann Laird for her irrepressible encouragement.
Lynne Carson Rickards for her faithful editorial assistance.
The authors of *Wolfert's Roost* for their inspiration.

Duncan Urquhart, Patricia Urquhart Mesick and the late Hector Urquhart for a memorable (and historical!) childhood.
Janet, Ross and Callum Urquhart for their boundless patience.
The late Dr Harper W. Boyd,
without whose support this work would not have been possible.